HALPERN'S
GUIDE
TO THE
ESSENTIAL
RESTAURANTS
OF
ITALY

HALPERN'S
GUIDE
to the Essential
RESTAURANTS
of
I·T·A·L·Y

*From Milan to Rome
with Notes on the Food
and Wine*

DANIEL HALPERN
with Jeanne Wilmot Carter

ADDISON-WESLEY PUBLISHING COMPANY

*Reading, Massachusetts • Menlo Park, California • New York
Don Mills, Ontario • Wokingham, England • Amsterdam • Bonn
Sydney • Singapore • Tokyo • Madrid • San Juan*

FOR MARK STRAND,
BROTHER IN THINGS ITALIAN

Library of Congress Cataloging-in-Publication Data

Halpern, Daniel, 1945–
    [Guide to the essential restaurants of Italy]
    Halpern's guide to the essential restaurants of Italy : from Milan
to Rome with notes on the food and wine / by Daniel Halpern with
Jeanne Wilmot Carter.
        p.   cm.
    Includes bibliographical references.
    ISBN 0-201-06247-X
    1. Restaurants. lunch rooms, etc.—Italy—Guide-books.   2. Italy—
Description and travel—1975—Guide-books.   I. Carter, Jeanne Wilmot.
II. Title.
TX907.5.I8H35   1990
647.9545—dc20   89-39242

Cover design by Copenhaver Cumpston

Text design by Richard Oriolo

Set in 10-point Galliard by Compset, Inc. Beverly, MA

A B C D E F G H I J – D O – 9 5 4 3 2 1 0

FIRST PRINTING, March 1990

ACKNOWLEDGMENTS

I wish to thank the many people without whose help and generous support this book would not have been possible, especially Enza Cirrincione, Carla Gaita, and the CIGA hotel chain; Nancy Galler of Humbert Travel; Jo Inzerillo and Silverio Nardone of the Italian Government Tourist Office; Giorgio Lulli, Doreen Schmid, and the Italian Trade Commission; Karen Preston and the Leading Hotels of the World chain; and Tina Gebel-Kiser and Utell International. Thanks also to Pier Luigi Magrini and the Grand Hotel Baglioni in Bologna; Vittorio Spicciani, Giuseppe Azzerboni, and the Savoy Hotel in Florence; Giorgio Daina, Sarah Jane Battersby, and the Hotel Principe di Savoia in Milan; Maurizio Ferrante and the Hotel Brufani in Perugia; Nadio Benedetti and the Hotel Excelsior in Rome; Nushin Mozaffari and the Hotel d'Inghilterra in Rome; Roberto Wirth and the Hassler Hotel in Rome; Antonio Esposito and the Park Hotel in Siena; Paolo Danieli and the Hôtel des Îles Borromées in Stresa; A. Braggion and the Hotel Continental in Treviso; Raimondo Giavarini and the Hotel Due Torri in Verona; and Natale Rusconi, Alfredo Cavallaro, Mariano Mastel, and the Hotel Cipriani in Venice. To Trans World Airlines, for their support. And to the keepers of the flame, the many restaurant owners and chefs who spent endless amounts of time explaining to me their native cuisine, with constant patience, goodwill, and love for their art. And for his discussion regarding the wines of Italy, Brian Larky and the vineyards of Ca' del Bosco.

I am also indebted to the authors of two books that served as primary references: Burton Anderson, for his definitive work on the wines of Italy, *The Simon and Schuster Pocket Guide to Italian Wines;* and Fay Sharman and Brian Chadwick, for their carefully researched *The Taste of Italy.*

I am grateful to Jennifer Griffin and Jennifer Novick for their work in assembling this guide. And to William Sheehan of the Vatican Library for his *spiritual* contribution.

Finally, I wish to thank those whose seemingly tireless work saw this book through to its publication: my agent, Bob Cornfield, for his commitment to this project; my editor, Martha Moutray, for her enthusiasm, good sense, and endless patience; John Fuller and Cope Cumpston, who *produced* the book; Anna Jardine, for her acute eye and skilled reading of the manuscript; and Richard Oriolo, whose design so masterfully translated that manuscript into type.

—D.H.

CONTENTS

INTRODUCTION

I've been going to Italy for twenty-five years—my first trip was in the winter of 1964. I had it in mind to become a poet and felt a trip was necessary training, so I went to Venice in search of the artistic side of the *dolce vita,* and of Ezra Pound, whom as it turns out I encountered briefly on the *vaporetto* between San Marco and Accademia. He sat down next to me, and when I looked over I immediately recognized the face, the intense blue eyes I had seen in a recent feature in *Life* magazine, which described his life in Venice as one of the great literary figures of the twentieth century, once again in Italy, in voluntary exile. Not knowing what, exactly, to say, I asked him if he spoke English. "Nope," he said in perfect American, keeping it simple between us.

It was on that winter trip that I first discovered the glories of Italian cuisine—although, it must be admitted, in those days my needs were somewhat less ambitious than the enterprise of this book. It was my first experience with the simple, fresh, unprocessed ingredients that go into the dishes served throughout Italy: the inimitable cream; the fresh fruits and vegetables; the seafood from the Mediterranean; the salad lettuces such as *radicchio di Treviso* of the Veneto and *puntarelle* of Rome; the roast pork called *porchetta,* which the Umbrians cook with herbs; the baby lamb of Lazio; the risotto and veal of Lombardy; the *fiorentina* of Tuscany, a T-bone steak cut from Chianina beef—to make a short list of what comes immediately to mind.

As I've traveled through Italy these past twenty-five years, I have continued to pursue the possibilities of the regional cuisine of northern Italy because the itinerary I have most often followed has been along the roads that run from Milan to Rome—and thus the geographical range of this book. My purpose is to document some of the happy discoveries I've made wandering along this magical route, through the foothills of the Alps around Lake Maggiore, the undeniable maze of Venice, the elegant city of Verona, the hill towns of Umbria and Tuscany, the treacherous and beautiful mountains of the Abruzzi, the languid seaside towns along the Adriatic, and the streets in which lie the immortal and infinite puzzles of Rome. It's also my purpose to make an argument for traveling beyond the holy triangle of Venice, Florence, and Rome.

I have not included two regions of northern Italy, Trentino–Alto Adige and Friuli–Venezia Giulia, because they lie outside my defined geographical scope of that part of Italy between Milan and Rome, with the understanding that these boundaries are informal and flexible, ranging as far northwest as Aosta and as far northeast as Treviso. On the other hand, I have included two regions that are not, properly speaking, part of northern Italy—Lazio, or Latium, and the Abruzzi. I have covered these because they *are* situated within the boundaries of the itinerary that this book is all about.

To be sure, everyone has an idea of what to do when traveling in Italy—which paintings of the Renaissance are the "great paintings," which churches are the grandest, the most moving to experience, which hill towns are worth that extra fifty kilometers, and so on. But regardless of opinion and individual preference as to how time might be best spent, the one thing all travelers must do—beyond seriously contemplating the overwhelmingly bountiful history and art of Italian civilization—is to partake of another of Italy's great traditions: that is, to eat. That tradition, however, is a complicated one; as you move from meal to meal you'll encounter a variety of ideas about what Italian cooking should be, from the most regionally oriented *cucina* of a restaurant such as Picci in Cavriago to the flash-and-glitz *alta cucina* of Gualtiero Marchesi in Milan, which participates in the French model of *nouvelle cuisine*. There's also the belief held by many in Italy that something in between is the answer, that the old ways should be honored but with more attention paid to the presentation of the food, although these proponents are quick to add they do not want dishes to become overly fussy. Another aspect of tradition is the institution of Mamma in the kitchen, and it's cheering, at least to me, to find that regardless of the direction a restaurant decides to go, more often than not Mamma remains part of the act, carrying on the old ways—for example, you'll find her very much on the scene at Guido in Costigliole d'Asti—also at Scaletta in Milan and La Mora in Ponte a Moriano. In fact, Italian restaurants are still very much a family affair, which accounts in part for their magic and longevity.

Anyone who has dined in Italy with some thought has dined well—has discovered that *trattoria* with the finest *penne all 'amatriciana* (pasta with tomatoes, onions, bacon, and hot pepper); the table in a certain out-of-the-way village where one is guaranteed to find *lepre in salmì* (a rabbit stew) as God intended it; the silver cart in Bologna that serves an inimitable *bollito misto* (an assortment of boiled meats), with pungent green sauce and preserved fruits suspended in the mustard, honey, and white wine sauce called *mostarda*; or the perfect ending to a meal during the Christmas season: *montebianco* (a dessert of chestnuts and cream).

Certainly, there are plenty of guidebooks that go to extraordinary lengths to map out the lay of the land in terms of museums, churches, statues, paintings, and other works of artistic endeavor; and hotels, shopping areas, itineraries and walks, and so on. And yet there hasn't really been a publication that attempts to guide visitors to Italy in a focused way to the restaurants that offer the very finest and traditional *cucina italiana*.

This book is addressed to casual diners who are interested in eating well as they move through Italian townscapes and landscapes. It is also for those whose ambition, when it comes to gastronomy, is slightly higher, those who are willing to go an extra distance to consume something special, who travel in Italy partly to experience Italian cuisine at its best—those discriminating gourmands in obsessive pursuit of the perfect restaurant.

I have selected the most frequently visited towns and cities between Aosta and Treviso in the north, and Rome and L'Aquila in the south—basically, the well-traversed part of the map that extends from Milan to Venice by way of Parma and Verona, to Florence via Bologna, and on to Rome through Siena and Perugia, with various attendant diversions along the way. These are the places where most travelers are likely to find themselves following any number of possible innovative itineraries. I have also included lesser-known towns that house important restaurants worthy of a day trip for lunch, or an overnighter with the promise of an important dinner. Part of the magic of traveling through Italy is that the occasion is more frequent than not that one discovers that in the tiny hill town with its outstanding *cucina,* there is, perhaps, a little-known Piero della Francesca hanging on a local wall.

A few cities or towns are included even though they do not have a restaurant of the same high quality as other restaurants reviewed here; these towns have been listed for the obvious reason that they are major stops on many itineraries. My suggestions for dining in these cities attempt to make the best out of what is available, which in Italy is never anything to worry overly about.

In reviewing the restaurants, I have tried to evoke a sense of what it's like to be there: the atmosphere and decor, the way the food is prepared and presented, the kind of food the restaurant is engaged in serving. The recommended dishes listed are meant to give you an idea of what a particular restaurant is interested in presenting—and because the ever-changing Italian menu is responsive to the seasons and creativity, it's likely some of the dishes I've listed under this category will no longer be found on the restaurant menu.

Over the past several years, some of the more serious restaurants in Italy have formed groups to help promote Italian cuisine. The two most important are Linea Italia in Cucina and Le Soste.

Linea Italia in Cucina
A group of northern Italian restaurateurs, headed by Franco Colombani (from Albergo del Sole in Maleo), formed this association in 1980. The members of the "Italian Line in Cooking" established five basic principles:

1. To use and respect the traditional recipes of regional Italian cooking.
2. To change those recipes only when modern alimentary methods make it imperative, without destroying the great richness of tastes, traditions, and historical memories.
3. To present dishes in which the vegetables are in natural harmony with the meats.
4. To limit the number of dishes on the menu.
5. Not to invent just for the sake of it, not to play games, and not to follow fashions slavishly.

The eighteen members are:

*Albergo del Sole, in Maleo (Franco and Silvana Colombani)

*Al Bersagliere, in Goito (Roberto and Massimo Ferrari)

Dall'Amelia–Alla Giustizia, in Mestre (Dino and Mara Boscarato)

*Dal Pescatore, in Canneto sull'Oglio (Antonio and Nadia Santini)

*Il Cigno, in Mantua (Gaetano and Alessandra Martini)

Romano, in Viareggio (Romano and Franca Franceschini)

*Vecchia Lugana, in Lugana di Sirmione (Pierantonio Ambrosi)

*A member of Linea Italia in Cucina and Le Soste.
†Outside the area covered in this book.

La Mora, in Ponte a Moriano (Sauro and Angela Brunicardi)

Manuelina, in Recco (Gianni and Maria Rosa Carbone)

*†Antica Trattoria Boschetti, in Tricesimo (Giorgio Trentin and Rinaldo and Roberto Krcivoj)

Il Faro, in Oristano (Giovanni and Giovannina Brai)

La Casanova, in Chianciano Terme (Carlo Doricchi and Leonardo Falvo)

Locanda dell'Amorosa, in Sinalunga (Carlo Citterio)

La Contea, in Neive (Tonino and Claudio Verro)

Vecchio Mulino, in Certosa di Pavia (Luca and Christina Bolfo)

Da Giovanni, in Cortina Vecchia di Alseno (Renato Besenzoni and Mamma Carolina)

Ceresole, in Cremona (Rino and Saverio Botte)

Da Toni, in Gradiscutta di Varmo (Aldo and Lidia Morassutti)

Le Soste

"Le Soste (founded in 1983) is a guide that groups together restaurateurs who have in common a particular sensitivity to food, wine and hospitality. Although they follow diverse 'cuisine creeds,' they feel associated due to qualitative choices. Some faithfully interpret traditional cusine, while others create according to their imaginations. Each accomplishes a creative gesture that arises from an intuitive capacity to project a cuisine with love" (*Guida ai ristoranti de le Soste*).

The twenty-seven Italian members are:

Cavallo Bianco, in Aosta (Paolo and Franco Vai)

Al Rododendro, in Boves (Mary Barale)

†*Balzi Rossi,* in Ventimiglia (Giuseppina and Andrea Beglia)

Al Sorriso, in Soriso (Luisa and Angelo Valazza)

Il Griso, in Malgrate (Roberto and Bruno Gobbi)

Antica Osteria del Ponte, in Cassinetta di Lugagnano (Renata and Ezio Santin)

Emiliano, in Stresa (Romano and Corrado Felisi)

Del Sole, in Ranco (Carlo and Itala Brovelli)

Gualtiero Marchesi, in Milan (Gualtiero Marchesi)

Aimo e Nadia, in Milan (Aimo and Nadia Moroni)

**Albergo del Sole,* in Maleo (Franco and Silvana Colombani)

**Vecchia Lugana,* in Lugana di Sirmione (Pierantonio Ambrosi)

Il Desco, in Verona (Natale Spinelli and Elia Rizzo)

**Al Bersagliere,* in Goito (Massimo and Roberto Ferrari)

**Il Cigno,* in Mantua (Gaetano and Alessandra Martini)

**Dal Pescatore,* in Canneto sull 'Oglio (Nadia and Antonio Santini)

†*Andrea,* in Merano (Peppi Nothdurfter)

Antica Osteria del Teatro, in Piacenza (Filippo Chiappini Dattilo and Franco Ilari)

San Domenico, in Imola (Gian Luigi Morini)

La Frasca, in Castrocaro Terme (Gianfranco Bolognesi)

Dolada, in Pieve d'Alpago (Enzo and Rossana de Prà)

*†*Antica Trattoria Boschetti,* in Tricesimo (Giorgio Trentin and Rinaldo and Roberto Krcivoj)

Enoteca Pinchiorri, in Florence (Giorgio and Annie Pinchiorri)

**La Mora,* in Ponte a Moriano (Sauro and Angela Brunicardi)

La Chiusa, in Montefollonico (Dania and Umberto Lucherini)

†*Don Alfonso 1890,* in S. Agata sui due Golfi (Alfonso e Livia Iaccarino)

Gambero Rosso, in San Vincenzo (Fulvio Pierangelini)

HOW
TO USE
THIS
GUIDE

GENERAL ORGANIZATION

I've tried to provide as much practical information as possible so that readers might get the most out of restaurant eating in Italy. In addition to information relating directly to the restaurants, I've included a sampling of seasonal food and regional specialties, as well as a listing of wines within each region section, to serve as a general guide. The General Index at the back of the book contains wine entries to help you locate descriptions of the various wines recommended under individual restaurant reviews. With some exceptions, in the restaurant reviews I've suggested only wines that come from the region of the restaurant.

Although the body of the book is devoted to the restaurant reviews, the lists summarized below provide a great deal of information in a concise format. Refer to the table of contents to locate each of the lists:

1. *A Few Essential Words for the Restaurant.* Italian food words you are likely to encounter on the menu.

2. *Seasonal Foods.* A list of seasonal ingredients and preparations.

3. *Regional Food and Wine Specialties.* A select list of important and traditional regional specialties, presented alphabetically by region. After the descriptions of specific foods and typical cheeses are listings of the wines produced in each region, the grapes cultivated, and the leading producers.

4. *A Few Essential Wine Terms.* A good base for your wine vocabulary, to help in ordering wine.

5. *A Ranking of the Essential Restaurants of Italy.* A list of all the restaurants reviewed in this book, ordered by star category, and alphabetically within each category. This will provide you with an "easy reference" comparison among restaurants.

6. *A General Listing of the Restaurants of Italy by City.* The restaurants named here include three categories: all those I've reviewed as "Essential Restaurants"; those listed by city as "Other Recommended Restaurants"; and a number of other restaurants worthy of your attention.

7. *Italian–English Gastronomic Glossary.* This contains food terms for the most part. Actual dishes are described under "Regional Food and Wine Specialties" and may also be described as recommended dishes in the restaurant reviews.

8. *A Reading List.* If you fall hopelessly in love with Italy and you're serious, you'll want each of these books in your library. If you participate in moderation (but would you be reading this book?), make a list of the five or six titles that most appeal to you and read them before casting off for the good country. It's a varied list—history, art, fiction, poetry, food and wine. Is there anything left?

9. *Index.* A comprehensive index to food and wine reviewed in this guide. If you're looking for the term for a particular food, you will find it in English here, followed by the Italian equivalent and text page-number references. Entries for "Essential" and "Other Recommended" restaurants are also given here.

These lists, especially "Seasonal Foods" and "Regional Food and Wine Specialties," will enable you to prepare for the region or regions in your itinerary. They will familiarize you with the food and wine of that region, thus making more enjoyable your experience with the menu and wine list—and most important, with the meal itself.

EXPLANATION OF RATINGS AND CATEGORIES

Towns and Cities

Restaurants are reviewed under their towns or cities, which are presented in alphabetical order in the section beginning on page 121. For some cities I've provided a brief description or noted a few sightseeing possibilities. Below each city/town heading is a list of other localities, with distances in kilometers, to help with geographical orientation (1 kilometer = .6 mile).

Restaurant Reviews

Within each city or town section, restaurants are reviewed in order of star ranking and, within that, order of importance.

Overall Rating: The Stars ★-★ ★ ★ ★

Primarily a food rating, but something from all the categories—class, atmosphere, service, wine—has been taken into consideration.

★ ★ ★ ★ ★

Great on every count, every step of the way. Serving the best food with the greatest skill and imagination, in the best possible circumstances. For a restaurant to get this rating, everything must work.

★ ★ ★ ★

One of the very best, but just missing true greatness. The ambition is a degree or so lower, but the food is very close to the highest rating.

★ ★ ★

A good, solid restaurant, serving tasty, reliable food in reasonably comfortable surroundings.

★ ★

Capable, with unrealized potential, but still not up to the more serious three-star category; nevertheless, two-star restaurants do have something of interest to recommend them.

★

Only when there's no other choice. Better than nothing, and better than the worst when nothing's better.

Class Rating: 1–5

This rating is based on how *formally* the restaurant presents itself—in terms of decor, glassware, china and cutlery, service, presentation of food and wine, and so on.

5 The height of elegance, with a little something beyond the call of the expected, or even the imagined, thrown in—all stops out.

4 Formal and successfully so—very fine dining. Serious, elevated, and elegant, if not "outrageous."

3 Solid comfort; a restaurant tastefully put together, just the high side of casual, but serious nonetheless.

2 Rustic; not uncomfortable, but nearly so.

1 A place in which to eat quickly, for survival only. Basic.

Atmosphere Rating: 1–5

The general feeling of the restaurant: how well it works, whether formal or informal. This rating measures the spirit of the place, ambience, affect . . . atmosphere.

5 Perfect. Everything is harmonious and you're in gastronomical heaven. Serious magical airs.

4 Compellingly comfortable with a fine prevailing spirit hovering; memorable, if without the ultimate magic of a 5.

3 Very pleasant in the fine Italian fashion—that is, everything in good taste.

2 Just passable, nothing terrible. It could, on a good night, even be fun, but you'd probably go elsewhere if you had other options.

1 Raw and basic and even *un*comfortable. Only for an amazing specialty dish—or emergency hunger.

Service Rating: 1–5

This category describes the quality of attention you're likely to receive in the restaurant, the skills of the waiters and dining room staff, and the way the proprietor has seen fit to train and oversee his staff.

5 Perfect, flawless. Professional waiters whose goal is to please *you* if it's your night at their table: to anticipate your needs and execute your dining event with precision, while remaining nearly invisible.

4 Almost great, but just the lower side of perfect. The distinction between 4 and 5 is subtle, and a 4 certainly represents serious service; but it's the extra English (as in "spin") that makes the difference.

3 Workable. Fine service, nothing special—but on the other hand, nothing negative either. A utilitarian performance.

2 Minimal help, just enough to get the food to your table.

1 The kind of place where you can't be sure whether the waiters are waiters or other diners who have dressed that day in the same outfit.

Wine Rating: 1–5

This rating is based on the depth of the wine list, especially the representation of wines from the region of the restaurant, with price a secondary factor.

5 One of the great cellars; a fully rounded list: a large selection of the particular region's wines, as well as representative wines from around the country, with a good sampling of more obscure wines from the smaller vineyards and newer producers.

4 A serious list, large and representative, substantial—with a happy number of pleasing surprises.

3 A solid wine list, not large, but well selected. You'll likely find what you're looking for or even something you've never sampled, but you won't daydream in this *lista dei vini*.

2 Adequate, but barely. You'll come across a bottle or two to drink, but more likely than not it will be something that seems obvious—which is to say, a serviceable list and no more.

1 A watering hole.

Price: Inexpensive to Very Expensive

The price category indicates the per-person cost of a full meal: a first course (appetizer or pasta), a main dish, a moderately priced bottle of wine (around 15,000 lire), dessert, and an additional 5 percent tip.*

Very expensive (VE)	Above 100,000 lire ($71)
Expensive (E)	70,000–100,000 lire ($50–$71)
Moderate (M)	40,000–70,000 lire ($28–$50)
Inexpensive (I)	Below 40,000 lire ($28)

Suggested Dishes

Under this category I've listed a selection of the better dishes I sampled in the restaurant. As the Italian menu changes sea-

*Dollar amounts have been calculated at the rate of 1,400 lire to the dollar.

sonally in a significant way—and daily, less dramatically, and occasionally, as the restaurant develops new dishes—many of the recommendations may not be on the menu when you arrive. I've tried to include offerings from each of the seasons, but keep in mind that these listings are meant as a guide only. Names of dishes are given first in Italian (or regional dialect) and then in English, to help with the identification of menu entries, to convey how a particular restaurant goes about presenting its food, to provide a frame of reference when ordering to get the most out of your meal, and finally, to acquaint you with the vocabulary of Italian cuisine.

When a restaurant does not use a menu, as with Scaletta in Milan, or when a dish the restaurant prepares does not appear on the menu, I have used "generic" Italian to describe it.

When a dish is extraordinary and absolutely should not be missed, I've marked it with an asterisk (*).

Suggested Wines

I've selected wines from the region of the restaurant, making an exception to this practice only when it was impossible or imprudent to do otherwise. As the vintages are constantly changing, generally I have not given them, but have selected from what was available on the current wine list; this means that the wines reviewed are of recent vintage, and have been reviewed accordingly. On a few occasions, however, I have suggested a vintage, either because the depth of the wine list offered a large selection of vintages of a given wine or because the year made a major difference. A number of the suggested wines are on the expensive side, but they should be sampled at some point on your Italian journey: many are wines that aren't easily come upon. Although house wines are more often than not satisfactory, and are especially effective in keeping your bill down, I have suggested them only rarely. I have tried to recommend wines that are not readily available in the United States—especially wines from the newer vineyards or wines made by small producers whose output is too small for export.

Italians like to begin their meals with an *aperitivo,* which is meant to stimulate the appetite and alert the body that a meal is about to come. It's often a glass of sparkling wine, or *spumante,* which in the better restaurants is poured at your table. Sometimes, it's poured before you know it—and don't be surprised if on occasion it turns up on your bill.

Other Recommended Restaurants

This is a list of other worthwhile restaurants that aren't quite up to the level of the restaurants I've reviewed for a particular city or town. This doesn't mean that they're not very fine, but that I've reviewed only the top restaurants there; it's often the case that a restaurant placed under "Other Recommended Restaurants" in a city with a number of important restaurants is better than a restaurant that receives a primary review in a town with few such restaurants. It should also be pointed out that many of the restaurants in the general listing (pages 101–120)—are neither reviewed nor listed under "Other Recommended Restaurants"; they are listed because they can provide decent meals.

Restaurants to Avoid

On the rare occasion when a restaurant has gone out of its way to underwhelm its patrons, I have warned against eating there. For an establishment to achieve this distinction, there must, in my view, be a *serious* problem with it—impressively poor food at outrageous prices, complete indifference on the part of the staff and proprietor, or something approaching dishonesty.

Hotels

I've suggested hotels where you can feel assured of *at least* a comfortable bed. The recommended hotels range from comfortable to luxury (see page 19).

Food and Wine Shops, Markets

For some of the larger cities I've selected food and wine stores that will interest those interested in food—whether from a cook's perspective or simply as a consumer. I've mentioned food markets of special note, such as the Rialto market in Venice and Rome's famous market in the Campo dei Fiori, which should not be missed. Visiting marketplaces will also give you the chance to preview seasonal specialties.

TRAVELING

IN

ITALY

DRIVING IN ITALY

Renting a car in Italy and being your own conductor is by
far the most convenient method of travel. Your own car allows you to make all the necessary or desired detours and,
most important, to operate on *your* schedule. Also, on the
highways it's a pleasure to drive with Italians—yes, they drive
fast, but they drive correctly and well. If you like speed, this
is your country. If not, stay to the right and enjoy the passing
countryside. You'll notice that Italians *always* signal to announce their intentions, and while they may lack patience,
they do follow the laws of the road.

Car Rentals

After trying a number of international car rental groups that
operate in Italy, I have found Kemwel (which subcontracts
Eurodollar and Budget/Italy by Car) to be the most consistently reliable. Be sure to make your bookings in advance and
in the United States, so that you can qualify for rates lower
than those you'll obtain in Italy. Budget in the U.S. also has
very good weekly rates and is trustworthy. Check with either
company about a collision damage waiver (CDW), which
American Express pays for if you *use* that card. If not, note
that the Budget CDW comes with a zero deductible, as op-
posed to Kemwel's $100 deductible. Drive carefully.

Speed Limits

Only in Italy could there be speed limits that change depending on the particular day of the week or year, and the size of
your engine. Naturally, it's complicated—and since the laws
are constantly changing, they should be checked when you
pick up your car. In general, the speed limits are: 50 kilometers per hour inside city limits; 90 outside city limits; and 130
on the larger highways. There are exceptions: The speed limit
on the highways goes down to 110 kilometers per hour on
Saturdays and Sundays; from the Thursday before Easter to
the following Wednesday; from the second Sunday of July
through the first Sunday of September; from December 20
to January 7; and on April 25 (Liberation Day), May 1 (In-

ternational Workers' Day), November 1 (All Saints' Day), and December 8 (Immaculate Conception).

The Italians have come up with another invention worth bearing in mind: Autoveloxe. This controversial hidden radar system takes photographs of the license plates of speeding cars. Violators then receive a ticket in the mail—fines, it should be added, can be as high as $300.

A last piece of useful information: The car entering a traffic circle has precedence over those already in the circle. The general rule of thumb is: regardless of the situation, yield to cars on your right.

TRAINS AND BUSES

Traveling by bus or train is practical and economical and can be pleasant and reliable; keep in mind, however, that strikes are a primary Italian institution. Although it will not allow you the flexibility of a car, train or bus travel offers the opportunity to relax between cities—to read, to talk with the local people, or if you're on the right train, to take a casual meal while the countryside races along outside. Check with your travel agent about tickets, passes, schedules, and so on.

HOTELS

I've recommended hotels for those places where you're most likely to spend a night. For the smaller towns—where it's more probable you'll be stopping just for lunch—I've mentioned a hotel only if there's something special to make an overnight visit worthwhile, as in Torgiano at Le Tre Vaselle, Soriso at Al Sorriso, and Ranco at del Sole. The hotels suggested here are excellent establishments that will assure your comfort, regardless of the time of year—a consideration when you're traveling in off-season weather or after a long day's drive, when you want to *know* that a comfortable retreat awaits you.

It is worth asking when you check in if breakfast is included; coffee, a few rolls and packets of jam and butter can cost as much as 25,000 lire ($18). Keep in mind also that dry cleaning, pressing, and laundry can be very expensive in hotels. There are a number of hotel chains in Italy, but the most consistently reliable are those in the CIGA and the Leading Hotels of the World chains. For a listing of their member hotels and other information, call their 800 numbers in the United States.

The following categories are based on the price of a double room per night:*

Very expensive—Luxury above 300,000 lire ($214)

Expensive 200,000–300,000 lire ($143–$214)

Moderate 100,000–200,000 lire ($71–$143)

Inexpensive below 100,000 lire ($71)

PAYING IN ITALIAN

The Italians have a particular way of paying in many cafés and bars, sometimes referred to as the *scontrino* method. You first decide what you want—an *espresso,* a sandwich—and then go to the cashier, at the *cassa,* to pay. You will be given a receipt, which you bring back to the barman, who in turn will give you your order.

TIPPING

Allow common sense to guide you. Generally, 1,000 to 2,000 lire is adequate for the small things; 2,000 lire for room service (a service charge is usually already added); an additional 3 to 7 percent at restaurants, depending on how much service is built into or added to your check; loose change for a cab ride; 1,000 to 2,000 lire a bag to the porter, depending on the class of hotel; for hotel maids, 2,000 to 3,000 per diem; and if the concierge has been helpful, 10,000 to 20,000 lire, dependin: on just how helpful he was. When in doubt about those miscellaneous helping hands, a thousand lire or two will keep you on good terms.

SHOPPING HOURS

In general, stores are open Tuesday through Saturday, 9:00 A.M. to 7:30 P.M., with a lunch break from 12:30 or 1:00 to 3:00 or 4:00. On Mondays food stores are open mornings and afternoons, and nonfood stores, afternoons only. Many food markets are open in the mornings only, Monday through Saturday. Most shops are closed Saturday afternoons during the summer. Banks are open Monday through Friday

*Dollar amounts have been calculated at the rate of 1,400 lire to the dollar.

USEFUL INFORMATION

DAYS OF THE WEEK

Monday	*lunedì*
Tuesday	*martedì*
Wednesday	*mercoledì*
Thursday	*giovedì*
Friday	*venerdì*
Saturday	*sabato*
Sunday	*domenica*

THE SEASONS

winter	*inverno*
spring	*primavera*
summer	*estate*
autumn	*autunno*

NATIONAL HOLIDAYS

January 1	New Year's Day
April 25	Liberation Day (1945)
(varies)	Easter Sunday and Monday
May 1	International Workers' Day
August 15	Ferragosto (Feast of the Assumption)
November 1	All Saints' Day
December 8	Immaculate Conception
December 25	Christmas
December 26	St. Stephen's Day

THE MOST IMPORTANT
WORD IN ITALIAN:
CHIUSO

If you forget every word of Italian you ever knew, you will still be left with the *c* word lingering—smoldering?—in your memory. *Chiuso*, the word for "closed," the word that announces disappointment. It's a word you'll soon have as part of your permanent Italian vocabulary—as it's part of the experience. In the end, it's impossible to keep track of the ever-shifting day of rest (*giorno di chiusura*) and days of closing for restoration (*per restauro*), holiday (*ferie*), and strike (*sciopero*).

8:30 A.M. to 1:30 P.M., and in some cities from 2:45 to 3:45 P.M. as well.

Note that shopping hours (and days) vary from city to city and from region to region.

GUIDEBOOKS AND MAPS

There are endless guides to select from, but the time-proven books in my opinion (I travel light, so the selection is small) are:

Burton Anderson, *The Simon and Schuster Pocket Guide to Italian Wines* (revised edition). Simon and Schuster, 1987. The single best reference work on Italian wines—mandatory equipment.

Italia (red edition). Michelin, 1990. A useful guide for all the practical information about hotels and restaurants.

Italy (green edition). Michelin, 1983. Concise, and very good for quick reference.

Macadam, Alta (ed.) *Northern Italy* (Blue Guide, 8th ed.). Ernest Benn/W. W. Norton, 1984. A detailed guide to northern Italy.

You'll find maps at the back of this book which indicate the locations of all the restaurants reviewed here. When working out your itinerary, be sure to refer to them so you won't miss an important restaurant in a small town on your route.

Aside from these maps, you'll need a good detailed road map, whether you are traveling by car, train, or bus. The most efficient is the (red) Michelin map, available in most better bookstores. If you want serious detail with an exhaustive index, there is only one map set to own, the *Atlante stradale d'Italia,* published by the Touring Club Italiano. You'll want two of the three volumes: *Nord* (north: Emilia-Romagna, Liguria, Lombardy, Piedmont, Valle d'Aosta, the Veneto), and *Centro* (central: the Abruzzi, Lazio, The Marches, Tuscany, Umbria). A new collection of maps of Italy that's easier to handle than the large volumes of the TCI is the *Atlante stradale de Agostini.* Published by the Instituto Geografico de Agostini, it is quite popular with Italians and can be found in any good bookstore in Italy.

EATING

IN

ITALY

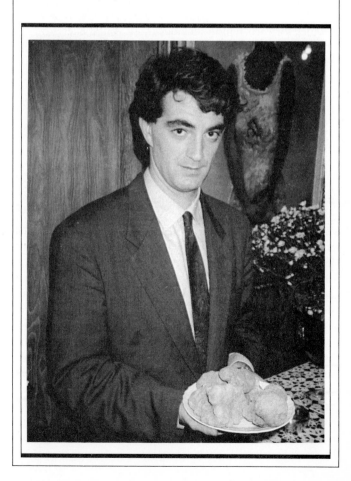

> Spaghetti can be eaten successfully if you inhale it like a vacuum
> cleaner . . . Everything you see I owe to spaghetti.
>
> —SOPHIA LOREN

What follows is basic information about eating in Italian restaurants: an explanation of restaurants and their menus, a list of seasonal foods, a section on regional food and wine specialties, and a basic wine vocabulary. I've provided these lists to convey the ever-changing richness of Italian cuisine and help the diner make the critical decisions about what to order, in part according to the time of year and the regional location. It should be kept in mind that what is called by one name in Tuscany, for instance, is more than likely called something different in Lombardy—and such differences in nomenclature can be the case even from town to town within the same region. The general list of wines for each region includes those you're likely to find on restaurant wine lists; many of these are described in the individual restaurant reviews. To locate descriptions of the various recommended wines, refer to the Index.

THE RESTAURANT
IL RISTORANTE

Traditionally, the categories *ristorante, trattoria, osteria,* and *taverna* addressed size more than anything else. *Ristorante* referred to an establishment that provided all the services expected of a restaurant; *trattoria* to a smaller, more informal restaurant; and *osteria* and *taverna* to local tavern-restaurant places. Today, however, the categories tend not only to overlap but even to lose entirely their traditional definitions, so that a very fancy restaurant might call itself an *osteria*—as does one of Italy's very best restaurants, Antica Osteria del Ponte, in Cassinetta di Lugagnano.

You'll also encounter the *pizzeria,* which serves pizza; the *rosticceria,* basically a take-out store for roasted meats and various other dishes, which sometimes also operates as a snack bar; the *tavola calda* ("hot table"), which serves quick lunch and snack items, both hot and cold, cafeteria style; the *latteria,* which sells cheese, milk, yogurt, pudding, and so on; and the *gelateria,* which serves ice cream, and sometimes cof-

fee and pastries—although you're sure to find the latter in a
bar or *pasticceria.*

Dining Hours/*Ore di Apertura*

Generally, Italians eat their meals later than Americans. Most
of the lunch crowd arrives between 1:00 and 2:00 P.M.; the
dinner crowd, between 8:30 and 10:00 P.M.

Breakfast—*Colazione* (sometimes *prima* or *piccola colazione*) 7:00 to 10:00 A.M.
Italians don't eat much in the morning. On their way
to work they might stop at a bar for coffee and a
brioche—the Italian equivalent of a croissant. Freshly
baked brioches are delivered every morning, so if you go
early you will find them still warm. If you order a *caffè*,
you'll be given *espresso;* if you prefer a less concentrated
coffee, something closer to American coffee, ask for *caffè
americano* (see page 28). Like all Italian coffees, it will
taste different from American coffee because the coffee
beans are roasted differently: it has a bite, and is more
aromatic and bitter than American coffee.

Lunch—*Pranzo* (sometimes *colazione*) 12:00 to 3:00
P.M.

Dinner—*Cena* 7:30 to 10:00 P.M.

Reservations/*Prenotazioni*

To avoid disappointment, it's worth taking a minute to make
a reservation, especially for dinner at well-known restaurants;
and it's a good idea to call ahead to reconfirm in the smaller
towns. The concierge of your hotel will happily make the call
for you.

Waiters/*Camerieri*

One of the numerous pleasures of eating in Italy is to find
that waiters here *are* waiters—and will continue to be waiters
until they kick back into retirement. As is not the case in the

U.S., there is a *class* of professional waiters in Italy; it's not uncommon to find waiters who have worked in the same restaurant for twenty or thirty years. If you frequent a particular restaurant over the years, it's more than reassuring to know a familiar face—a friend!—will be there to welcome you back no matter how long it's been since your last trip.

THE MENU
LA CARTA, IL MENÚ

Pane e coperto This is the cover charge added into the bill. It applies to your silverware, plates, glasses—and the bread that always attends the meal.

Acqua minerale Mineral water. Soon after you're seated the waiter will ask if you want *acqua minerale;* if you say yes, he'll want to know if you want it *gassata* or *non gassata,* which is to say, carbonated or not.

Antipasti Appetizers, hors d'oeuvres. Here you'll find *prosciutto,* fish salads, various dressed vegetables, artichokes, olives, and so on.

Minestre or primi piatti *Minestra* means "soup," but this category includes pastas, *gnocchi,* and *risotto* as well as soups, also called *zuppe.* You'll also find as first courses various pastas served in a broth, such as *tortellini in brodo.* Pastas are sometimes listed as *pasta asciutta* (or *pastasciutta*), which is dry pasta, or *farinacei.*

Uova Egg dishes, such as *frittate,* or omelettes, and *uova strapazzate con la salsiccia,* scrambled eggs with sausage.

Pesce Fish—from the Mediterranean and various lakes and rivers—typically grilled, *ai ferri,* or baked, *al forno.* Usually more expensive than meat.

Piatti del giorno or *secondi piatti* Dishes of the day, second courses. You'll generally find the main dishes of meat and poultry here. Sometimes they are listed under individual categories: *carne* for meats; *arrosti* for roasted meats; *bolliti* for boiled meats; and *ferri, griglia,* or *grigliate* for grilled meats and fish.

Piatti da farsi Dishes that are prepared to order and therefore take a longer time.

Piatti pronti Dishes that are ready to be served.

Piatti freddi Cold dishes.

Cacciagione or *selvaggina* Wild game: for example, *capriolo,* venison; *cinghiale,* wild boar; *coniglio,* rabbit; and various game birds: *beccaccia,* woodcock; *fagiano,* pheasant; *pernice,* partridge; *quaglia,* quail.

Contorni, legumi, or *verdure* Side dishes, namely vegetables. Salads are sometimes listed here as well, and sometimes as *insalate.*

Insalate Salads.

Formaggi Cheeses.

Frutta Fruit.

Dolci Desserts.

Gelati Ice creams.

Caffè Although Italians may not have quite as many ways of serving it as Eskimos have words for *snow,* they do take their coffee very seriously. The box on page 28 should serve as a guide for the uninitiated.

Tasting Menu/*Menú Degustazione*

In better restaurants the tasting menu is a well-thought-out grouping of dishes, designed to give you a sample of the chef's finest work. It's the best way to get a sense of what a particular restaurant is capable of producing. Not to be confused with the fixed-price (*prezzo fisso*) menu—and especially not the "tourist menu," which should be avoided whenever possible.

Bill and Tip/*Conto e Mancia*

The tip, anywhere from 12 to 20 percent, is almost always added into the bill; *servizio incluso* or *servizio compreso* indicates that service is included. The custom is to leave a little change as an additional tip; 5 percent is adequate if your service has been good. Be sure to keep a copy of your bill; Italian law requires you to have it on your person when you leave the restaurant.

COFFEE

espresso What you receive when you order *un caffè*—a small amount of dark, rich coffee served in a demitasse. *Doppio espresso* is a double *espresso*.

caffè americano or *caffè molto lungo* American-style coffee, served in an American-sized coffee cup.

caffè corretto An *espresso* "corrected" with a spot of rum, *grappa*, *sambuca*, brandy, or other liquor.

caffè freddo *Espresso* chilled and mixed with cold water in a glass.

caffè Hag This is the most often used brand of decaffeinated coffee in Italy. Caffè Hag can be used to make all the coffees listed here.

caffelatte *Espresso* with milk, served in a large cup at breakfast.

caffè lungo A weaker coffee, made with more water than a regular *espresso*. Served in a demitasse.

caffè macchiato An *espresso* "stained" with a little steamed milk.

caffè marocchino An *espresso* served with a little milk; darker than *caffelatte*, and served in a smaller cup.

caffè con panna An *espresso* with whipped cream.

caffè ristretto A stronger coffee made with less water than a regular *espresso*. Served in a demitasse. A *doppio ristretto* is a double *ristretto*.

cappuccino *Espresso* topped with frothy steamed milk, served in an American-sized coffee cup—so named because it's the color of the robes of Capuchin monks. *Con cacao* denotes a sprinkling of cocoa powder on top. This coffee is usually served at breakfast or as a pick-me-up during the morning or afternoon; it's not considered hip to order it after a meal.

A FEW ESSENTIAL WORDS FOR THE RESTAURANT

This brief, practical guide will assist you when you first arrive and find yourself confronted with a battery of gastronomical terms that will have direct impact on what finally arrives at your table. The words are grouped according to category. See "Seasonal Foods," "Regional Food and Wine Specialties," and the glossary in the back for more complete listings.

aceto   Vinegar.

bicchiere   Glass.

bottiglia   Bottle.

coltello   Knife.

cucchiaio   Spoon.

forchetta   Fork.

olio   Oil.

piatto   Plate.

pepe   Pepper.

sale   Salt.

sedia   Chair.

tavola   Table.

tazza   Cup.

tovaglia   Tablecloth.

tovagliolo   Napkin.

dal (al) carrello   From the food cart.

casalingo, fatto in casa   Homemade.

doppio   Double.

misto   Mixed, assorted—of salads, meats, and so on.

all'olio   With oil.

a piacere   As you like it.

a scelta   Of your choice.

di stagione   Of the season.

A GUIDE TO SEAFOOD IN ITALIAN

aragosta Spiny lobster (clawless), rock lobster, sea crayfish.

astice, astaco Lobster.

calamaretti Baby squid.

calamari Squid.

canestrelli Scallops. (But also a type of cookie.)

canocchie Mantis shrimp.

cannolicchi, cannelli Razor clams.

cappe Various shellfish.

cape lunghe, cappe longhe Razor clams.

cap(p)e sante, capesante Scallops.

cozze Mussels.

datteri di mare Date mussels, date shells.

gamberetti Shrimps.

gamberi di fiume Freshwater crayfish.

gamberi Prawns. Sometimes crayfish, sometimes shrimp. Singular is *gambero*.

gambero di mare Lobster.

gamberoni Giant shrimp.

granceola, grancevola, granseola Spider crab.

caldo Hot.

freddo Cold.

tiepido Tepid, slightly warm—served at about or just above room temperature.

arrosto Roasted.

bollito Boiled.

granchio   Shore crab.

granciporro   Crab.

*mazzancolle, gamberi imperiali, mazzancu-
ogni, sparnocchi, spannocchi*   Large prawns.

mitili   Mussels.

moleche   Soft-shelled crabs.

moscardino   Small octopus.

muscoli   Mussels.

peoci   Mussels.

polpo   Octopus.

poveracce   Small clams.

scampi   Scampi, Dublin Bay prawns. Despite the popular belief, scampi are crustaceans of the lobster family,
not large shrimps or prawns; also called Dublin Bay
prawns, langoustines, Norway lobsters, or salt-water
crayfish.

sepiole, seppiette   Small squid.

seppie   Cuttlefish.

seppioline   Small cuttlefish.

sparnocchi   Jumbo shrimp or prawns.

telline, arselle   Wedge-shelled clams.

totano   Flying squid.

vongole   Clams.

alla brace   Charcoal-grilled.

al carbone   Charcoal-grilled.

ai ferri   Grilled.

alla griglia, grigliato   Grilled.

lesso, lessato   Boiled.

allo spiedo   Roasted on a spit; skewered.

in umido Stewed.

al vapore Steamed.

cotto Cooked.

ben cotto Well-cooked.

crudo Raw or uncooked.

al dente "To the tooth"—cooked until *just* done, still firm.

alla diavola Usually referring to a method of cooking chicken: cut in half, flattened, and grilled over coals.

mezzo cotto Half cooked.

punto, cotto a puntino Medium.

al sangue Rare.

A NOTE ON *INSALATA*

You'll find many a dish on the Italian menu called *insalata*. This can mean a salad as we know it, with lettuce greens, *radicchio*, chicory, and so on. It can also refer to a dish composed of various ingredients, served at about room temperature (*tiepido*) as a first course; for example, *insalata di mare*, a seafood plate, or *insalata di pollo*, made of pieces of chicken, usually dressed with oil and other ingredients; sometimes lettuce is used as a base or garnish, sometimes not. A *macedonia* is a fruit salad.

arista   Loin of pork.

braciola   Cutlet, steak, or chop; slice of meat.

bracioletta   Chop, stuffed veal roll, lamb cutlet, or steak.

braciolina   Lamb cutlet, steak.

braciolone   Rolled slice of beef or veal, stuffed and braised.

costata   Cutlet, steak, rib, or chop.

costoletta, cotoletta   Lamb or pork chop, veal cutlet or scallop, beefsteak, and so on.

involtino   Thin slice of meat rolled around some kind of stuffing.

lombata, lombatina   Steak, loin chop.

medaglione   Medallion, thick slice of meat.

paillard   Veal or beef steak, pounded thin.

polpettone   Ground meat made into a loaf or sausage.

scaloppa, scallopina   Thin slice of meat.

sella   Saddle, as of rabbit.

trancia, trancio   Thick slice.

P.V., prezzo da vedere   Price to be seen.

S.G., secondo grandezza   According to size.

S.Q., secondo quantità   According to quantity.

S.S., secondo stagione   According to season.

UCCELLETTI:
BIRDS AND ITALIANS

Of particular note in Italian cuisine is the relationship between skewered veal and birds—what Spike and Charmian Hughes call "the veal-bird obsession." For example, you'll find such dishes as *quagliette di vitello*, "little quails of veal"; *uccelli scappati*, literally "escaped birds," which is really a dish of skewered pieces of meat; and *tordi matti*, which again are pieces of skewered veal and not "mad thrushes." And throughout Italy you'll run into dishes described as *all 'uccelletto*, "cooked like little birds," on skewers as in *spiedini all 'uccelletto*, skewered veal with bacon and sage. Also *fagioli all 'uccelletto*, white beans stewed with oil and tomatoes, and *vitello all 'uccelletto*, veal cooked with white wine and herbs. Basically, Italians love birds—on the wing and on the plate.

SEASONAL FOODS

As in any country that takes its cuisine seriously, Italy's menus are composed to highlight what each season can offer to the table. To eat well anywhere, it's more than useful to know what ingredients have arrived at *their* time: there's no sense in ordering asparagus, for example, in October, when you should be looking to begin your meal with a little squid or the wonders of simply grilled fresh *porcini* mushrooms, and proceed to a preparation of fresh game. The following lists indicate what you might expect to find in Italian restaurants at various times of the year.

Winter—*Inverno*

arancie, aranci   Oranges.

bagna cauda (caôda)   A hot dipping sauce for vegetables, especially cardoons, made with oil, butter, anchovies, garlic, and in season, white truffles (Piedmont).

bianchetti, gianchetti, schiuma di mare   A specialty of Liguria: newly hatched (neary fetal) red mullet, sardines, or anchovies, which appear on menus in February and March. They are so small and young that they look more like interconnected pieces of shredded fish without skin than like fish; they are boiled for a fast second and served with a little lemon and oil.

broccoletti di rape   Turnip tops.

castagne   Chestnuts.

cavolfiore   Cauliflower.

fagioli   Beans.

finocchio   Fennel.

lenticchie   Lentils.

mandaranci   Clementines.

mandarini   Tangerines, mandarins.

olive   Olives.

piccione   Pigeon.

pompelmo   Grapefruit.

radicchio   A slightly bitter red chicory that comes in four varieties: *radicchio di Treviso* (*spadone*) has long thin red and white leaves and is the tastiest; *radicchio di Verona* is round like a head of lettuce; and *radicchio di Chioggia* and *Castelfranco* are leafier than the others, with green as well as red leaves. People from Treviso recognize only their own *radicchio* as the real thing; according to Waverley Root, the locals term their variety *un fiore che si mangia*, "a flower that is eaten."

tartufi bianchi   White truffles, available from October till about mid-January.

Christmas—*Natale*

Every region in Italy has its own gastronomical ways of celebrating this holiday—based on history, location, and tradition. I've listed a few of the more obvious and delicious dishes, but understand that the "complete" list—as if there could ever be general agreement as to *what* is complete with regard to the Italian *cucina*—is a long one.

capitoni   Large eels. On Christmas Eve, these are prepared with oil, wine, garlic, and herbs (Lazio).

mazzafegato   A spicy pork liver sausage, usually made with pine nuts and raisins (The Marches, Umbria).

TRUFFLES

The white truffle (*tartufo bianco; tuber magnatum*) is a fungus that grows half a foot or more under the surface of the ground, taking sustenance from the root systems of various trees, including chestnut, walnut, hazelnut, willow, poplar, and most important, oak: it's believed that hardwood trees produce the most pungent truffles. White truffles are found in all their glory in Piedmont, although they're also found in Tuscany, Umbria, and Emilia-Romagna. They're gathered at night, when their smell is strongest, by dogs specially trained at the "dog university" in the town of Roddi, near Alba. Certainly the white truffle is one of the most famous and beloved foodstuffs in Italy. The classic *tartufo bianco* is harvested around Alba, in Piedmont—thus its regional appellation, *trifola d'Alba*. White truffles are in season from the beginning of October to the middle of January (December truffles are considered the best).

"Gray" or "summer" truffles may be found throughout the year. They are called by different names in different places—*martzoli, martsoli, marzaili; bianchetti; grigi d'Alba;* and *crostoni di Monferrato*. These truffles are sometimes mistakenly and confusingly referred to as "black truffles" (*tartufi neri*), truffles altogether different from the white or gray. The true black truffle is found in Umbria, specifically near Norcia and Spoleto. The gray truffle is clearly related to the white truffle, which bears no resemblance at all to their nearly tasteless black relative. I should stress that although gray truffles are similar to white truffles—they possess the same unmistakable and inimitable aroma—they do not have the amazing intensity, depth, and power, a scent that has an almost benzene headiness, of the great white Piedmont truffle.

At any time of the year, the Piedmontese can find an excuse to shave a few truffle slices or more onto just about anything, from pasta to *risotto* to sautéed turkey breast to their famous *fonduta*, made with *fontina* cheese, eggs, milk, and butter. You'll pay dearly for this white gold—about 3 million lire per kilogram (2.2 pounds) for truffles in high season, which comes in at about $1,000 per pound.

pandoro   A high cake, similar to *panettone,* but made with a slightly heavier dough. The cake itself is plain inside and is covered with a sprinkling of powdered sugar (Veneto).

panettone   A dome-shaped bread-cake made with raisins and candied fruit (Lombardy).

panforte   "Strong bread"; actually, a very tasty cake made with almonds, walnuts, honey, preserved fruit, and spices (Siena, Tuscany).

spongata   A pie filled with various nuts, candied fruits, raisins, nutmeg, wine, and honey (Emilia-Romagna).

torrone   Hard white nougat candy with almonds or hazelnuts (Piedmont, Lombardy).

Spring—*Primavera*

agnello   Baby lamb.

asparagi   Asparagus.

carciofi   Artichokes.

castraure   Baby eggplants.

cee, cie, cieche   Newborn elvers (eels).

chiacchiere   Sweets made of thin layers of flaky dough shaped into twisted bows that are fried in oil, cooled, and covered with powdered sugar. They are found only around the time of Carnevale, or Carnival, which ends on *martedì grasso,* the day before Ash Wednesday (Lombardy).

ciliege   Cherries.

fave   Broad beans.

fragoline di bosco   Wild strawberries.

piselli   Peas.

risi e bisi   The well-known rice and pea soup, consumed with plenty of Parmesan.

le virtù   The famous *minestrone* from the Abruzzi.

Easter—*Pasqua*

frittelle di riso, frittelle di San Giuseppe alla toscana   Little rice fritters with pine nuts and lemon, traditionally made for Palm Sunday (Tuscany).

OLIVE OIL

An Italian gentleman never eats salad when travelling in foreign countries, for his palate, used to the finest oil, revolts against the liquid fit only for the lubrication of machinery he so often is offered in Germany, England and France.

—COLONEL NEWNHAM DAVIS

Virgin Olive Oils—*Oli d'Oliva Vergini*

Naturally, no one in Italy agrees on which region produces the finest olive oil. There is, however, some accord that the three regions at the top of the list are Liguria, Tuscany, and Umbria (that order is mine). The virgin olive oils listed below, made from the first pressing (*olio di prima spremitura*), contain the lowest acidity and are probably the only oils you'll find in the restaurants reviewed in this book. In order to qualify as virgin, an oil must satisfy a number of requirements, which include:

1. The oil must be obtained through only mechanical or physical processes.
2. The oil must be processed at temperatures that do not cause its alteration.
3. The only treatments allowed are cleaning, decanting, centrifuging, and filtering.

Oils that employ solvents, that are mixed with other oils, or that have been "esterified" (in a process that adds fragrance to the oil) are excluded from this category.

Grades of Virgin Olive Oil

Olio d'oliva extra vergine Extra virgin olive oil. Its acidity can't exceed 1 gram of oleic acid per 100 grams of oil—or 1 percent. This is 100 percent olive oil, and the very best available.

Olio d'oliva sopraffino vergine Superfine virgin olive oil with up to 1.5 percent acidity.

Olio d'oliva fino vergine Fine virgin olive oil. The acidity of this class must not exceed 2 percent.

Olio d'oliva corrente vergine Common virgin olive oil. Up to 3.3 percent acidity is allowed.

Olio d'oliva vergine lampànte "Clear" virgin
olive oil that is not as pure as the other oils in this
category; its acidity is greater than 3.3 percent.

Non-Virgin Olive Oils

The oils listed below may be acceptable, but you're not
likely to encounter them in serious Italian restaurants.

Olio d'oliva raffinato Refined olive oil, obtained
by refining virgin olive oils.

Olio d'oliva Olive oil obtained by blending refined
olive oil and virgin olive oils other than clear oil.

Olio di sansa d'oliva greggio Crude oil of olive
husks, obtained through treatment with solvents of olive husks.

Olio di sansa d'oliva raffinato Refined oil of
live husks, obtained through the refining of crude oil
from olive husks.

Olio di sansa d'oliva Oil of olive husks obtained
through the blending of oil of refined olive husks and
virgin oils other than clear oil.

Types of Olives

Carboncello	Frantoio	Moraiolo	Rosciola
Casaliva	Gentile	Pendolino	Sargano
Dritta	Leccino	Raggiolo	Taggiasca

My Ten Favorite Olive Oils

1. Ardoino (Liguria)
2. Marvaldi (Liguria)
3. Pallanca (Liguria)
4. Mancianti (Umbria)
5. Lungarotti (Umbria)
6. Brisighello (Emilia-Romagna)
7. Badia a Coltibuono (Tuscany)
8. Castellare (Tuscany)
9. Castello di Volpaia (Tuscany)
10. Incisa della Rocchetta (Tuscany)

colomba pasquale A dove-shaped cake studded with almonds, preserved fruits, and raisins (Emilia-Romagna, Lombardy).

torta pasqualina A pie filled with a mixture of artichokes, possibly chard, eggs, milk, and ricotta; traditionally made with thirty-three ultrathin layers of dough for each of the crusts (Liguria).

torta sbrisolana A "crumbly" almond cake-cookie (Lombardy).

Summer—*Estate*

albicocche Apricots.

fagiolini String beans.

fichi Figs.

fragole Strawberries.

lamponi Raspberries.

melanzane Eggplants.

melone Melon, cantaloupe.

nespole Loquats.

peperoni Bell peppers.

pesche Peaches.

pomodori Tomatoes.

prugne, susine Plums.

zucchine, zucchini Zucchini.

Fall—*Autunno*

cacciagione, selvaggina Wild game: boar, rabbit, pheasant, partridge, and so on.

cachi Persimmons.

calamari Squid (late fall).

funghi Mushrooms: *porcini* (*cèpes, boletus*); *ovoli* (imperial agaric); *spugnoli* (morels); *galletti, gallinacci, giallini, cantarelli, finferle* (chanterelles); *prataioli* (field mushrooms).

mele Apples.

melagrane Pomegranates.

pane dei morti "Bread of the dead": a large oval cookie, made with ground nuts and crushed fruit. This sweet is found around All Saints' Day, the day of the dead, celebrated on November 1; on this day Italians visit the graves of their loved ones.

pere Pears.

schie Baby shrimp, a specialty of Venice, available from October to January.

uva Grapes: *bianca* (green), *nera* (red).

REGIONAL FOOD AND WINE SPECIALTIES

As mentioned earlier, one of the notable qualities about eating in Italy is the changeability of the menu, according to the time of year—what's *in season*—and the climate and geographical location. Regionalism, although not as fiercely delineated as it was perhaps fifty years ago, still very much characterizes the cuisine of Italy. The problem with providing even a selective list of regional specialties is in getting Italians to agree on what is of their region and what isn't—in other words, what the specialties of a given region *are*. The number of dishes that could be listed given time and space is vast; to see in what way this is true, treat yourself to a copy of Waverley Root's definitive (if now slightly dated) *The Food of Italy*, which remains the bible for English readers of Italian cuisine.

In this section I've included the dishes you're most likely to find on the menus of the restaurants reviewed later in the book. These regional lists are in no way meant to be exhaustive; they should simply give you a sense of what to expect in a particular part of the country.

The ancient Greeks called Italy Enotria, "Land of Wine," and wine has remained one of Italy's most important commodities. Many of the wines I've listed for each region have been described under individual restaurants. To find the description of a wine, refer to the Index at the back of the book. Note the information on DOC and DOCG wines (page 91). Unclassified table wine, or *vino da tavola*, doesn't qualify for these two categories; producers of such wine don't subscribe

subscribe to DOC/DOCG regulations, or their vineyards are beyond a prescribed winegrowing area. *Vini da tavola* can also be excellent—in fact, many of the best Italian wines are not DOC or DOCG. As my primary reference, I have used the revised *Simon and Schuster Pocket Guide to Italian Wines* by Burton Anderson, which is the single best quick-reference work on Italian wines and a must for anyone traveling in Italy with an interest in consuming this beverage.

Abruzzi

Cities and Towns

L'Aquila   Chieti   Pescara   Teramo

agnello alla diavola Lamb cooked with hot chili peppers (*peperoncini*) and wine.

cacioricotta A sheep's-milk junket, blended with coffee and lemon.

escabecio, scapece Fried fish marinated in vinegar, olive oil, garlic, and saffron. Called *scabecio* in Liguria.

fiadone A tart filled with layers of eggs, ricotta, sugar, cinnamon, and lemon.

maccheroni alla chitarra A thin square noodle cut into this shape with a *chitarra,* an implement with strings like a guitar's. Typically served with a lamb and/or tomato sauce.

'ndocca 'ndocca A powerful stew made of pork parts such as the feet, ears, snout, skin, and chops, cooked with bay leaves, garlic, vinegar, pimientos, rosemary, and tomatoes.

panarda Legendary Abruzzi feast, at which more than twenty—the number can run to sixty!—dishes might be offered and consumed.

parrozzo An almond cake covered with chocolate.

peperoncino Hot red pepper, ubiquitous in Abruzzese cuisine.

pincisgrassi Sheets of pasta layered with various ingredients, including sausage, chicken livers, onions, sweetbreads, truffles, ham, butter, and cream, then baked with grated cheese over the top. In The Marches this is called *vincisgrassi;* we'd probably call it busy lasagne.

polpo in purgatorio Octopus "in purgatory," stewed in a tomato sauce spiced with hot red peppers and garlic.

rosticcini Skewered lamb or pork grilled over coals; sold in street stands.

scripelle 'mbusse Pancakes layered with cheese and ham, traditionally served with chicken broth.

stracci, fregnacce Baked pancakes served with meat, vegetables, cheese, and sometimes a béchamel sauce.

timballo all'abruzzese Sheets of pasta layered with meatballs, chicken livers, *scamorza* cheese, and tomato sauce and then baked.

ventricina A well-spiced pork sausage.

le virtù The famous *minestrone* from Teramo, made with pork, *fava* beans, peas, and various other fresh vegetables; traditionally made with seven ingredients in seven pots and cooked for seven hours—or seven days, depending on who's passing the recipe along. (See page 44.)

zeppole Sweet fritters, made sometimes with cinnamon, sometimes with chestnuts and chocolate.

CHEESES

pecorino abruzzese A hard, dry cheese made from sheep's milk. Sharp, and used here in place of Parmesan.

scamorza A soft pear-shaped cheese not unlike mozzarella, often grilled (*scamorza ai ferri*).

WINES

The Abruzzi has two wine zones, Montepulciano d'Abruzzo and Trebbiano d'Abruzzo. The wines are simple and rustic, reflecting the nature of the Abruzzi—a rough, mountainous landscape placed between the Apennines and the Adriatic, which offers the wine grower a variety of microclimates. The best wines from this region can be very appealing, hearty and direct.

LE VIRTÙ
OF THE ABRUZZI

Le virtù ("the virtues") appears in the month of May, since that is the season when the fresh young vegetables providing one of its series of ingredients become available. These must include fava beans and peas, but you can add any other spring vegetable that may be available; they are boiled along with dried beans, lentils, and chick peas in pot number one. In pot number two, you boil together endives, leeks, young beet leaves, celery and fennel. In pot number three, you boil ham, cut into substantial chunks, and pig's crackling, ears and feet. In pot number four (which is a pan), you fry bacon with parsley, fresh onions and fresh garlic. In pot number five, you cook some factory-made pasta (macaroni, spaghetti or any other kind) and some homemade egg pasta. In pot number six (a saucepan), you fry meatballs.

You now have six pots and pans bubbling, steaming and sizzling on the stove, and things are about to get complicated.* Take pot (pan) number four (bacon, etc.), pour its contents into pot number one, and add salt, marjoram and mint. Take the pig's feet out of pot number three, bone them, return them to their pot, and then add its contents to pot number one. After a decent interval, empty the greens from pot number two into pot number one, add tomato, and let everything stew together for a while in what is becoming a pretty crowded vessel. Now empty pot number five, whose pasta you have timed to be still a little undercooked at this juncture, into pot number one. You still have pot (pan) number six waiting with its meatballs. They go in last. And serve.

—WAVERLEY ROOT

*It's not clear why Mr. Root used six pots instead of the traditional seven and didn't prescribe the seven hours (or days!) of cooking required. It's seven, for the total seven cardinal and theological virtues.

Spinello   *Cerasuolo d'Abruzzo (rosé)*
Trebbiano d'Abruzzo

The Reds

Montepulciano d'Abruzzo   *Rustico*
Rubino

The Grapes

WHITE   *Moscato Bianco, Trebbiano*
RED   *Montepulciano, Sangiovese*

Reliable Producers

Casal Thaulero, Barone Cornacchio, Dino Illuminati, Camillo Montori, Emidio Pepe, Edoardo Valentini

---

Emilia-Romagna

Cities and Towns

Alseno (Cortina Vecchia)   Argenta   Bologna   Brisighella
Caorso   Castrocaro Terme   Cavriago   Chianciano Terme
Faenza   Ferrara   Forlì   Imola   Modena   Nonantola
Parma   Piacenza   Ravenna   Reggio nell'Emilia
Rimini   Rubiera   Scandiano   Tossignano
Trebbo di Reno

anatra (anitra) in creta   Duck baked in clay.

anolini   Small *ravioli*-like pasta stuffed with meat.

bensone   Lemon cake.

bollito misto   Mixed boiled meats, served with *salsa verde,* a green sauce, and *mostarda,* a mustard sauce with preserved fruits suspended in it.

alla bolognese   In the style of Bologna; with *ragù,* a hearty meat sauce.

> The *zampone* came, I have eaten it up.
> The Lambrusco came, I have just drained the cup.
> Of Rossini was worthy the exquisite first,
> While the second was fit to quench Homer's gods' thirst.
>
> —PAOLO FERRARI
> (attributed to Gioacchino Rossini)

bomba di riso A baked rice and pigeon dish.

brodetto A variety of fish soup, typically made with fish from the Adriatic.

budino di pollo in brodo A soup of puréed chicken, eggs, and cheese.

burlenghi Pastry fritters prepared with bacon, rosemary, garlic, and cheese.

canestrelli di pollo Chicken fillets stuffed with smoked ham and onion.

cappellacci di zucca Little *ravioli* stuffed with pumpkin and cheese.

capretto alla piacentina Kid (young goat) stewed in white wine.

chizze Squares of bread dough fried and served with butter and cheese.

coppa (capocollo) Salt-cured pork sausage.

cotechino A large boiled pork sausage. Traditionally served with lentils at New Year's.

culatello The rump, or "heart," as the Italians say, of *prosciutto*.

erbazzone, scarpazzone A baked cheese and spinach tart.

garganelli Ridged, quill-shaped pasta tubes.

lasagne al forno Lasagne baked with meat and béchamel sauces.

lumache alla bobbiese Snails stewed with vegetables and white wine.

mortadella   The well-known large smooth pork sausage from Bologna, laced with pieces of fat and peppercorns. The father of what we call bologna.

padellete   Pork ribs baked with white beans.

alla parmigiana   In the style of Parma; with Parmesan cheese.

piadina (romagnola)   A flat, pitalike bread from Romagna, also known as *pie,* usually served with cheese and ham.

pisarei e fasö   Little bread dumplings served with a tomato and bean sauce.

prosciutto   Salt-cured ham, especially good from Langhirano and Parma.

salame da sugo   Sausage made of various pork cuts, spices, and wine; served warm with mashed potatoes.

spalla di San Secondo   Cured shoulder of pork.

spongata   A pie filled with various nuts and candied fruits, honey, and raisins.

tagliatelle, taitadei   Long flat strips of pasta slightly wider than *fettuccine.*

tigelle   Rounds of deep-fried bread served with bacon and herbs.

torta di tagliatelle   A crunchy cake made with thin noodles, nuts, and candied fruit.

tortelli all'erbetta   *Ravioli*-like pasta stuffed with ricotta and *erbetta,* a green similar to Swiss chard.

tortelli di zucca   Large *ravioli*-like pasta stuffed with puréed pumpkin, preserved fruit (*mostarda*), crumbled *amaretti,* nutmeg. Served with a little butter and Parmesan.

tortellini   Small rings of pasta, usually stuffed with meat—ham, chicken, pork, sausage.

zampone   A rich fresh pork sausage placed in a pig's foot and boiled, and served with lentils or mashed potatoes; from Modena.

zuppa inglese   A dessert consisting of sponge cake soaked in liqueur, and cut into layers with custard between.

CHEESES

crescenza   Similar to *stracchino* but slightly milder.

grana   Similar to Parmesan.

grana padano   *Grana* from the Po Valley.

mascarpone   A rich, thick creamy cheese, softer and much sweeter than our cream cheese.

parmigiano-reggiano   Parmesan cheese made within a prescribed region and aged for at least eighteen months. *Tenero* refers to the fresh, unripened cheese. When the cheese is two years old it's called *vecchio;* after three years it's *stravecchio,* and after four, *stravecchione.* Each maker is given a number, which is stamped on every wheel of cheese. The lower the number, the closer that producer is to the center of the original production area.

pecorino   A pungent sheep's-milk cheese, sharp when aged, gentler when fresh.

puina   The local name for ewe's-milk ricotta.

stracchino   A soft, full, slightly bitter cheese.

WINES

Emilia-Romagna is the largest wine-producing region in Italy, with Lambrusco its mainstay. This is really two regions, each quite distinct from the other—Emilia to the west, Romagna to the east, Bologna the fulcrum. Lambrusco hails from Emilia, and in its dry DOC incarnation can be a decidedly pleasing drink and must be sampled while you're in the region; in spite of its local reputation, it may take some getting used to (the best is Lambrusco di Sorbara). Romagna is known for its Sangiovese di Romagna, Trebbiano, and Albana di Romagna; in fact, Albana was the most recent addition to the ranks of DOCG—only the sixth member of that elite group, and the first white to achieve this distinction. Also very fine are the wines from the Colli Bolognesi, and anything from Terre Rosse (Vallania) has something to recommend it.

The Spumanti

Bruno Negroni Brut, Negroni
Tarsallo

Trabense, Valentino
Migliorini

The Whites

Albana di Romagna (Italy's
  only DOCG white wine)

Chardonnay

Malvasia, Colli di Parma

Monterosso Val d'Arda

Pagadebit (also sweet)

Pinot Bianco, Colli Bolognesi

Pinot Grigio, Colli Piacentini

Riesling Italico, Colli
  Bolognesi

Ronco del Re

Sauvignon, Colli Bolognesi

Trebbiano di Romagna

The Reds

Barbarossa di Bertinoro

Barbera, Colli Bolognesi

Boldo

Bonarda

Cabernet Sauvignon, Colli
  Bolognesi

Favagello

Gutturnio dei Colli
  Piacentini

Lambrusco Grasparossa di
  Castelvetro

Lambrusco Reggiano

Lambrusco Salamino di
  Santa Croce

Lambrusco di Sorbara

Merlot, Colli Bolognesi

Ronco Casone

Ronco dei Ciliegi

Ronco delle Ginestre

Rosso Armentano

Rosso di Rivergaro

Rosso di Vignazzo

Sangiovese di Romagna

The Grapes

WHITE   Albana, Chardonnay, Malvasia, Moscato, Ortrugo,
Pagadebit, Pinot Grigio, Riesling Italico, Sauvignon,
Trebbiano

RED   Barbera, Bonarda, Cabernet Sauvignon, Lambrusco,
Merlot, Sangiovese

Reliable Producers

Gian Matteo Baldi (Casteluccio), Cavicchioli, Chiarli, Contessa
Matilder, Fratelli Conti, Corovin, Fattoria Paradiso,
Ferrucci, Giacobazzi, Valentino Migliorini, Bruno Negroni,
Pusterla, Riunite, Romagnoli, Spalletti, La Stoppa, Tenuta
Zerbina, Terre Rosse (Vallania), Tre Monti, Fratelli
Vallunga, Ziano

Lazio/Latium

Cities and Towns

Frosinone   Latina   Rieti   Rome   Velletri   Viterbo

abbacchio   Milk-fed baby lamb, cooked with wine, garlic, vinegar, anchovies, and rosemary.

brodettato   A lamb stew with a sauce of lemon and egg yolks.

carciofi alla giudia   Artichokes that are first flattened, then fried in oil until brown and crisp. A Jewish specialty.

carciofi alla romana   Artichokes cooked with olive oil and mint.

ciriole alla fiumarola   Tiny eels cooked with white wine, garlic, anchovies, and capers.

coda alla vaccinara   Oxtail prepared with wine, celery, tomatoes, onions, pine nuts, and sultanas.

fagioli con le cotiche   Beans cooked for many hours with pieces of pork skin.

fave al guanciale (alla romana)   Broad beans cooked with pork cheek.

filetti di baccalà alla romana   Fillets of dried salt cod dipped in batter and fried in oil. Sometimes cooked with tomatoes, pine nuts, and raisins.

maccheroni alla ciociara   Pasta tubes cooked with ham and sausage.

mazzancolle   Large prawns.

penne all'arrabbiata   Quill-shaped pasta with a fiery ("rabid") sauce made with tomatoes and hot red peppers.

pinzimonio   Olive oil spiked with salt and pepper, used as a dip for raw vegetables.

pollo alla diavola   Chicken that has been cut in half, flattened, and grilled.

puntarelle   A chicorylike green used in salads. Often dressed with oil, vinegar, and mashed anchovies.

saltimbocca   Thin slices of veal layered with *prosciutto* and fresh sage, sautéed in butter and wine.

spaghetti all'amatriciana   Spaghetti made with bacon, tomatoes, onions, and hot pepper.

spaghetti alla carbonara   Spaghetti made with bacon, onions, and raw eggs.

spaghetti alla carrettiera   Spaghetti "cart drivers' style," prepared with tuna and mushrooms.

stracciatella   A light soup made with chicken stock, Parmesan cheese, and "rags" of beaten eggs and semolina. (Also Italian for "chocolate chip ice cream.")

supplì al telefono   Rice balls stuffed with mozzarella and ham, and fried in oil. It's the strands of melted cheese—"telephone wires"—that give this dish its name.

testarella d'agnello   A lamb's head, roasted with rosemary.

trippa alla romana   Tripe cooked with a meat sauce, mint, and *pecorino* cheese.

C H E E S E S

mozzarella di bufala   Mozzarella made with buffalo's milk.

pecorino romano   A Parmesan-type cheese made from sheep's milk, sometimes called simply *romano*.

provatura   A cheese similar to mozzarella, mild.

W I N E S

Although they are not all that well-known outside Italy, there are some wonderful discoveries to be made among the wines of Lazio. Some of the best come from the area known as Castelli Romani, "Roman Castles."

The Whites

Colle Picchioni	*Falerno*	*Trebbiano (Aprilia)*
Colli Albani	*Fiorano Bianco*	*Velletri Bianco*
Colli Lanuvini	*Frascati Superiore*	*Aleatico di Gradoli*
Est! Est!! Est!!!	*Marino*	*(sweet)*

The Reds

Cesanese di Affile
Cesanese di Olevano Romano
Cesanese del Piglio
Colle Picchioni
Falerno

Fiorano Rosso
Merlot (Aprilia)
Sangiovese (Aprilia)
Torre Ercolana
Velletri Rosso

The Grapes

WHITE *Malvasi, Trebbiano*

RED *Aleatico, Cabernet Sauvignon, Cesanese, Merlot, Montepulciano, Sangiovese*

Reliable Producers

Boncompagni Ludovisi, Cantina Colacicchi, Cantine G. Mazziotti, Casale del Giglio, Consorzio Produttori Vini Velletri, Paola Di Mauro, Fontana Candida (Vigneti Santa Teresa), Villa Simone

Liguria

Cities and Towns

Ameglia   Chiavari   Cinque Terre   Genoa   Imperia
La Spezia   Leivi   Lerici   Rapallo   Recco
San Remo   Savona

bagioi Snails served with a tomato and mint sauce.

bianchetti, gianchetti, schiuma di mare Newly hatched (nearly fetal) red mullets, sardines, or anchovies, so small and young they look more like interconnected pieces of shredded fish without skin than fish. Prepared by boiling for a fast second, and served with a little lemon and oil; found in restaurants in February and March.

buddego A variety of fish stew.

buridda A fish stew made with salt cod, tomatoes, anchovies, and dried mushrooms.

cappon magro   This cold dish is literally a pyramid of various fish, shellfish, and vegetables, topped with a sauce of garlic, anchovies, and oil. Typical at New Year's.

castagnaccio   A flat cake made with unleavened chestnut flour, and various herbs, raisins, and pine nuts.

cima   Cold breast of veal rolled around various ingredients including chopped veal, brains, sweetbreads, eggs, cheese, peas, and herbs.

ciuppin   A fish stew served on slices of bread.

condiggion   Mixed salad served on bread.

corzetti   Pasta in the shape of a figure eight.

cozze pelose   Mussels whose shells are covered with "hair."

datteri di mare stufati alla ligure   Date mussels braised with tomatoes, parsley, and garlic.

farinata   Fried or baked crepes made with chickpea flour; served as a snack.

focaccia   Flat bread often made with sage. Also made with various toppings or fillings—onions, cheese, tomatoes.

lumache alla genovese   Snails sautéed in olive oil with a little lemon, and sometimes other ingredients: basil, anchovies, white wine.

macchettaia   A type of pizza.

mesciua   A soup that employs the unusual combination of chickpeas, beans, and wheat.

minestrone alla genovese (condito col pesto)   A very hearty soup with a generous dollop of famous Genovese *pesto* added when served.

mitili   Mussels. Sometimes called *muscoli*.

paniccia, panissa   A *polenta* of sorts, made with chickpea flour and onions, first boiled, then baked or fried until crisp, and served with grated cheese. Similar to *farinata*.

pansôti   Ravioli-like pasta stuffed with ricotta, spinach, chard, and sometimes brains and/or sweetbreads, usually served with a creamy walnut sauce (*salsa di noci*).

pesto   Genoa's claim to fame: the inimitable green sauce made of basil, garlic, *pecorino* and/or Parmesan cheese, pine nuts (sometimes walnuts), and olive oil.

ravioli Pasta envelopes stuffed with meat or cheese. This famous pasta is said to have originated in Genoa.

ravioli di magro "Thin" or "lean" *ravioli*, stuffed with something other than meat—spinach and ricotta, for example.

riso arrosto alla genovese Rice baked with sausage, various vegetables, including artichokes and peas, and Parmesan cheese.

sardenaira, pissaladeira Flatbread, usually covered with onions, tomatoes, black olives, herbs, garlic, and anchovies.

scabecio Fried fish, marinated and served at room temperature. Called *scapece* or *escabecio* in the Abruzzi, *saor* in the Veneto.

tocco, tuccu A pasta sauce, usually made with meat or mushrooms.

tomaxelle Veal rolls stuffed with minced veal, eggs, mushrooms, pine nuts, garlic, and herbs, and braised in wine.

torta pasqualina A traditional Easter pie made with artichokes and possibly chard, eggs, and ricotta. The classic version would have thirty-three ultrathin layers of dough, for the thirty-three years of Jesus' life.

trenette Narrow pasta strips, often served with potatoes, string beans, and *pesto*.

troffie al pesto Small twists of pasta with a *pesto* sauce.

vitello all'uccelletto Pieces of veal sautéed in wine and herbs.

in zimino Cooked in a casserole with various vegetables, usually spinach, and herbs.

CHEESES

formaggella A soft fresh white cheese.

pecorino A sheep's-milk cheese that is either soft and mild, or dry, sharp, and salty, used for grating. *Pecorino fiore sardo* is one sturdy version.

This region, beautifully located on the Riviera, curled along the sea, with the added scenery of the Ligurian Apennines and Maritime Alps, is not known as good wine country—in fact, only the Valle d'Aosta produces less wine. Nevertheless, there are some wines to look for when dining in Genoa or other Ligurian towns. Most of these wines come from the mysterious area between Genoa and La Spezia called Cinque Terre ("Five Lands"). Some very fine wine is now produced in the Riviera Ligure di Ponente DOC wine zone (west of Genoa) and around the town of Dolceacqua, where Rossese di Dolceacqua, a fine red in a region noted for its whites, is produced. There are many local wines that are worth trying. Burton Anderson guides us: "Local wines to look for are Coronata and Polcevera on the outskirts of Genoa; the whites and reds of Piematone (near Bordighera); and the red Granaccia of Quiliano near Savona."

The Whites

Buzzetto di Quiliano

Cinqueterre

Coronata

Lumassina

Pigato di Albenga

Polcevera

Verici

Vermentino

Cinqueterre Sciacchetrà
(sweet; rare)

Rosa di Albenga (rosé)

The Reds

Barbarossa

Dolceacqua (Rossese di
Dolceacqua)

Granaccia di Quiliano

Ormeasco (Dolcetto)

Rossese

Terizzo

The Grapes

WHITE   Albarola, Bosco, Buzzetto, Lumassina, Pigato, Vermentino (Malvasia)

RED   Barbarossa, Cabernet Sauvignon, Dolcetto, Granaccia, Rossese, Sangiovese

Reliable Producers

Anfossi, Cascina Fèipu dei Massaretti, La Colombiera, Cooperativa Agricoltura di Cinqueterre, Emilio Croesi, Bruna Donato Francesco, Enzo Guglielmi, Michele Guglielmi, Liana Rolandi, Scarrone

Lombardy/Lombardia

Cities and Towns

Bergamo   Brescia   Canneto sull'Oglio   Cassinetta di Lugagnano (Abbiategrasso)   Certosa di Pavia   Chiavenna   Como   Cozzo Lomellina   Crema   Cremona   Gardone Riviera   Goito   Iseo   Lugana di Sirmione   Maleo   Malgrate   Mantua   Milan   Pavia   Quistello   Ranco   Sondrio   Trescore Cremaseo   Varese   Villa Poma

agnoli, agnolini   Ravioli-like pasta stuffed with a variety of items, including chicken, bacon, chicken liver, cheese, eggs, and different spices, and generally served in a chicken broth.

agone   A flat, freshwater lake fish related to shad, cooked in butter with sage.

asparagi alla milanese   Asparagus served with Parmesan, butter, and fried eggs.

bresaola   Air-cured beef cut in thin slices, like *prosciutto*, sometimes served with a little lemon and olive oil.

busecca   A richly flavored tripe soup—an important part of the Milanese cuisine. In fact, the Milanese are sometimes called *busecconi*, "tripe eaters."

busecchina   A dessert made with boiled chestnuts, wine, and cream.

casoncelli, casonsei   Ravioli-like pasta stuffed with, among other things, sausage, spinach, and cheese.

cassoeula   A stew prepared with different cuts of pork, cabbage and other vegetables, herbs, and white wine. Usually accompanied by *polenta*.

ceci con la tempia di maiale   A soup made with chickpeas and pieces of pork head.

colomba pasquale A dove-shaped cake studded with almonds, candied or dried fruits, including raisins, eaten in celebration of Easter. *Colomba* means "dove."

costoletta alla milanese A veal loin chop dipped in egg and bread crumbs, fried in butter, and served on the bone. A classic Milanese dish.

foiolo alla milanese Tripe stewed with garlic, onions, and white wine, and served with Parmesan.

lenticchie e cotechino Lentils and *cotechino,* a rich, pork sausage, boiled and sliced. Traditional for New Year's.

lesso misto Boiled meats. Better cuts of meats are used than in Emilia-Romagna's *bollito misto.*

minestrone alla milanese Milanese classic: a rich, hearty vegetable soup with rice and *pancetta* (bacon). Served with a sprinkling of Parmesan.

mondeghili Breaded meatballs fried in butter.

nervetti A salad of calf's trotters (feet and shins), julienned and dressed.

ossobuco Veal shin braised in butter and then cooked in a variety of ways, depending on whose family recipe you have in hand. The ingredients usually include many of the following: parsley, garlic, crushed anchovies, rosemary, sage, tomato, white wine, lemon peel. Traditionally finished with a sprinkling of *gremolata*—parsley, lemon peel, and garlic—and served with *risotto alla milanese.*

panettone A dome-shaped bread-cake made with raisins and candied fruit. Usually associated with Christmas.

pizzoccheri A specialty from Valtellina: short, wide buckwheat pasta, typically boiled with potatoes, leeks, and cabbage, and served with melted cheese.

polenta Boiled cornmeal (maize), which can be baked, or in its thicker incarnation, grilled or fried and served in a solid cake with butter and cheese. Of Etruscan origin, it arrived in Lombardy by way of Rome.

polenta e osei alla bergamasca Small birds (*osei*) wrapped in bacon and cooked with sage over a grill (or with butter in the oven), and served on slices of grilled *polenta*. A specialty of Bergamo.

polenta pasticciata A baked dish featuring layers of sliced *polenta*, a meat sauce, cheese, and butter.

ris e ran A soup made with rice and frog legs.

riso al salto A *risotto* pancake sautéed in butter until crisp and brown.

risotto alla certosina A lively rice dish that can include freshwater crayfish, frogs, and perch, as well as vegetables such as mushrooms and peas, rice, and white wine.

risotto alla milanese A Milanese classic: rice cooked with onions, chicken stock, beef marrow, saffron, and white wine, topped with butter and Parmesan. Traditionally served with *ossobuco*—the only time *risotto* is served with another dish.

risotto alla pilota A *risotto* with sausage and cheese.

risotto alla valtellinese A *risotto* made with beans, cabbage, and sage.

rostin negaa Veal chops cooked in white wine.

sciatt Buckwheat fritters containing a little *grappa* and served with cheese. *Sciatt* means "tails," in dialect.

stufato A stew of beef or other meat, vegetables, various herbs and spices, and perhaps red or white wine.

stufato di cavallo Horse meat prepared in the manner for *stufato*.

tinca carpionata A fish, tench, first fried in oil, then marinated in wine, vinegar, onions, garlic, and various herbs, and then served at room temperature.

torta sbrisolona   A "crumbly" almond cake-cookie, found at Easter.

torta di tagliatelle   A crunchy cake made with noodles, nuts, chocolate, and sometimes candied fruit.

tortelli di zucca   A large ravioli-like pasta stuffed with puréed pumpkin, preserved fruit (*mostarda*), crumbled *amaretti,* and nutmeg, served with a little butter and Parmesan.

vitello tonnato   Sliced braised veal with a tuna, mayonnaise, anchovy, and caper sauce. Served cold.

zuppa pavese   Consommé served with bread fried in butter, and Parmesan and a raw egg yolk set afloat on the toast to poach in the soup.

CHEESES

bagoss   A hard, sharp grainy cheese.

bel paese   A mild but flavorful cheese, not to be confused with the cream cheese–like version sold under this name.

bitto   A creamy cheese with some body, made from cow's and goat's milk.

branzi   A soft, full-bodied cheese, similar to *taleggio.*

crescenza   A soft, mild, *stracchino*-like cheese, made from cow's milk.

gorgonzola   King of the blue cheeses—rich, big, full.

grana, grana padano (val padano), grana lodigiano   A Parmesan-like cheese, grainy and nutty.

groviera, gruviera   A relative of Gruyère.

mascarpone   A rich, fresh, creamy cheese vaguely similar to our cream cheese.

pannerone   A cheese similar to *stracchino*.

provolone   A smooth cheese not unlike mozzarella, which ranges from quite mild to something fuller and stronger.

quartirolo   A mild and smooth cheese that comes in a square form.

robiola   A soft, rich, creamy cheese.

stracchino, certosa, certosino   A soft, full, slightly bitter cheese made from the milk of "tired" cows.

taleggio   A smooth, creamy, full-bodied cow's-milk cheese with plenty of power.

WINES

Lombardy is a region of many guises—from the flat plain of the Po Valley to the imposing Alps and peaceful lakes to fast-paced industrial cities. There are three primary winegrowing areas in Lombardy: the Valtellina, in the north, around Son-drio; the Oltrepò Pavese ("across the Po"), in the southwest, around Pavia; and Franciacorta, in the northeast, in the province of Brescia. Especially impressive are the *spumanti*, white and red, from Maurizio Zanella's Ca' del Bosco vineyards.

The Spumanti

Ballabio Brut, Ballabio

Ca' del Bosco, Brut, Dosage Zero, Cremant, Ca' del Bosco

Cristal Pinot Brut, Maggi

Cuvée Imperiale Berlucchi Brut, Guido Berlucchi

Gran Cuvée Bellavista, Bellavista

Gran Spumante La Versa Brut, La Versa

Monsupello Spumante Brut Classese, Monsupello (Boatti)

The Whites

Chardonnay

Clastidium

Cortese dell'Oltrepò

Lugana

Malvasia

Müller Thurgau

Pinot Bianco di Franciacorta

Riesling dell'Oltrepò

Tocai di San Martino della Battaglia

Uccellanda (Chardonnay)

Moscato (sweet)

Riviera del Garda Bresciano Chiaretto (rosé)

The Reds

Ballabio

Barbacarlo (frizzante)

Barbera di Montù Beccaria

Barbera dell'Oltrepò

Bonarda dell'Oltrepò

Botticino

Buttafuoco

Casotte

Cellatica

Il Felicino

Franciacorta Rosso

Frecciarossa

Maurizio Zanella

Monsupello (Oltrepò Pavese)

Narbusto

Pinero

Pinot Nero

Riviera del Garda Bresciano

Ronco di Mompiano

Rosso (Oltrepò Pavese)

Sangue di Giuda

Sfursat (Sforzato)

Solesine

Valtellina Superiore
  Grumello   Inferno   Sassella   Valgella

The Grapes

WHITE   *Chardonnay, Cortese, Garganega, Müller Thurgau
  (a cross of Riesling and Sylvaner), Pinot Bianco, Pinot Grigio,
  Riesling (Italico, Renano), Sylvaner, Tocai Friulano,
  Trebbiano*

RED   *Barbera, Bonarda, Cabernet Franc, Croatina, Gropello,
  Marzemino, Merlot, Molinara, Nebbiolo (called
  Chiavennasca in Valtellina), Negrara Trentina, Pinot Nero,
  Prugnola, Rondinella, Rossanella, Rossolo, Sangiovese,
  Schiava Gentile, Terzi, Ughetta, Uva Rara, Vespolina*

Reliable Producers

*Giacomo Agnes, Bianchina Alberici, Bellavista, Fratelli
  Berlucchi, Ca' del Bosco, Ca' Longa, Cavalleri, Clastidio
  (Angelo Ballabio), Enologica Valtellinese, Fratelli Fraccaroli,
  Frecciarossa (Odero), Maga Lino, Monsuppello (Boatti), La
  Muirighina, Nino Negri, Andrea Pasini, A. Pelizzatti,
  Rainoldi, San Carlo, Tona, Luigi Valenti, Vilide, Visconti,
  Zenato*

The Marches/Le Marche

Cities and Towns

Ancona   Ascoli Piceno   Borgo Pace   Fano   Macerata
                  Pesaro   Urbino

brodetto   Fish soup. There are endless local versions, all
  made with a variety of Adriatic fish and shellfish, parsley,
  garlic, onions, tomatoes, and oil.

brodetto all'anconetana   One of the most famous fish
  soups, employing no fewer than thirteen different types of
  fish. From the city of Ancona.

calcioni   What they call *ravioli* here (sometimes *ravioli all'ascolana*); they are typically stuffed with cheese, egg, and lemon and baked with a topping of cheese.

ciarimboli   Pieces of pork innards cooked with cabbage, garlic, and rosemary.

coniglio in porchetta   Rabbit spit-roasted with rosemary, fennel, garlic, and olive oil.

faraona in potacchio   Guinea fowl stewed with tomatoes, hot peppers, onions, garlic, rosemary, and wine.

lasagne incassettate   Lasagne made with meat, chicken, cheese, and truffle.

mazzafegato   A spicy pork liver sausage, usually made with pine nuts and raisins and sometimes coriander and garlic. Served at Christmas.

olive all'ascolana, olive alla marchigiana, olive ripiene   Deep-fried giant green olives stuffed with meat and Parmesan.

piadina   A pizza-like flat bread that's filled with many different items, including *prosciutto,* cheese, and sausage.

piccioni ripieni   Baked pigeons stuffed with a chestnut purée.

pizza di Pasqua, pizza al formaggio, crescia di Pasqua, crescia di cascia   An Easter pizza starring a variety of cheeses—usually including fresh and aged *pecorino,* ricotta, and Parmesan—and spices.

porchetta   Suckling pig spit-roasted with fennel, rosemary, garlic, and olive oil.

in potacchio   Stewed with tomatoes, onions, garlic, hot peppers, rosemary, and white wine. Fish, fowl and meat can all be prepared this way.

stoccafisso (stocco) all'anconetana   Dried cod cooked with herbs, tomatoes, garlic, anchovies, white wine, and oil.

tornedo alla Rossini   A steak traditionally cooked with ham, mushrooms, parsley, pepper, and lemon. A specialty of Pesaro, the birthplace of the composer.

triglie all'anconetana   Marinated red mullet baked in a slice of raw ham.

uccelletti di mare allo spiedo   Small spit-roasted fish from the Adriatic.

vincisgrassi   Sheets of pasta layered with various ingredients, including sausage, chicken livers, onions, sweetbreads, truffles, ham, butter, and cream, then baked in the oven with grated cheese over the top. In the Abruzzi this is called *pincisgrassi*. We'd probably call it fancy lasagne.

CHEESES

caciofiore, caciotta   A semihard cheese made from cow's milk.

pecorino dolce   A sweet version of this sheep's-milk cheese, eaten as a dessert.

raviggiolo   A soft, full-bodied cheese made from sheep's milk.

WINES

The Marches is known more for its Adriatic beaches and mountainous terrain than for its wines. There is, however, one wine synonymous with this region—Verdicchio. And there are many other wines being made here that are worth trying.

The Spumanti

Colonnara Brut, Verdicchio dei Castelli di Jesi, Cantina Sociale di Cupramontana

Verdicchio Pian delle Mura, Brut Nature Spumante, Fabrini

Vernaccia di Serrapetrona, Fabrini (red)

The Whites

Antico di Casa Fosca

Bianchello del Metauro

Bianco dei Colli Maceratesi

Falerio dei Colli Ascolani

Gallia Togata

Jubilè

San Secondo

Tristo di Montesecco

Verdicchio dei Castelli di Jesi

Verdicchio di Matelica

Verdicchio di Montanello

Verdicchio Pian delle Mura

Vernaccia di Matelica

The Reds

Montepulciano delle Marche	Sangiovese dei Colli Pesaresi
Pongelli	Tenuta di Pongelli
Rosso Cònero	Vernaccia di Pergola
Rosso di Corinaldo (Merlot)	Vernaccia di Serrapetrona
Rosso Piceno	(frizzante, dry to sweet)

The Grapes

WHITE Bianchello, Ciliegiolo, Maceratino, Malvasia di Candia, Malvasia Toscano, Passerina, Pinot Bianco, Pinot Grigio, Riesling Italico, Trebbiano Toscano, Verdicchio

RED Balsamina, Cabernet Sauvignon, Merlot, Montepulciano, Sangiovese, Vernaccia di Serrapetrona

Reliable Producers

Fratelli Bisci, Brunori, Bucci, Cocci Grifoni, Cantina Sociale di Cupramontana, Cantina Sociale Val di Nevola, Attilio Fabrini, Fattoria di Montesecco (Massimo Schiavi), Fazi-Battaglia, Garofoli, Enzo Macella, Marchetti, Monte Schiavo, Tattà, Umani Ronchi, Villa Bucci, Villamagna, Villa Pigna

---

Piedmont/ Piemonte

Cities and Towns

Alba   Alessandria   Arona   Asti   Barolo
Borgomanero   Boves   Bra   Carmagnola   Casale
Monferrato   Caselle Torinese   Castiglione Torinese
Centallo   Cioccaro   Costigliole d'Asti   Cuneo   Isola
d'Asti   Moncalvo   Monforte d'Alba   Neive   Novara
San Bernardino   Soriso   Stresa   Turin   Vercelli

agnolotti Pasta envelopes stuffed with some combination of meat, spinach, cheese, and nutmeg. Served with various sauces, or simply with a little melted butter.

---

amaretti   The famous almond cookies, somewhat reminiscent of macaroons.

bagna cauda (caôda)   A hot dipping sauce ("hot bath") for raw vegetables, especially cardoons (edible thistles). Made with olive oil, butter, anchovies, garlic, and in season, white truffles; served in a bowl placed over a flame to keep the mixture hot.

bagnet verd   A green sauce with plenty of garlic, used with boiled meats.

bonet   A rich custard pudding, spiked with rum and flavored with crumbled *amaretti*.

brasato al barolo   Beef marinated in Barolo wine and herbs and then braised slowly in the marinating liquid.

bue al barolo   Sirloin steak cooked in Barolo wine.

caponet   Cabbage leaves or zucchini flowers stuffed with various herbs, veal, and sausage.

castellana di peperoni   Bell peppers baked with *prosciutto* and cheese.

cisra   Chickpea soup.

crumiri   A type of cookie.

faseui a la tofeja, fasoeil al furn   Red beans with pork rind or bacon, garlic, and spices.

finanziera   A rich, hearty, even elaborate stew of chicken, chicken liver and giblets, mushrooms, cocks' combs, sweetbreads, and truffles; traditionally, leftover meats are used. Supposedly a favorite dish of nineteenth-century businessmen—hence the name.

fonduta   Melted *fontina* cheese with eggs, butter, milk, and slices of white truffle when available. Served as a sauce for a variety of things, including vegetables and mushrooms, or just over a little toasted bread. Called *fondue* in the Valle d'Aosta.

fritto misto alla piemontese   Mixed fried food: sausage, brains, beef, veal, liver, chicken, lamb, sweetbreads, eggplant, zucchini, mushrooms—that is, almost anything the chef can lay his hands on. A typical dish of the region, and slightly on the heavy side.

gnocchi di patate alla bava   Potato dumplings served with cheese and cream blended together.

grissini   Breadsticks, Turin's world-famous contribution to the Italian table.

lepre al sive   Jugged hare, first marinated in red wine and then stewed until tender.

paniscia   A rice dish, containing white beans and sometimes tomatoes, onions, and bacon.

panna cotta   A rich cream topped with carmelized sugar—similar to *crème caramel.*

pollo alla babi   A young chicken sautéed in oil; sometimes, chicken grilled over coals.

puccia   An unusual dish composed of pork, stewed vegetables, *polenta,* and Parmesan. Sometimes served cooled, sliced, and fried in a little butter.

rane dorate   Fried frog legs.

ris in cagnon   Boiled rice finished by frying it with sage, garlic, and a great deal of butter and cheese. Waverley Root writes of this dish: "So called because a minute drop of the butter blackened in the frying clings to each grain of rice, making it resemble a certain type of small worm called in the local dialect *cagnott.*"

risotto al barolo   *Risotto* cooked with chicken broth, Barolo wine, butter, and cheese.

salamin d'la duja   A special Piedmont salami, mild-flavored and soft, that is kept in a clay pot called a *duja.*

tajarin al tartufo, ceresolini   Noodles tossed with butter and Parmesan and topped with white truffles.

tapulon   Donkey meat, typically stewed with red wine and various herbs and spices.

tortini di tartufi alla piemontese   Fried or toasted bread with ground game and sliced truffle on top.

trota alla Savoia   Trout that's floured and pan-fried in butter, placed on a bed of mushrooms, sprinkled with butter and bread crumbs, and then baked.

vitello tonnato   Braised veal sliced thin and covered with a sauce composed of mayonnaise, tuna, anchovies, and capers. Served cold.

zabaione, zabaglione   A dessert made of beaten egg yolks, sugar, and Marsala or other sweet wine. Served as a sauce and on its own.

CHEESES

capra   A soft goat cheese with a mild but present flavor.

castelmagno   A strong, reasonably hard cheese, similar to *pecorino*. Produced in the town of Pradleves and evidently favored by the popes of Avignon, as well as by Charlemagne. Popular among restaurant owners, who seem quite proud of it.

fontina   A soft, buttery, and rich cheese, full of delicate flavor.

formaggetta   A small, soft, intensely flavored white cheese, made with milk from cows and ewes. In Tuscany it's called *formaggetta di zeri,* and it may be related to the Ligurian *formaggella.*

paglierino, pagliarino   A cheese made from cow's milk.

robiola di Roccaverano   A creamy, rich, goat's-milk cheese.

toma   A yellow cheese with a rich, full flavor—nutty when young, more subtle when aged. Served often in Piedmontese restaurants.

WINES

In the Piedmont the Nebbiolo grape rules supreme. It's employed here to father Barolo, the "king of wines, the wine of kings"—one of only six wines in Italy to receive the prestigious DOCG ranking. Other stars of this region include Barbaresco, also in the DOCG category, Gattinara, Carema, and of course, Asti Spumante. Piedmont is not known for its whites, of which there are very few of note.

The Spumanti

Asti Spumante

Banfi Brut, Villa Banfi-Strevi

Bruno Giacosa Extra Brut, Bruno Giacosa

Gran Cuvé Carlo Gancia, Chardonnay Brut and Gancia di Gancia, Fratelli Gancia

Marone Cinzano Pas Dosé, Cinzano

Spumante Pados, Soldati–La Scolca

Valentino Brut, Podere Rocche dei Manzoni-Valentino

The Whites

Arneis

Bianco dei Roeri

Chardonnay

Gaia & Rey (Chardonnay)

Erbaluce di Caluso

Gavi (Cortese di Gavi)

Moscato d'Asti (frizzante, sweet)

The Reds

Barbaresco

Barbera d'Alba

Barbera d'Asti

Barbera del Monferrato

Barolo

Boca

Bramaterra

Bricco del Drago

Bricco Manzoni

Bricco dell'Uccellone (Barbera)

Carema

Darmagi (Cabernet)

Dolcetto d'Acqui

Dolcetto d'Alba

Dolcetto d'Asti

Dolcetto di Diano d'Alba

Dolcetto di Dogliani

Dolcetto di Ovada

Freisa

Gattinara

Ghemme

Grignolino d'Asti

Grignolino del Monferrato Casalese

Lessona

Nebbiolo d'Alba

Nebbiolo delle Langhe

Roero

Ruchè di Castagnole Monferrato (also Rouchet, Roché)

Sizzano

Spanna

Villa Pattono

Vinot

Barolo Chinato (sweet; rare)

Brachetto d'Acqui (frizzante, semisweet)

Caluso Passito (sweet)

The Grapes

WHITE   Arneis, Chardonnay, Cortese, Erbaluce, Moscato Bianco, Moscato di Canelli

RED   Barbera, Bonarda, Brachetto, Cabernet Sauvignon, Croatina, Dolcetto, Freisa, Grignolino, Nebbiolo (called Spanna in the Novara-Vercelli area), Uvalino, Vespolina

KING BAROLO

Although it has always been too scarce, too dear, too much of a mouthful to become anyone's everyday beverage, Barolo has always been the one red wine to turn to in Italy when one looked for grandeur, for a wine able to temper force with refinement. When its credentials are impeccable—a fortunate vintage year, a choice vineyard, thoughtful vinification, well-husbanded maturation—Barolo has few peers among the world's great wines.

Its first address to the nose and palate is undeniably powerful. The initial impression of alcohol, which makes one think of cognac, gives way to an intricate succession of odors. A heavy, dense, rubbery scent of tar muscles past the ethereal ones of faded rose, violet, and almond. The intriguing alternation of light and heavy aromas, flowery and tarry, is one through which we learn to identify not only Barolo, but most wines from the nebbiolo grape. In a fully mature Barolo it is accompanied by other sensations that may recall tree bark, leather, pepper, or tobacco.

The impact in the mouth is large, but not ponderous. The drama of Barolo's power is that it manages its great girth with supple and buoyant grace. The flavors bloom in the palate, conveying even in very advanced age an opulent and delectable impression of fruit. The aftertaste fades with haunting slowness, releasing as it retreats a seemingly indelible last emanation of flavor.

—VICTOR HAZAN

Reliable Producers

Antoniolo, Bera, Giacomo Bologna, Boratto, Braida-Bologna, Bricco Asili, Castello di Neive, Ceretto, Quinto Chionetti, Clerico, Elvio Cogno, Aldo Conterno, Giacomo Conterno, Paolo Cordero di Montezemolo, Redento Dogliotti, Ferrando, Fontanafredda, Gaja, Bruno Giacosa, Malvirá, Marchesi di Gresy, Marchesi Incisa della Rochetta, Giuseppe Mascarello, Pio Cesare, Podere Rocche dei Manzoni, La Porta Rossa, Produttori Nebbiolo di Carema, Alfredo Prunotto, Renato

Ratti, Scarpa, La Scolca, Tenuta San Pietro, Vallana, Vietti, Voerzio

Tuscany / Toscana

Cities and Towns

Anghiari   Arezzo   Carrara   Cetona   Cortona
Florence   Forte dei Marmi   Grosseto   Livorno   Lucca
Massa   Montecatini Terme   Montefollonico
Montepulciano   Monteriggioni   Pieve Santo Stefano
Pisa   Pistoia   Ponte a Moriano
San Casciano in Val di Pesa   San Gimignano   Sansepolcro
San Vincenzo   Siena   Sinalunga   Viareggio   Volterra

acquacotta   Literally, "cooked water." A thick soup of seasonal vegetables poured over slices of toasted bread.

arista all'aretina   Roasted or spit-roasted pork loin, cooked with garlic and rosemary.

arista alla fiorentina   Pork loin roasted in water with garlic and rosemary.

asparagi alla fiorentina   Asparagus prepared with butter and Parmesan and presented with a fried egg on top.

bistecca alla fiorentina   The king of steaks, often referred to simply as *fiorentina*. For purists, it must be a very thick T-bone steak cut in Florence from Chianina beef, grilled over coals and served *very* rare (*al sangue*) with olive oil, salt, and pepper.

cacciucco alla livornese   A spicy fish stew composed of a number of "junk" fish—the local recipes call for at least as many types of fish as there are "C"s in *cacciucco*—as well as shellfish, tomatoes, hot peppers, and herbs. Served with garlic toast. A precursor to French bouillabaisse.

cantucci, biscotti(ni) di Prato   Tuscan almond biscuits, often dipped in Vin Santo.

castagnaccio   A flat cake made with unleavened chestnut flour, and pine nuts or walnuts, rosemary, and raisins.

cenci   Little "rags" of dough—sometimes tied into knots, sometimes cut into ragged squares—fried and dusted with sugar.

cibreo An unusual Tuscan stew, starring one of Tuscany's favorite ingredients: chicken livers. The livers are cooked along with chicken giblets, cocks' combs, eggs, and lemon.

cieche (cee, cie) alla pisana After the Leaning Tower and Galileo, Pisa's claim to fame is this dish of tiny eels, or elvers, from the Arno. They are cooked in oil with a little sage, lemon, and garlic and served with Parmesan.

crostini di fegato Slices of toast or fried bread with a topping of chicken-liver pâté.

fagioli al fiasco Beans, traditionally cooked in a flask to hold in their flavor. Now they're simply boiled and dressed with oil, garlic, salt, pepper, and sometimes a little sage.

fagioli alla fiorentina Beans cooked with various herbs and served with an oil, egg, and lemon sauce.

fagioli all'uccelletto Literally, "beans like little birds." The beans are flavored with sage, garlic, and tomato, which according to Waverley Root "is supposed to make them taste like small game."

fegatelli di maiale all'uccelletto Cubed pork liver skewered with bay leaves and cooked "like little birds" over coals.

fettunta Toasted sliced bread rubbed down with plenty of garlic and bathed in the finest olive oil. Called *bruschetta* in other regions.

finocchiona A pork sausage similar to salami, spiced with fennel seeds.

fricassea A light stew of meat, poultry, or vegetables, served with a sauce of eggs and lemon.

frittelle di riso, frittelle di San Giuseppe alla toscana Little rice fritters with pine nuts and lemon, traditionally made for Palm Sunday.

fritto misto alla fiorentina A combination of deep-fried foods, including brains and sweetbreads, chunks of lamb and chicken, and artichokes, cauliflower, and zucchini.

garmugia, gramugia, garmucia A hearty soup made with *fava* beans, peas, artichokes, asparagus, onions, and bacon.

infarinata Sometimes resembling a soup, sometimes prepared more like *polenta*, this dish combines *polenta*, various seasonal vegetables, beans, and a little bacon for flavor.

alla maremmana In the style of the Maremma, a region along the coast. The Maremma, once marshland, is rich in game such as birds, rabbits, wild boar, and deer.

panforte "Strong bread"; actually, a very tasty Sienese cake made with almonds and walnuts, honey, preserved fruit, and spices. Associated with Christmas.

panzanella A bread salad, made by moistening pieces of stale bread with a little water or stock, combining them with tomatoes, cucumbers, onions, anchovies, and basil, and tossing it all with a little oil and vinegar.

pappa A thick souplike dish made with fresh tomatoes, garlic, olive oil, and bread.

pappardelle alla lepre Wide flat noodles served with a rich rabbit sauce.

peposo A spicy beef stew, made with tomatoes, wine, and plenty of black pepper.

pici A type of homemade noodles.

pollo alla diavola Chicken that has been split and flattened, then grilled. Sometimes called *pollo al mattone*, flattened with a "brick."

ribollita Literally, "reboiled." A soup with beans and cabbage, thickened with bread, then reheated and charmed with a little olive oil at the table.

ricciarelli Soft little almond cakes that come coated with edible rice paper.

risotto nero Black rice: a *risotto* cooked with cuttlefish and their ink.

salsiccia di cinghiale di Maremma Wild-boar sausage from the Maremma region.

scottiglia A stew that uses all sorts of meats—game, chicken, pork, veal—cooked with wine, garlic, tomatoes, onions, and various herbs.

stracotto Beef stewed with red wine, tomatoes, and herbs; basically a pot roast.

telline, arselle Wedge-shell clams.

tonno con fagioli A simple, very Tuscan dish of tuna and beans.

tordi allo spiedo Spit-roasted thrushes.

tortino alla toscana A thick omelette with artichokes, cooked in the oven.

triglie alla livornese Red mullet cooked with olive oil, tomatoes, and herbs.

trippa alla fiorentina Tripe cooked in a tomato sauce with herbs and Parmesan.

uccelletti, uccellini Small birds that the Italians eat with considerable relish—larks, thrushes, and so on. Usually spit-roasted.

all'uccelletto Referring to food prepared as small birds would be: spit-roasted, often with sage.

ventresca di tonno con fagioli A Tuscan favorite, the stomach of a tuna served with white beans.

zuccotto A dome-shaped cake with numerous ingredients, including chocolate, whipped cream, candied fruit, nuts, and often ice cream.

zuppa di datteri alla viareggina A spicy soup made with date mussels, tomatoes, garlic, and hot peppers.

zuppa di fagioli A thick soup of beans and other vegetables.

CHEESES

brancolino A soft, fatty cheese from the town of Brancoli.

caciotto di pecorino del Chianti A semihard sharp cheese.

formaggetta di zeri A small-form soft cheese made with cow's and ewe's milk.

giuncata Curds, junket.

marzolino A strong cheese, similar to *pecorino*.

mucchino   A cheese similar to *pecorino*, but milder and sweeter.

pecorino dolce di Siena   Sweet *pecorino*, made from sheep's milk.

raveggiolo   A full-bodied sheep's-milk cheese.

WINES

Mention Tuscany to wine lovers and their first association will be Chianti, one of the six Italian wines to achieve the coveted DOCG status. In Tuscany, the Sangiovese grape is king, and is the author of all the great classified Tuscan wines—Brunello di Montalcino, Chianti, Vino Nobile di Montepulciano (all three DOCG wines), and Carmignano.

The Spumanti

Antinori Brut Nature,
   Marchesi Antinori

Brut di Capezzana, Villa di
   Capezzana

The Whites

Bianco di Pitigliano

Bianco di Toscana

Bianco Vergine della
   Valdichiana

Chardonnay
   Cabreo
   Colline di Ama
   Fontanelle
   Le Grance
   Marzocco
   Meriggio

Galestro

Grattamacco Bianco

Libaio

Montecarlo

Pinot Grigio

Pomino

Spera

Terre di Tufo (Vernaccia)

Trebianco

Vernaccia di San Gimignano

Villa Antinori Bianco

Sassolato (sweet)

Torricella (sweet)

Vin Ruspo (rosé)

Vin Santo (dry to sweet)

The Reds

Alicante

Barco Reale

Borgo Amorosa

Borro Cepparello

Brunello di Montalcino

Bruno di Rocca

Brusco dei Barbi

Ca' del Pazzo

Cabreo

Capannelle Rosso

Carmignano

Cetinaia

Chianti Classico

Chianti Colli Aretini

Chianti Colli Fiorentini

Chianti Colli Senesi

Chianti Colline Pisane

Chianti Montalbano

Chianti Rufina

Colline Lucchesi (Rosso delle Colline Luchesi)

Coltassala

Concerto

La Corte

Elba

Elegia

Flaccianello della Pieve

Fontalloro

Ghiaie della Furba

Grattamacco Rosso

Grifi

Grosso Senese

Montesodi

Morellino di Scansano

Palazzo Altesi

Percarlo

Le Pergole Torte

Pomino

Querciagrande

Rosso di Cercatoia

Rosso di Montalcino

Sammarco

Sangioveto di Coltibuono

THE TWENTY BEST PRODUCERS OF CHIANTI CLASSICO

Badia a Coltibuono

Capannelle

Castellare di Castellina

Castello di Ama

Castello di Fonterutoli

Castello di Querceto

Castello dei Rampolla

Castello di San Polo in Rosso

Castello Vicchiomaggio

Castello di Volpaia

Fattoria Querciabella

Fontodi

Isole e Olena

Monte Vertine

Peppolì

Podere Il Palazzino

Poggio al Sole

Riecine

Rocca delle Macie

Villa Antinori

Sassicaia

Secentenario

Il Sodaccio

I Sodi di San Niccolò

Solaia

Solatio Basilica

Tavernelle

Tignanello

Vigorello

Vinattieri Rosso

Vino Nobile di Montepulciano

The Grapes

WHITE   Albarola, Aleatico, Ansonica, Canaiolo Bianco,
Grechetto (Pulcinculo), Greco, Malvasia, Pinot Bianco,
Roussanne, Sauvignon, Traminer, Trebbiano (Procanico),
Verdicchio, Vermentino, Vernaccia di San Gimignano

RED   Cabernet Sauvignon, Canaiolo, Ciliegiolo, Colorino,
Malvasia Nera, Mammolo, Merlot, Occhio di Pernice, Pinot
Nero, Sangiovese (the important strains of this grape include
Brunello, Morellino, Prugnolo Gentile, Sangiovese Grosso, and
Sangioveto) Sirac

Reliable Producers

Altesino, Marchesi Antinori, Artimino, Avignonesi, Eric Banti,
Biondi-Santi, Capannelle, Castelgiocondo, Castellare di
Castellina, Castello di Ama, Castello di Fonterutoli, Castello
dei Rampolla, Castello di San Polo in Rosso, Castello di
Volpaia, Emilio Costanti, Riccardo Falchini, Fassati, Fattoria
dei Barbi, Fattoria del Buonamico, Fattoria di Felsina,
Fattoria di Fognano, Fattoria di Fubbiano, Fattoria dei
Pietrafitta, Fattoria Il Corno, Fattoria Le Pupille, Fattoria
di San Giusto a Rentennano, Fattoria Vetrice, Fontodi,
Marchesi de Frescobaldi (Castello di Nipozzano), Marchesi
Incisa della Rocchetta, Isole e Olena, Lisini, Lunaia, Monte
Vertine, Podere Capaccia, Podere di Grattamacco, Podere Il
Palazzino, Poderi Boscarelli, Poderi Emilio Costanti, Poggio
alla Sala, Poliziano, Ruffino, San Felice, Selvapiana, Tenuta
Caparzo, Tenuta di Capezzana, Tenuta La Chiusa, Tenuta

Il Poggione, Teruzzi & Puthod, Vecchie Terre di Montefili, Villa Banfi, Villa Cafaggio, Villa di Capezzana, Villa Cilnia, Villa di Trefiano, Vinattieri

Umbria

Cities and Towns

Arrone   Assisi   Baschi   Deruta   Foligno
Isola Maggiore   Gubbio   Norcia   Orvieto
Passignano sul Trasimeno   Perugia   Spello   Terni
Todi   Torgiano   Trevi

bruschetta   Toasted bread exposed to plenty of garlic and olive oil.

cardi alla perugina   Cardoons dipped in batter and fried in oil.

carne ai capperi e acciughe   Veal cooked with capers, anchovies, and herbs.

cicherchiata   A deep-fried cake made with pine nuts, almonds, candied fruit, and honey. Traditional for Carnival.

fichi bianchi   White figs, often stuffed with walnuts and/or almonds.

gobbi alla perugina   Cardoons cooked the same way as the *cardi* above, but served with a meat sauce.

imbrecciata   A soup made with beans, lentils, and chickpeas.

lasca   A fish from Lake Trasimeno; roach in English.

mazzafegato   A spicy pork liver sausage, usually made with pine nuts and raisins, and sometimes with coriander and garlic. Served at Christmas.

minestra di farro   A typical country soup, made with emmer (a type of wheat) and various vegetables, usually including tomatoes and onions, and most important, a ham bone.

palombacce alla ghiotta   Spit-roasted wood pigeons presented in a wine sauce typically enriched with ham and capers.

piccione alla perugina   Roast pigeon made with a sauce of black olives.

pizza al testo   A flat pizza baked with a cheese filling.

piconi   Ravioli.

pinoccate   Little pine-nut Christmas cakes, a specialty of Perugia.

porchetta   Spit-roasted suckling pig that's cooked with garlic, fennel, rosemary, and various other herbs, depending on where you find it.

regina in porchetta   Lake Trasimeno carp cooked in a wood oven with pork fat, fennel, rosemary, and garlic. Sometimes the carp is stuffed with vegetables.

salume di Norcia   The important charcuterie of this Umbrian town. The pigs here feed on acorns, which make their meat so memorable.

sedano di Trevi in umido   The famous celery of Trevi stewed (*in umido*) in a tomato sauce.

serpentone   A cake that's shaped to look like a snake, composed of dried fruit and almonds.

spaghetti ai tartufi neri   Spaghetti with a sauce of black truffles, which are found in the area around Norcia.

stringozzi, ceriole   A country-style short-noodle pasta, prepared with a sauce containing a good quantity of garlic and olive oil, and sometimes tomatoes.

tegamaccio   A hearty soup of lake fish, made with local white wine and a variety of herbs.

torcolo   A ring-shaped cake made with nuts and fruits, typically dipped into Vin Santo.

torta al testo   A flat pizza-like bread that's cooked on a hot stone or modern griddle.

trifole   Black truffles, in Umbria; white truffles in Piedmont; also called *tartufi*.

CHEESES

caciotto   A semi-hard cheese. It's said that the best *caciotto* is fresh from Norcia.

pecorino   Made from ewe's milk, the Umbrian variety runs the range from sweet to sharp.

raveggiolo   A full-bodied sheep's-milk cheese.

WINES

Umbria is one of the most magical of Italy's regions. Happily, it's not on many tourists routes, as it has no access to the sea and appears somewhat behind the times in terms of entertainment. The fine art found here, the landscape, and the excellent food and wine give this area an atmosphere unlike any other part of the country. Umbria isn't a large wine producer, but it does have two wines that have established international reputations: Orvieto (white) and Rubesco (red), the latter produced by the most important winemaker in this region—and one of the most important in Italy—Giorgio Lungarotti.

The Spumanti

Decugnano dei Barbi Brut,
Decugnano dei Barbi

Lungarotti Brut, Lungarotti

The Whites

Bianco d'Arquata

Castello della Sala

Cervaro della Sala

Chardonnay di Miralduolo

Colli Altotiberini Bianco

Colli del Trasimeno Bianco

Grechetto

Orvieto (also sweet)

Torre di Giano

Muffato della Sala (sweet)

Orvieto Classico, Pourriture Noble, Decugnano dei Barbi (sweet)

Vin Santo (dry to sweet)

The Reds

Cabernet Sauvignon di Miralduolo

Castello di Montoro

Colli Altotiberini Rosso

Colli Perugini

Colli del Trasimeno Rosso

Decugnano dei Barbi Rosso

Merlot

Montefalco Rosso

Rosso d'Arquata

Rubesco (Torgiano Rosso)

Rubino

Sagrantino di Montefalco
(also sweet)

San Giorgio

The Grapes

WHITE   Chardonnay, Drupeggio, Garganega, Grechetto,
Malvasia, Pinot Blanc, Procanico, Sauvignon Blanc, Tocai,
Traminer, Trebbiano, Verdello, Verdicchio

RED   Barbera, Cabernet Sauvignon, Cannaiolo, Ciliegiolo,
Cometta, Corvetta, Gamay, Merlot, Montepulciano,
Sagrantino, Sangiovese

Reliable Producers

Adanti, Antinori, Barberani, Bigi, Caprai, Castello della Sala,
Decugnano dei Barbi, Dubini Locatelli, Angelo Fongoli,
Lungarotti, Montoro

Valle d'Aosta

Cities and Towns

Aosta   Courmayeur   Gignod   Saint-Vincent   Verrès

boudin   Blood sausage. The best comes from Morgex.

caffe valdostano   A powerful coffee made with lemon
rind and grappa. Served in a special wooden pot, called a
coppa dell'amicizia (friendship cup), which comes with a
spout for everyone at the table.

camoscio in salmì   Chamois, marinated and then stewed
in red wine, garlic, oil, and herbs.

camoscio stufato alla valdostana   Chamois marinated in wine and then stewed with vegetables, garlic,
herbs, wine, and a splash of *grappa*. Traditionally served
with *polenta*.

capriolo alla valdostana Venison stew, made with a variety of vegetables, garlic, herbs, wine, *grappa,* and a little cream.

carbonade, carbonata Beef stew; a variation on the French stew, but made with wine instead of beer.

costoletta di vitello alla valdostana A breaded veal chop, first stuffed with *fontina* cheese, ham, and sometimes the undeniable white truffle, then fried in oil.

fiandolein The local version of *zabaione,* with rum added.

kanostrelle A round cake.

mocetta di camoscio Dried, salted, and spiced leg of chamois, served in very thin slices, like *prosciutto.*

polenta alla valdostana, polenta cunsa Polenta layered with Parmesan, *fontina,* and *toma* cheese and butter.

tegole Little almond or hazelnut cookies shaped, as the name suggests, like roof tiles.

trote Trout. Those from the high mountain streams of Valle d'Aosta have a great reputation among trout aficionados. Sometimes served *al vino rosso* (cooked in red wine), but best when simply sautéed in butter.

zuppa valpellinentze A soup-stew specialty of this region, made with *fontina* cheese, ham, rye bread, cabbage, and a personal selection of herbs and spices.

CHEESES

aostino The consistency of a goat cheese, although made from cow's milk. Rich and full in favor.

caprino A creamy goat's-milk cheese, sometimes fresh, sometimes preserved in oil.

fontina A dense, whole-milk cheese, subtly rich, delicate, and mild.

toma A firm, yellow cheese, sometimes with holes, made from cow's milk.

tomino A small-form round cheese that tastes like fresh goat cheese. Made from cow's or goat's milk, or both, and sometimes enclosed in a layer of herbs.

WINES

The vineyards of Italy's smallest region, Valle d'Aosta, on the slopes of the spectacular valley beneath Mont Blanc and the Matterhorn, produce wines of modest accomplishment. Although this region is usually linked to the Piedmont, the wines here do have their own identity and are well worth sampling along with the rugged mountain landscape. The vineyards at Morgex are the highest classified vineyards in Europe.

The Whites

Blanc de Cossan

Blanc de Morgex

Chardonnay de Moncenis

Müller Thurgau

Vin du Conseil

Chambave Moscato (a dry and a sweet)

Passito di Chambave (sweet)

The Reds

Chambave Rouge

La Colline de Sarre et Chesallet

Donnaz

Enfer d'Arvier

Nus Rouge (Rosso)

Petit Rouge

Pinot Noir

La Sabla (Aymaville)

Sang des Salasses

Sirah

Torrette

The Grapes

WHITE Blanc de Valdigne (also called Blanc de Morgex), Moscato, Müller Thurgau, Petite Arvine, Pinot Gris (called Malvoisie locally)

RED Dolcetto, Fumin, Gamay, Grenache, Nebbiolo, Petit Rouge, Pinot Noir, Vien de Nus

Reliable Producers

Co-Enfer, Costantino Charrère, La Crotta di Vegneron, G. Gabriele, Filippo Garin, Institut Agricole Régional Aoste, Don Augusto Pramotton, Alberto Vevey, Ezio Voyat

Veneto

Cities and Towns

Mestre   Padua   Pieve d'Alpago   Rovigo   Treviso
Valeggio sul Mincio   Venice   Verona   Vicenza

anatra (anitra) col pien   Boiled duck that's been stuffed with sausage, mushrooms, pistachios, and various herbs.

asparagi alla bassanese   Asparagus from Bassano del Grappa, steamed with lemon, oil, and spices.

baccalà mantecato   Salt cod that's first steamed, then puréed with a little olive oil. Served with sliced *polenta*.

baccalà alla vicentina   Salt cod braised slowly in milk with olive oil, onions, anchovies, Parmesan, and herbs—and sometimes spices, garlic, and wine. Served with *polenta*.

bigoli (bigoi) in salsa   A thick, homemade whole-wheat spaghetti, at fifteen inches said to be the longest pasta in Italy. Made with an instrument called a *bigolo*, a traditional pasta press (*torchio*). Typically served with an onion and anchovy sauce. *Bigoli con l'anara* is the pasta served with a duck sauce.

bisato   Eel. In this region often cooked with vinegar, oil, and bay leaves.

bisato sull'ara   Eel baked with bay leaves.

bottarga   Tuna roe, dried, pressed, and salted.

bovoloni   Snails.

capon (cappone) alla canevera   A capon cooked in an ox or pig bladder. *Canevera* means straw, which is used as a vent to let the steam out during the cooking.

casunziei   Venetian ravioli filled with a variety of ingredients, ranging from pumpkin, spinach, and cheese to ham and beets.

faraona in tecia   Guinea hen cooked in a clay pot.

fegato alla veneziana   One of the Venetian claims to fame: calf's liver sliced and fried in butter and oil with onions. Served with the ever-present slices of *polenta*.

granceole, grancevole, granseole Spider crabs, served cold with oil and lemon.

lucanega, luganega A very spicy sausage made in the Treviso area. Called also *iuganega* or *xuganega* in dialect.

masanette Female crabs.

moleche Soft-shelled crabs.

paeta (arrosto) al malgaragno Spit-roasted turkey basted with pomegranate sauce.

pasta e fasoi The Venetian version of pasta and bean soup, made with a little pork rind or bacon, and sometimes rosemary.

pastissada, pastizzada A rich sauce made with beef or horse meat, vinegar, wine, and various herbs and spices. Often served with *gnocchi* or *polenta*.

peverada A highly spiced sauce from Treviso made with oil, vinegar, lemon juice, garlic, anchovies, Parmesan cheese, chicken livers, bread crumbs, peppercorns, lemon peel, and ginger (this list according to Waverley Root). Served with game and boiled or roasted meats.

polenta The ubiquitous accompaniment to the Venetian plate: boiled cornmeal served "soft" like mashed potatoes, with butter and cheese, or in a cake, grilled or fried.

polenta e osei (oseleti, uccelli) Spit-roasted game birds served on grilled slices of *polenta*.

polenta con oseleti scampai *Polenta* served with skewered chunks of meat and mushrooms.

pollo alla padovana Chicken sometimes fricasseed with egg yolks and lemon, and sometimes grilled with herbs.

radicchio di Treviso, di Verona, di Chioggia, di Castelfranco A slightly bitter red chicory, in four varieties; *Treviso (Spadone)* has long thin red and white leaves and is the tastiest; *Verona* is round like a head of lettuce; and *Chioggia* and *Castelfranco* are leafier heads with green as well as red leaves. People from Treviso recognize only their own *radicchio* as being the real thing; according to Waverley Root, the locals term their variety *un fiore che si mangia,* "a flower that is eaten."

rafoi A dialect word for *ravioli*.

risi e bisi   The well-known rice and pea soup, which is consumed with plenty of Parmesan.

riso alla luganega   A rice soup made with the spicy sausage from Treviso.

risotto   This essential rice dish reaches heavenly heights in the Veneto. Made with an endless list of ingredients, the rice is prepared using the same basic method as for *risotto alla milanese*. First, the long-grained rice is sautéed in butter, oil, and a little chopped onion. Then it's cooked with a rich stock, added a little at a time as the liquid is absorbed. The rice is then ready to receive other ingredients such as meat or fish. Served with Parmesan and additional butter.

risotto nero   Cuttlefish and their ink combine to make this "black *risotto*."

risotto alla sbirraglia   A *risotto* made with pieces of finely chopped chicken.

sarde in saor   Sardines first fried, then marinated in vinegar, oil, onions, raisins, pine nuts, and other ingredients.

seppie alla veneziana   Cuttlefish stewed in white wine, oil, garlic, and their own ink; sometimes tomatoes are added.

sopa coada   A stew made with layers of pigeon and bread and wine.

soppressa   Pork sausage.

tiramisù   One of the best desserts in Italy. Made with *mascarpone*, eggs, *espresso*, liqueurs, ladyfingers, and chocolate. An undeniable piece of work.

torresani al spiedo   Spit-roasted pigeons wrapped in bacon and seasoned with various spices.

zuppa scaligera   An odd but traditional Venetian dish created in honor of the ruling family of Verona. Made with chicken broth, pigeon, turkey, Parmesan, and bread, which are arranged in layers, and baked.

CHEESES

asiago   A semi-fat, hard cow's-milk cheese; softer and more delicate when young, spicy and sharper when aged.

casatella   A white, creamy cheese.

montasio A cheese similar to *asiago;* firm and smooth when young, but harder and sharper when aged.

vezzena stravecchio An aged soft cheese, smooth and rich.

WINES

It's not surprising that with such international stars as Soave, Valpolicella, and Amarone, the Veneto is one of Italy's most important winegrowing regions. It produces more DOC wine than any other region and is fourth in total wine projuction.

The Spumanti

Accademia Brut, Maculan

*Venegazzù Brut, Conte
  Loredan Gasparini*

Zardetto Brut, Pino Zardetto

The Whites

Bianco di Custoza

Breganze Bianco

Capitel San Rocco

Colli Berici Garganega

Colli Berici Pinot Bianco

Gambellara Bianco

Masianco

Piave Tocai Italico

Pinot Bianco

Pinot Grigio

*Prosecco di Conegliano-
  Valdobbiadene (Cartizze)*

Soave

Tocai di Lison

Vespaiolo

*Villa Dal Ferro
  Bianco del Rocolo
  Busa Calcara
  Costiera Granda*

Bardolino Chiaretto (rosé)

Costa d'Olio (rosé)

*Recioto Bianco di Campociesa
  (sweet)*

Recioto di Soave (sweet)

Torcolato (sweet)

Vin dela Fabriseria (sweet)

The Reds

*Amarone (Recioto della
  Valpolicella Amarone)*

Bardolino

Breganze Cabernet

Breganze Rosso

Cabernet

Campo Fiorin

Capitel San Rocco

Castello Guerrieri

Castello di Roncade–Villa
  Giustiniani

Catullo

Colli Berici Cabernet

Colli Berici Tocai Rosso

Colli Euganei Rosso

Grola

Lison-Pramaggiore Cabernet

Merlot, Colli Berici

Merlot, Lison-Pramaggiore

Piave Cabernet

Piave Raboso

Pinot Nero

Le Sassine

Valpolicella

Venegazzù della Casa

Villa Dal Ferro
  Cabernet, Le Rive Rosse
  Merlot, Campo del Lago
  Pinot Nero, Rosso del
  Rocolo

Recioto della Valpolicella
(sweet)

The Grapes

WHITE   Chardonnay, Durello, Garganega, Pinot Bianco,
Pinot Grigio, Prosecco, Renano, Riesling, Trebbiano, Tocai,
Verduzzo, Vespaiolo

RED   Barbera, Cabernet Franc, Cabernet Sauvignon, Corvina
Veronese, Malbec, Marzemino, Merlot, Molinara, Negrara,
Petit Verdot, Pinot Nero, Raboso, Refosco, Rondinella,
Sangiovese, Tocai Rosso, Veronese

Reliable Producers

Allegrini, Anselmi, Arvedi d'Emilei, Bassetti, Bertani, Bolla,
Boscani, Campagnola, Cantine Nino Franco, Carpenè
Malvolti, Cavalchina, Cescon, Barone Ciani Bassetti, La
Fattoria, Gasparini, Guerrieri-Rizzardi, Conte Loredan,
Maccari, Maculan, Masi, Pieropan, Giuseppe Quintarelli, Le
Ragose, Santa Sofia, Fratelli Tedeschi, Le Vigne di San
Pietro, Villa Dal Ferro, Villa Sceriman, Pino Zardetto,
Fratelli Zenato

A FEW ESSENTIAL
WINE TERMS

abboccato   Slightly sweet.

alcool   Alcohol.

amabile   A little sweeter than *abboccato*.

amaro   Bitter.

annata   Year of vintage.

asciutto   Very dry, bone dry.

azienda (agricola, vinicola)   Farm; estate winery; winemaking company.

barrique   A 225-liter oak barrel used for aging wine.

bianco   White.

bicchiere   Glass.

bottiglia   Bottle.

brut   Dry; dry sparkling wine.

cannellino   Moderately sweet. Wine grown in the Castelli Romani (Lazio), from Frascati and Morino. The reference is to cinnamon (*cannello*).

cantina   Winery; wine cellar.

castello   Castle.

cépage   Variety of grapevine.

cerasuolo   Cherry-red color, used to describe the color of rosés.

charmat   Method of making sparkling wines in sealed, temperature-controlled vats. (See *metodo champenois*.)

chiarello   Light-colored red wine.

chiaretto   Deep-colored rosé wine.

classico   Term used for central, well-established vineyards or growing areas within a controlled appellation district, and the wine from those areas.

colli   Hills.

colline   Low hills.

DOC AND DOCG

Denominazione di Origine Controllata (DOC)
Controlled Appellation of Origin. The DOC system of controlling the production of wine, modeled after the *appellation contrôlée* laws of France, began in Italy in 1963. Through DOC law, various aspects of wine production are governed—watched over—by an official panel of wine experts. Among these aspects are the location and condition of vineyards, and the types of grapes and the quantity in which they are used in the wine. All matters related to production, aging, and labeling of bottles are regulated to promote quality and consistency. After wines are approved by the tasting panel, they receive their official DOC status from the government.

Denominazione di Origine Controllata
e Garantita (DOCG)
Controlled and Guaranteed Appellation of Origin. This category is reserved for a few outstanding wines, "guaranteed" by the government. Only six wines have achieved this status: Barolo and Barbaresco in Piedmont; Brunello di Montalcino, Vino Nobile di Montepulciano, and Chianti in Tuscany; and Albana di Romagna, the only white DOCG, in Emilia-Romagna.

cru "Growth"; referring to a wine grown in a particular defined area or vineyard.

dolce Sweet.

DOC (Denominazione di Origine Controllata) Controlled Appellation of Origin.

DOCG (Denominazione di Origine Controllata e Garantita) Controlled and Guaranteed Appellation of Origin

enologia Enology, the study of wine.

enoteca "Wine library"; wine shop or premises with wines on display.

fattoria Farm.

fermo Still, as in a still wine. Also wine that is stable, which has completed all its fermentation.

FOOD STORES

alimentari A grocery store. Sells cheese, *salumi* (salted and cured meat cuts), bottled water, among other items.

bottiglieria A wine store.

caseificio A cheese shop.

drogheria A general grocery and dry goods store. Doesn't usually stock cheese, *salumi,* or fresh produce.

enoteca A wine shop, usually stocked with a wide variety of wines, both regional and national.

frutteria, frutta e verdura A fruit and vegetable store.

gastronomia A delicatessen or general food store.

gelateria An ice cream shop.

latteria A milk shop, which also sells yogurt, cream, and other dairy items.

macelleria A butcher's shop.

norcineria A butcher who specializes in pork products. The name refers to the Umbrian town of Norcia, famous for its *salumi.*

panetteria, panificio A bread shop.

pasticceria A pastry shop.

pastificio A store that sells fresh pasta.

pescheria A fish store. A *mercato ittico* is a fish market.

rosticceria A delicatessen that sells prepared dishes, including roasted meats.

salumeria A store specializing in *salumi—salame, prosciutto, mortadella,* and other meats, both raw and cured.

salsamenteria A delicatessen that often sells many of the items of a *salumeria.*

torrefazione A store that sells coffee (ground or whole beans). Tea, spices, and chocolate may also be found here.

vini e olii A store selling wine and olive oil.

fresco Fresh; cool.

frizzante Frizzy, bubbly, but not "sparkling"; such a wine.

governo The addition of dried grapes to wine that is already fermented, which produces a second fermentation.

liquoroso Referring to a wine, often fortified, with a high alcohol content.

metodo classico or metodo champenois (méthode champenoise, m.c.) The process of fermenting sparkling wine in bottles. Named after the classic French method of making champagne. (See *charmat.*)

netto Clean.

ossidato Oxidized.

passito Semidried; sweet wine made from semidried grapes.

pastoso Moderately sweet; "mellow."

perlage Bubbles in a glass of sparkling wine.

podere   Small farm or estate.

raccolta, raccolto   Harvest.

Recioto   Wine produced from semidried grapes picked from the *recie,* the upper and outer part of grape bunches, where the most sunlight hits. *Recie* means "ears" in a Venetian dialect.

ripassare   To referment a wine on the lees another in order to create a fuller, more complex one. Examples: Campo Fiorin (Masi) and Catullo (Bertani) are both refermented on lees of Recioto Amarone.

riserva   Reserve; referring to a wine aged for a specified period of time, according to DOC and DOCG regulations.

riserva speciale   Referring to a wine aged longer than a *riserva.*

rosato   Rosé.

rosso   Red.

rubino   Ruby-colored.

secco   Dry, *sec.*

semisecco   Semisweet, *demisec.*

spumante   Sparkling; such a wine.

superiore   Referring to a DOC wine that goes beyond what's required by DOC law—higher alcohol content, longer aging, and so on.

tappo   Top, as of cork (*sughero*); "corked."

tenuta   Farm or estate.

uva   Grapes.

vendemmia   Grape harvest or vintage.

vigna, vigneto   Vineyard.

vino novello   A new wine, usually in a Beaujolais style.

vino da tavola   A table wine. Unclassified, not a DOC or DOCG.

A RANKING

OF THE

ESSENTIAL

RESTAURANTS

OF ITALY

Restaurants are listed
alphabetically within each
star category.

★ ★ ★ ★ ★

Antica Osteria del Ponte, Cassinetta di Lugagnano / 156
Enoteca Pinchiorri, Florence / 170
Guido, Costigliole d'Asti / 163
La Mora, Ponte a Moriano / 254
Al Sorriso, Soriso / 294

★ ★ ★ ★ ½

Aimo e Nadia, Milan / 209
Fini, Modena / 225
Al Rododendro, Boves / 150
Scaletta, Milan / 211
La Smarrita, Turin / 306
Del Sole, Ranco / 260

★ ★ ★ ★

Alberto Ciarla, Rome / 270
Antica Osteria del Teatro, Piacenza / 249
Cavallo Bianco, Aosta / 125
La Frasca, Castrocaro Terme / 159
Gambero Rosso, San Vincenzo / 286
Gualtiero Marchesi, Milan / 213
Locanda della Colonna, Tossignano / 301
Al Moro, Rome / 266
Nuovo Marconi, Verona / 332
Patrizia e Roberto del Pianeta Terra, Rome / 272
Picci, Cavriago / 161
Romano, Viareggio / 340

San Domenico, Imola / 190
Il Trigabolo, Argenta / 129
Da Vittorio, Bergamo / 137

★ ★ ★ ½

Albergo del Sole, Maleo / 199
Alfredo-Gran San Bernardo, Milan / 215
Ambasciata, Quistello / 257
Antico Brolo, Padua / 236
Arche, Verona / 336
Al Bersagliere, Goito / 186
La Carmagnole, Carmagnola / 154
Ceresole, Cremona / 167
La Chiusa, Montefollonico / 228
Cibreo, Florence / 172
Il Cigno, Mantua / 204
Al 59-da Giuseppe, Rome / 274
La Contea, Neive / 230
Il Desco, Verona / 333
Gener Neuv, Asti / 133
Il Griso, Malgrate / 201
L'Oca Bianca, Viareggio / 341
Notai, Bologna / 142
Papagallo, Bologna / 144
Paracucchi–Locanda dell'Angelo, Ameglia / 122
Dal Pescatore, Canneto sull'Oglio / 152
Silverio, Bologna / 141
Taverna del Lupo, Gubbio / 189
Vecchia Lanterna, Turin / 308
Vecchia Lugana, Lugana di Sirmione / 196

★ ★ ★

Antica Trattoria Botteganova, Siena / 289
Checchino dal 1887, Rome / 275
Cinzia e Valerio, Vicenza / 346
Corte Sconta, Venice / 321
12 Apostoli, Verona / 337
Emiliano, Stresa / 297
Gran Gotto, Genoa / 184
Al Graspo de Ua, Venice / 322
Grill Casanova, Milan / 220

Locanda dell'Amorosa, Sinalunga / 292
Da Noi, Florence / 176
Osteria Da Fiore, Venice / 320
Peck, Milan / 218
Piperno, Rome / 277
La Rosetta, Perugia / 243
Sabatini, Florence / 177
Savini, Milan / 216
Sergio, Pisa / 251
Solferino, Lucca / 193
La Taverna del Bronzino, Florence / 174
Tre Marie, L'Aquila / 128
Le Tre Vaselle, Torgiano / 299
Umbra, Assisi / 131

★ ★ ½

Antico Martini, Venice / 324
Del Cambio, Turin / 310
Harry's Bar, Venice / 323
Locanda Cipriani, Venice / 326
Parizzi, Parma / 239
Da Rodolfo–La Diligenza, Borgo Pace / 148

Lo Scudiero, Pesaro / 247
Tre Spade, Ravenna / 263

★ ★

Alfredo–Relais El Toulà, Treviso / 303
Buca di Sant'Antonio, Lucca / 194
Nuovo Coppiere, Urbino / 315

★

Maurizio, Orvieto / 232

RESTAURANTS TO AVOID

La Caravella, Venice
Due Lampioni da Carlo, Turin
Papa Giovanni, Rome
Relais Le Jardin (in the Lord Byron Hotel), Rome
Ristorante M.R., Perugia
La Rosetta, Rome

A GENERAL LISTING OF THE RESTAURANTS OF ITALY BY CITY

Restaurants are listed
by city and within each
city by order of importance.

ALBARETTO DELLA TORRE

Dei Cacciatori da Cesare
via Romagna, 23
(0173) 520-141
Closed Tues, Wed, Jan, Aug

AMEGLIA

*Paracucchi–Locanda dell'Angelo
viale XXV Aprile 60 (strada provinciale Sarzana–Marinella)
(0187) 64-391
Closed Jan 10–31

ANCONA

Miscia
molo Sud
(071) 201-376
Closed Sun dinner, Dec 25–Jan 1

Passetto
piazza 4 Novembre
(071) 33-214
Closed Wed

ANGHIARI

†*Locanda al Castello di Sorci*
(See p. 243, under Perugia)
via San Lorenzo, 21
(0575) 789-066
Closed Mon

AOSTA

*Cavallo Bianco
via Aubert, 15
(0165) 362-214
Closed Sun dinner, Mon except July and Aug

L'AQUILA

*Tre Marie
via Tre Marie, 3
(0862) 20-191
Closed Sun dinner, Mon, Dec 25, Dec 31

AREZZO

†*Buca di San Francesco* (see p. 243, under Perugia)
piazza San Francesco, 1
(0575) 23-271
Closed Mon dinner, Tues, July

* Full review
† Other recommended restaurant

ARGENTA

Il Trigabolo
piazza Garibaldi, 4
(0532) 804-121
Closed Sun dinner, Mon,
July

ARONA

Taverna del Pittore
piazza del Popolo, 39
(0322) 3366
Closed Mon, June 15–30,
Dec 20–Jan 10

ASSISI

Umbra
vicolo degli Archi, 6
(075) 812-240
Closed Tues, Jan 10–Mar
15, Nov 15–Dec 15

Buca di San Francesco
via Brizi, 1
(075) 812-204
Closed Mon, Jan 7–Feb 28

Medio Evo
via Arco dei Priori, 4
(075) 813-068
Closed Wed, Jan 7–Feb 1,
July 3–21

ASTI

Gener Neuv
lungo Tanaro, 4
(0141) 57-270
Closed Sun dinner, Mon,
Jan or Dec, Aug

BASCHI

Vissani
(See p. 234, under Orvieto)
strada statale, 448
(in Civitella del Lago)
(0744) 950-206
Closed Wed, July

BERGAMO

Da Vittorio
viale Papa Giovanni XXIII,
21
(035) 218-060
Closed Wed, Aug 8–25

†*Gourmet*
via San Vigilio, 1 (Città
Alta)
(035) 256-110
Closed Tues

†*La Fontana*
piazza Vecchia, 2
(035) 220-648
Closed Wed, Jan

Tino Fontana
piazza della Repubblica, 6
(in the Hotel Excelsior
San Marco)
(035) 232-132
Closed Sun

BOLOGNA

Silverio
via Nosadella, 37a
(051) 330-604
Closed Mon, Aug

Notai
via de' Pignattari, 1
(051) 228-694
Closed Sun, Aug 15–30

Pappagallo
piazza della Mercanzia, 3c
(051) 232-807
Closed Sun dinner, Mon,
Jan 12–18, Aug 1–22

†*Diana*
via dell'Indipendenza, 24
(051) 231-302
Closed Mon, Jan 1–10,
Aug

†*Franco Rossi*
via Goito, 3
(051) 238-818
Closed Sun

Taverna 3 Frecce
strada Maggiore, 19
(051) 231-200
Closed Sun dinner, Mon,
    Aug, Dec 24–Jan 6

Rosteria Luciano
via Nazario Sauro, 19
(051) 231-249
Closed Tues dinner, Wed,
    Aug, Dec 24–Jan 1

BORGOMANERO

Pinocchio
via Matteotti, 147
(0322) 82-273
Closed Mon, Tues lunch,
    July 20–Aug 12

BORGO PACE

**Da Rodolfo–La Diligenza*
piazzetta del Paese
(0722) 89-124
Closed Wed, Sept 1–15

BOVES

*Al Rododendro
In San Giacomo
(0171) 680-372
Closed Sun dinner, Mon,
    Tues lunch, Jan 8–22,
    Aug 15–31

BRISIGHELLA

La Grotta
via Metelli, 1
(0546) 81-829
Closed Tues, Jan, June 1–
    15

Gigiolè
piazza Carducci, 5
(0546) 81-209
Closed Mon, Feb

CANNETO SULL'OGLIO

*Dal Pescatore
via Runate, 13
(0376) 70-304
Closed Mon, Tues, Jan 2–
    14, Aug 7–25

CARMAGNOLA

*La Carmagnole
via Sottotenente Chiffi, 31
(011) 971-2673
Closed Sun dinner, Mon,
    Aug 10–20

CASALE MONFERRATO

La Torre
via Garoglio, 3 (per salita
    Sant'Anna)
(0142) 70-295
Closed Wed, Aug 1–20

CASELLE TORINESE

†*Antica Zecca* (see p. 311,
under Turin)
via della Zecca, 9 (in the
    Jet Hotel)
(011) 996-3733
    (996-1403)
Closed Mon, Aug 3–19

CASSINETTA DI LUGAGNANO

**Antica Osteria del Ponte*
Near Abbiategrasso
(02) 942-0034
Closed Sun, Mon, Jan 1–
    15, Aug

CASTELFRANCO
EMILIA

Gaidello Club
via Gaidello, 18
(059) 926-806
Closed Sun, Mon, Aug

CASTIGLIONE
TORINESE

Villa Monfort's
strada del Luogo, 29
(011) 960-6214
Closed Sun dinner, Mon,
    Jan, Aug

CASTROCARO TERME

*La Frasca
via Matteotti, 34
(0543) 767-471
Closed Tues, Jan 2–20,
    Aug 1–15

CAVRIAGO

*Picci
via XX Settembre, 4
(0522) 57-201
Closed Mon dinner, Tues,
    Aug 5–25, Dec 26–Jan
    20

CENTALLO

Due Palme
via Busca, 2
(0171) 211-366
Closed Sun dinner, Wed

CERBAIA

La Tenda Rossa
piazza Monumento, 9 (near
    San Casciano in Val di
    Pesa)
(055) 826-132
Closed Wed, Thurs lunch,
    Aug 16–Sept 2

CERTOSA DI PAVIA

Vecchio Mulino
via al Monumento, 5
(0382) 925-894
Closed Sun dinner, Mon

CETONA

†*La Frateria di Padre Eligio*
(see p. 233, under Orvieto)
In the Convento di San
    Francesco
(0578) 238-015
Closed Tues, Jan 1–Feb 15

CHIANCIANO TERME

La Casanova
strada della Vittoria, 10
(0578) 60-449
Closed Wed, Jan, Feb

CIOCCARO DI
PENANGO
(MONCALVO)

†*Da Beppe* (see p. 136,
under Asti)
In the Locanda del
    Sant'Uffizio
(0141) 91-271
Closed Tues, Jan 3–25,
    Aug 10–20

COLLECCHIO

Villa Maria Luigia–Di Ceci
(0521) 805-489
Closed Thurs, Jan 11–31,
    Aug 9–24

CORTINA VECCHIA

Da Giovanni
via Cortina Centro, 79
    (near Alseno)
(0523) 948-113
Closed Tues, Jan 2–18,
    Aug 16–Sept 5

CORTONA

La Loggetta
piazza Pescheria, 3
(0575) 603-777
Closed Mon, Sun dinner
    Oct–March, Jan 2–Feb 2

COSTIGLIOLE D'ASTI

*Guido
piazza Umberto I, 27
(0141) 966-012
Closed every day lunch,
    Sun

COZZO LOMELLINA

Castello di Cozzo
via Castello, 20
(0384) 74-298
Closed Tues, Jan, Aug

CREMA

†Guada'l Canal (see p. 166
under Cremona)
via Crocicchio, 46 (near
    Santo Stefano)
(0373) 200-133
Closed Sun dinner, Mon,
    Aug

CREMONA

*Ceresole
via Ceresole, 4
(0372) 23-322
Closed Sun dinner, Mon,
    Jan 22–30, Aug 6–28

CUNEO

Tre Citroni
via Bonelli, 2
(0171) 62-048
Closed Wed, June 15–30,
    Sept 15–30

Le Plat d'Etain
corso Giolitti, 18
(0171) 61-918
Closed Sun

FAENZA

Amici Miei
corso Mazzini, 54
(0546) 661-600
Closed Mon, Aug

FANO

Trattoria Da Quinta
viale Adriatico, 42
(0721) 808-043
Closed Sun, Aug

FIESOLE

Trattoria le Cave di Maiano
via della Cave, 16 (near
    Malano)
(055) 59-133
Closed Sun dinner, Thurs,
    Aug

FLORENCE

*Enoteca Pinchiorri
via Ghibellina, 87
(055) 242-777
Closed Sun, Mon lunch,
    Aug, Dec 24–28

*Cibreo
via dei Macci, 118
(055) 234-1100
Closed Sun, Mon, Jan 1–7,
    Apr 4–10, Aug 1–Sept 5

*La Taverna del Bronzino
via delle Ruote, 25
(055) 495-220
Closed Sun, Aug 1–21

Da Noi
via Fiesolana, 46
(055) 242-917
Closed Sun, Mon, Aug

Sabatini
via de' Panzani, 9a
(055) 282-802
Closed Mon

†*Trattoria Le Quattro Stagioni*
via Maggio, 61
(055) 218-906
Closed Sun, Aug 9–31,
    Dec 21–Jan 4

†*Ottorino*
via delle Oche, 12–16
(055) 218-747
Closed Sun, Aug

†*Relais Le Jardin*
piazza Massimo d'Azeglio,
    3
(in the Hotel Regency)
(055) 245-247
Closed Sun

†*Al Campidoglio*
via del Campidoglio, 8
(055) 287-770
Closed Thurs

†*Antico Fattore*
via Lambertesca, 1
(055) 261-215
Closed Sun, Mon

†*Mamma Gina*
borgo San Jacopo, 37
(055) 296-009
Closed Sun, Aug 7–21

†*Sostanza detto Il Troia*
via della Porcellana, 25
(055) 212-691
Closed Sun, Sat dinner,
    Aug

†*Coco Lezzone*
via del Parioncino, 26
(055) 287-178
Closed Sun, Tues dinner;
    summer: closed Sun, Sat,
    open weekdays lunch and
    dinner

†*Cammillo*
borgo San Jacopo, 57
(055) 212-427
Closed Wed, Thur, Aug 1–
    21, Dec 20–Jan 15

†*Il Latini*
via dei Palchetti, 6
(055) 210-916
Closed Mon, Tues lunch,
    July 20–Aug 10

FOLIGNO

Villa Roncalli
via Roma, 25
(0742) 670-291
Closed Aug 8–28

FORTE DEI MARMI

†*Lorenzo* (see p. 343, under
    Viareggio)
via Carducci, 61
(0584) 84-030
Closed Mon, Dec 15–
    Jan 31

GARDONE RIVIERA

Villa Fiordaliso
(0365) 20-158
Closed Sun dinner, Mon

GENOA

Gran Gotto
via Fiume, 11
(010) 564-344
Closed Sun, Aug 10–31

Saint Cyr
piazza Marsala, 8
(010) 886-897
Closed Sun, Sat, Aug 6–31,
  Dec 23–Jan 7

Da Giacomo
corso Italia, 1
(010) 369-647
Closed Sun

Cardinali da Ermanno
via Assarotti, 60
(010) 870-380
Closed Sun, July 28–Aug
  22

Da Mario
via Conservatori del
  Mare, 35
(010) 297-788
Closed Sat

Da Genio
salita San Leonardo, 61
(010) 546-463
Closed Sun, Aug

GOITO

*Al Bersagliere
via statale Goitese, 258
(0376) 60-007
Closed Mon, Tues lunch,
  Jan 2–12, Aug 7–27

GUBBIO

Taverna del Lupo
via Ansidei, 21
(075) 927-1269
Closed Mon, Jan 7–Feb 6

†*Alla Fornace di Mastro
Giorgio*
via Mastro Giorgio, 2
(075) 927-5740
Closed Mon, Feb 4–28

Porta Tessenaca
via Piccardi, 21
(075) 927-2765
Closed Wed, Jan 10–Feb
  10

IMOLA

San Domenico
via Sacchi, 1
(0542) 29-000
Closed Mon, Jan 1–16,
  July 24–Aug 16

ISEO

†*Osteria il Volto* (see p. 139,
  under Bergamo)
via Mirolte, 33
(030) 981-462
Closed Wed, Thurs lunch,
  July (3 weeks)

Le Maschere
vicolo della Pergola, 7
(030) 982-1542
Closed Sun dinner, Mon

ISOLA D'ASTI

Il Cascinalenuovo
Strada Statale, 231 (Asti-
  Alba)
(0141) 958-166
Closed Sun dinner, Mon,
  Aug 1–20

ISOLA MAGGIORE

†*Sauro* (see p. 243, under
  Perugia)
Lago di Trasimeno
(075) 826-168
Closed Jan, Feb

LA MORRA

Belvedere
piazza Castello, 5
(0173) 50-190
Closed Sun dinner, Mon,
  Jan, Feb

LEIVI

†*Ca' Peo* (see p. 185, under
  Genoa)
strada Panoramica
(0185) 319-090
Closed Mon, Tues lunch,
  Jan 4–18, Nov

LUCCA

Solferino
Near San Macario in Piano
(0583) 59-118
Closed Wed, Thurs lunch,
  Jan 12–19, Aug 10–24

Buca di Sant'Antonio
via della Cervia, 1/5
(0583) 55-881
Closed Sun dinner, Mon,
  July 9–24

LUGANA DI SIRMIONE

Vecchia Lugana
piazzale Vecchia Lugana, 1
(Strada Statale Milano-
  Venezia)
(030) 919-012
Closed Mon dinner, Tues

MALEO

Albergo del Sole
via Trabbatoni, 22
(0377) 58-142
Closed Sun dinner, Mon,
  Jan, Aug

MALGRATE

Il Griso
via Provinciale, 51 (in the
  Hotel Il Griso)
(0341) 283-217
Closed Dec 20–Jan 6

MANTUA

Il Cigno
piazza d'Arco, 1
(0376) 327-101
Closed Mon, Tues, Aug 7–
  20

†*Aquila Nigra*
vicolo Bonacolsi, 4
(0376) 350-651
Closed Sun dinner, Mon

MESTRE

Dall'Amelia–Alla Giustizia
via Miranese, 113
(041) 913-951
Closed Wed, Oct–June

MILAN

Aimo e Nadia
via Montecuccoli, 6
(02) 416-886
Closed Sun, Sat lunch, Aug

Scaletta
piazzale Stazione Genova, 3
(02) 835-0290
Closed Sun, Mon, April 1–
  11, Aug, Dec 24–Jan 6

Gualtiero Marchesi
via Bonvesin de la Riva, 9
(02) 741-246
Closed Sun, Mon lunch,
  Sat in July, July 29–Aug
  29, Dec 23–Jan 9

Alfredo–Gran San Bernardo
via Borgese, 14
(02) 331-9000
Closed Sun, Aug, Dec 21–
    Jan 19

Savini
Galleria Vittorio Emanuele
    II
(02) 805-8343
Closed Sun, Aug 10–19,
    Dec 23–Jan 3

Peck
via Victor Hugo, 4
(02) 876-774
Closed Sun, July 3–24

Grill Casanova
piazza della Repubblica, 20
    (in the Palace Hotel)
(02) 6336
Closed Aug

†*Giannino*
via Amatore Sciesa, 8
(02) 545-2948
Closed Sun, Aug

†*Grattacielo*
via Vittor Pisani, 6
(02) 659-2359
Closed Fri dinner, Sat,
    Aug, Dec 26–Jan 8

†*Bagutta*
via Bagutta, 14
(02) 702-767
Closed Sun, Aug 7–31,
    Dec 23–Jan 5

Sadler
ripa di Porta Ticinese, 51
(02) 58-104-451
Closed Sun, Mon, Jan 1–
    10, Aug 12–Sept 5

Al Porto
piazzale Generale Cantore
(02) 832-1481
Closed Sun, Mon lunch,
    Aug, Dec 24–Jan 3

Canoviano
via Hoepli, 6
(02) 805-8472
Closed Sun, Sat lunch

Soti's
via Pietro Calvi, 2
(02) 796-838
Closed Sun, Sat lunch, Aug

A Riccione
via Taramelli, 70
(02) 668-6807
Closed Mon

Ascot
via Lentasio, 3–5 (in the
    Grand Hotel Brun)
(02) 862-946
Closed Sun, Aug

Gallia's
piazza Duca d'Aosta, 9 (in
    the Hotel Excelsior
    Gallia)
(02) 6277
Open every day

La Torre del Mangia
via Procaccini, 37
(02) 314-871
Closed Sun dinner, Mon

San Vito da Nino
via San Vito, 5
(02) 837-7029
Closed Mon, Aug

Osteria La Cagnola
via Cirillo, 14
(02) 331-9428
Closed Sun, Sat dinner,
    Aug

MODENA

*Fini
rua Frati Minori, 54
(059) 223-314
Closed Mon, Tues, July
    24–Aug 22, Dec 24–31

†Borso d'Este
piazza Roma, 5
(059) 214-114
Closed Sun, Aug

MONFORTE D'ALBA

Da Felicin
via Vallada, 18
(0173) 78-225
Closed Wed, Jan 1–Feb 5,
    June 28–July 5

MONTECATINI TERME

Gourmet
viale Amendola, 6
(0572) 771-012
Closed Tues, Aug 1–20

MONTEFOLLONICO

*La Chiusa
via della Madonnina, 88
(0577) 669-668
Closed Jan 6–March 15,
    Nov 5–Dec 5, lunch July
    and Aug

MONTEPULCIANO

†Fattoria Pulcino (see
    p. 230, under
    Montefollonico)
Strada Statale 146-via
    Chianciano Terme
(0578) 716-905
Closed Mon in winter

MONTERIGGIONI

Il Pozzo
piazza Roma, 2
(0577) 304-127
Closed Sun dinner, Mon,
    Jan 8–25, Aug 1–14

MONTIGNOSO

†Il Bottaccio (see p. 343
    under Viareggio)
via Bottaccio, 1 (near
    Massa)
(0585) 340-031
Always open

NEIVE

*La Contea
piazza Cocito, 8
(0173) 67-126
Closed Sun dinner, Mon
    except Sept, Oct, and
    Nov

NONANTOLA

Osteria di Rubbiara
via Risaia, 2 (in Rubbiara)
(059) 549-019
Closed Sun dinner, Tues,
    Aug, Dec 25–Jan 10

NORCIA

Grotta Azzurra
via Alfieri, 12
(0743) 816-513
Closed Tues

Dal Francese
(0743) 816-290
Closed Fri from Oct 1–
    May 31, June 10–22,
    Nov 10–22

ORVIETO

Maurizio
via del Duomo, 78
(0763) 41-114
Closed Tues, Jan

Cucina Monaldo
via Angelo da Orvieto, 7
(0763) 41-634
Closed Mon, July 15–30

Antica Trattoria dell'Orso
via della Misericordia,
18-20
(0763) 41-642
Closed Tues, Jan 15–Feb
15

PADUA

Antico Brolo
vicolo Cigolo, 14
(049) 664-555
Closed Sun, Aug 1–21

Da Artemio
Frazione Torre, via Fornaci,
128
(049) 625-153
Closed Tues, Wed, Aug

PARMA

Parizzi
strada della Repubblica, 71
(0521) 285-952
Closed Sun dinner, Mon,
July 21–Aug 17

†*La Greppia*
strada Garibaldi, 39
(0521) 33-686
Closed Thur, Fri, July, Dec
24–Jan 2

Angiol d'Or
vicolo Scutellari, 1
(0521) 282-632
Closed Sun, Mon lunch

Cocchi
via Gramsci, 16
(0521) 91-990
Closed Sat, Aug

PASSIGNANO SUL TRASIMENO

†*Cacciatore–Da Luciano* (see
p. 243, under Perugia)
lungolago Aganoor
Pompilj, 11
(075) 827-210
Closed Wed

PAVIA

Locanda Vecchia Pavia
via Cardinale Riboldi, 2
(0382) 304-132
Closed Mon, Wed lunch,
Aug

PERUGIA

La Rosetta
piazza Italia, 19
(075) 20-841
Closed Mon

†*La Lanterna*
via Rocchi, 6
(075) 66-064
Closed Sun, Aug 1–26

PESARO

Lo Scudiero
via Baldassini, 2
(0721) 64-107
Closed Thur, July

†*Da Teresa*
viale Trieste, 180 (in the
Hotel Principe)
(0721) 30-096
Closed Jan, Dec

PESCARA

†*Guerino* (see p. 129, under
L'Aquila)
viale della Riviera, 4
(085) 421-2065
Closed Tues except July and
  Aug

Duilio
via Regina Margherita, 11
(085) 378-278
Closed Sun dinner, Mon,
  Aug

PIACENZA

*Antica Osteria del Teatro
via Verdi, 16
(0523) 23-777
Closed Sun dinner, Mon,
  Jan 1–6, Aug 1–25

PIEVE D'ALPAGO

†*Dolada* (see p. 305, under
Treviso)
via Dolada, 9
(0437) 479-141
Closed Mon except July
  and Aug, Jan 9–Feb 3

PISA

*Sergio
lungarno Pacinotti, 1
(050) 48-245
Closed Sun, Mon lunch,
  Jan 15–31, July 15–31

†*Al Ristoro dei Vecchi Macelli*
via Volturno, 49
(050) 20-424
Closed Sun lunch, Wed, Jan
  1–8, Aug 10–24

†*Lo Schiaccianoci*
via Vespucci, 104
(050) 21-024
Closed Sun dinner
  (summer, all day), Mon,
  Aug, Dec 27–Jan 5

PONTE A MORIANO

*La Mora
via Sesto di Moriano, 1748
(0583) 57-109
Closed Wed dinner, Thurs,
  June 27–July 8, Oct 10–
  20

QUISTELLO

*Ambasciata
via Martiri di Belfiore, 33
(0376) 618-255
Closed Wed, Jan 7–23,
  Aug 4–21

RANCO

*Del Sole
piazza Venezia, 5
(0331) 976-507
Closed Mon dinner, Tues,
  Jan 1–Feb 11

RAVENNA

*Tre Spade
via Rasponi, 37
(0544) 32-382
Closed Mon, July 25–Aug
  28

Al Gallo
via Maggiore, 87
(0544) 23-775
Closed Mon dinner, Tues,
  July 1–15, Dec 20–Jan
  10

RECCO

Manuelina
via Roma, 278
(0185) 75-364
Closed Wed, Jan 10–Feb
   10, July 17–27

REGGIO NELL'EMILIA

Il Girarrosto
viale Nobili, 2 (in the
   Grand Hotel Astoria)
(0522) 35-245
Closed Sun, Aug 10–20,
   Dec 23–Jan 2

ROME

*Al Moro
vicolo delle Bollette, 13
(06) 678-3495
Closed Sun, Aug

*Alberto Ciarla
piazza San Cosimato, 40
   (in Trastevere)
(06) 581-8668
Closed every day lunch,
   Sun, Aug 12–29, Dec
   23–Jan 6

**Patrizia e Roberto del
Pianeta Terra*
via Arco del Monte, 94
(06) 686-9893
Closed every day lunch,
   Mon, Aug

*Al 59-da Giuseppe
via Brunetti, 59
(06) 361-9019
Closed Sun, Sat in June and
   July, Aug

*Checchino dal 1887
via di Monte Testaccio, 30
(06) 574-6318
Closed Sun dinner, all day
   Sun June–Aug; Mon, last
   week of July to the last
   week of Aug, Dec 25–
   Jan 1

*Piperno
Monte de' Cenci, 9
(06) 654-0629
Closed Sun dinner, Mon,
   Easter, Aug, Dec 23–Jan 2

†Dal Bolognese
piazza del Popolo, 1
(06) 361-1426
Closed Sun dinner, Mon,
   Sept–May, Aug 5–20

†Vecchia Roma
piazza Campitelli, 18
(06) 686-4604
Closed Wed

†Tavola d'Oro
via Marianna Dionigi, 37
(06) 312-317
Closed Sun, Aug

Camponeschi
piazza Farnese, 50
(06) 687-4927
Closed Sun

Nino
via Borgognona, 11
(06) 679-5676
Closed Sun

Passetto
via Zanardelli, 14
(06) 654-3696
Closed Sun, Mon lunch,
   Nov

Primavera (formerly *Leon d'Oro*)
via Cagliari, 25
(06) 861-847
Closed every day lunch

El Toulà
via della Lupa, 29b
(06) 687-3498
Closed Sun, Sat lunch,
    Aug, Dec 24–26

Tullio
via di San Nicola da
    Tolentino, 26
(06) 481-8564
Closed Sun, Aug

Il Buco
via Sant'Ignazio, 8
(06) 679-3298
Closed Mon, Aug 15–31

Taverna Giulia
vicolo dell'Oro, 23
(06) 686-9768
Closed Sun, Aug

Augustea
via della Frezza
(06) 360-6089
Closed Mon, Aug

RONCOLE VERDI

†*Guareschi* (see p. 168,
    under Cremona)
via Processione, 13 (near
    Busseto)
(0524) 92-495
Closed every day dinner,
    Fri, Feb, July, Dec

RUBIERA

*Arnaldo–Clinical
Gastronomica*
piazza XXIV Maggio, 3
(0522) 62-124
Closed Sun, Mon lunch

SAINT-VINCENT

Nuovo Batezar–Da Renato
via Marconi, 1
(0166) 3164
Closed Wed, Thurs lunch,
    Feb 20–Mar 10, July 1–
    15

SAN BERNARDINO

La Betulla
Near Trana
(011) 933-106
Closed Mon dinner, Tues,
    Jan

SAN CASCIANO IN VAL DI PESA

Antica Posta
piazza Zannoni, 1
(055) 820-116
Closed Mon, Aug

SAN GIMIGNANO

Le Terrazze
piazza della Cisterna (in the
    Hotel La Cisterna)
(0577) 940-328
Closed Tues, Wed lunch,
    Nov 10–March 10

SANSEPOLCRO

†*Ristorante Paola e Marco*
    (See p. 243, under
    Perugia)
via Palmiro Togliatti, 66 (in
    Pieve Vecchia)
(0575) 734-875
Closed Sun dinner, Tues

SANTA FRANCA

Da Colombo
Near Polesine Parmense
(0524) 98-114
Closed Mon dinner, Tues,
    Jan, July

SAN VINCENZO

Gambero Rosso
piazza della Vittoria, 13
(0565) 701-021
Closed Tues, every day
   lunch June 15–Sept 15,
   Nov

†*La Bitta*
via Vittorio Emanuele II,
   119
(0565) 704-080
Closed Mon, Oct 15–Nov
   15

SATURNIA

I Due Cippi-da Michele
piazza Vittoria Veneto, 26
(0564) 601-074
Closed Tues, Jan 7–30

SCANDIANO

Al Portone
piazza Boiardo, 4
(0522) 855-985
Closed Tues, July 15–Aug
   15, Dec 24–Jan 7

SIENA

*Antica Trattoria
Bottaganova*
via Chiantigiana, 29
(0577) 284-230
Closed Sun

*Ristorante dell'Hotel Certosa
di Maggiano*
strada di Certosa, 82 (in
   the Hotel Certosa)
(0577) 288-180
Closed Tues

Altri Tempi
via di Scacciapensieri, 10
   (in the Hotel Villa
   Scacciapensieri)
(0577) 41-442
Closed Wed, Nov 3–March
   25

Al Marsili
via del Castoro, 3
(0577) 47-154
Closed Mon

SINALUNGA

Locanda dell'Amorosa
2 km south of Sinalunga
(0577) 679-497
Closed Mon, Tues lunch,
   Jan 20–Feb 28

SORISO

Al Sorriso
via Roma, 18
(0322) 983-228
Closed Mon, Tues lunch,
   Jan 10–31

SPELLO

Il Molino
piazza Matteotti, 6
(0742) 651-305
Closed Tues

Il Cacciatore
via Giulia, 42
(0742) 651-141
Closed Mon, June 20–
   July 6

STRESA

Emiliano
corso Italia, 52
(0323) 31-396
Closed Tues, Nov 15–
   Dec 20

TARQUINIA

Il Bersagliere
via Benedetto Croce, 2
(0766) 856-047
Closed Sun dinner, Mon,
  Nov

TODI

Umbria
via San Bonaventura, 13
(075) 882-737
Closed Tues, Dec 19–Jan 8

TORGIANO

*Le Tre Vaselle
via Garibaldi, 48
(075) 982-447
Open every day

TOSSIGNANO

*Locanda della Colonna
via Nuova, 10–11
(0542) 91-006
Closed Sun, Mon, Jan 10–
  Feb 10, Aug 15–31

TREBBO DI RENO

*Il Sole-Antica Locanda del
Trebbo*
via Lame, 67
(051) 700-102
Closed Sun

TRESCORE CREMASCO

†Trattoria del Fulmine (see
p. 201, under Maleo)
via Carioni, 12
(0373) 70-203
Closed Sun dinner, Mon,
  Jan 1–10, Aug

TRESTINA

Mencuccio
(075) 854-409
Closed Sun, Aug

TREVISO

*Alfredo–Relais El Toulà
via Collalto, 26
(0422) 540-275
Closed Sun dinner, Mon,
  July 26–Aug 25

Le Beccherie
piazza Ancillotto, 10
(0422) 540-871
Closed Thurs dinner, Fri,
  July 14–31

TURIN

*La Smarrita
corso Unione Sovietica,
  244
(011) 390-657
Closed Mon, Aug 3–27

*Vecchia Lanterna
corso Re Umberto, 21
(011) 537-047
Closed Sun, Sat lunch,
  Aug 10–20

*Del Cambio
piazza Carignano, 2
(011) 546-690
Closed Sun, July 27–
  Aug 27

†Al Gatto Nero
corso Filippo Turati, 14
(011) 590-414
Closed Sun, Aug

'L Caval 'D Brons
piazza San Carlo, 157
(011) 553-491
Closed Sun

El Toulà
strada al Traforo del Pino,
    47 (in the Hotel Villa
    Sassi)
(011) 890-556
Closed Sun, Aug

Montecarlo
via San Francesco da Paola,
    37
(011) 541-234
Closed Sun, Sat lunch, Aug

Al Saffi
via Aurelio Saffi, 2
(011) 442-213
Closed Sun, Aug

Ostu Bacu
corso Vercelli, 226
(011) 264-579
Closed Sun, July 25–
    Aug 25

URBINO

*Nuovo Coppiere
via Porta Maja, 20
(0722) 320-092
Closed Wed, Feb

†*Vecchia Urbino*
via dei Vasari 3–5
(0722) 4447
Closed Tues Oct 1–Feb 28

VENICE

*Osteria Da Fiore
calle del Scaleter San Polo,
    2202
(041) 721-308
Closed Sun, Mon,
    Aug 1–22, Dec 25–
    Jan 6

*Corte Sconta
calle del Pestrin, Castello
    3886
(041) 522-7024
Closed Sun, Mon

*Al Graspo de Ua
calle dei Bombaseri, 5094
(041) 522-3647
Closed Mon, Tues,
    Dec 20–Jan 3

*Harry's Bar
calle Vallaresso, 1323
(041) 523-6797
Closed Mon, Jan 3–Feb 3

*Antico Martini
campo San Fantin, 1983
(041) 522-4121
Closed Tues, Wed lunch,
    Jan 10–Mar 15,
    Dec 12–21

*Locanda Cipriani
On Torcello Island
(041) 730-150
Closed Tues, March 19–
    Nov 20

†*Da Ivo*
calle dei Fuseri, 1809
(041) 528-5004
Closed Sun, Jan

†*La Colomba*
piscina di Frezzeria, 1665
(041) 522-1175
Closed Wed in winter

Antica Bessetta
calle Salvio, 1395 (Santa
    Croce)
(041) 721-687
Closed Tues, Wed, part of
    July and Aug

VERONA

*Nuovo Marconi
via Fogge, 4
(045) 595-295
Closed Sun

*Il Desco
via Dietro San Sebastiano, 7
(045) 595-358
Closed Sun, Jan 1–10,
    June 12–28

*Arche
via Arche Scaligere, 6
(045) 800-7415
Closed Sun, Mon lunch,
    June 25–July 17

*12 Apostoli
corticella San Marco, 3
(045) 596-999
Closed Sun dinner, Mon,
    June 16–July 6

VIAREGGIO

*Romano
via Mazzini, 120
(0584) 31-382
Closed Mon, Jan 9–27,
    July 3–10

*L'Oca Bianca
strada statale, 1 (Via
    Aurelia N)
(0584) 64-191
Closed Wed, Thurs lunch,
    lunch July and Aug,
    Nov 15–Dec 15

†Il Patriarca
viale Carducci, 79
(0584) 53-126
Closed Wed except
    June 14–Sept 15

Montecatini
viale Manin, 8
(0584) 962-129
Closed Mon except July–
    Sept 15

VICENZA

*Cinzia e Valerio
piazzetta Porta Padova,
    65–67
(0444) 505-213
Closed Mon, Aug

†Tre Visi
contrà Porti, 6
(0444) 238-677
Closed Sun dinner, Mon,
    July 15–Aug 8, Dec 25–
    Jan 1

Scudo di Francia
contrà Piancoli, 4
(0444) 228-655
Closed Sun dinner, Mon,
    Aug

Da Remo
via Caimpenta, 14
(0444) 911-007
Closed Sun dinner, Mon,
    July 25–Aug 22,
    Dec 27–Jan 12

VILLA POMA

Concorde
piazza Romano-Mazzali, 8
(0386) 566-667
Closed every day lunch,
    Mon

VOLTERRA

Etruria
piazza dei Priori, 6
(0588) 86-064
Closed Thurs, June 10–30,
    Nov

THE

ESSENTIAL

RESTAURANTS

OF

ITALY

BY CITY

Ameglia

PARACUCCHI–LOCANDA DELL'ANGELO
★ ★ ★ ½

REGION	Liguria
ADDRESS	viale XXV Aprile, 60 (strada provinciale Sarzana–Marinella)
PHONE	(0187) 64-391
CREDIT CARDS	AmX, Visa, Diners
CLOSED	Jan 10–31
37 ROOMS	Simple accommodations with a very comfortable country feeling. Moderate in price.

CLASS	ATMOSPHERE	SERVICE	WINE	PRICE
4	3.5	3	3	E

An open, appealing space, with large windows and plenty of light; the restaurant gives onto the lobby of the hotel itself. The fare is for the most part seafood, which the owner and chef, Angelo Paracucchi, will select for you from what's fresh that day. He has a reputation for being his own man and can be slightly eccentric in his cooking, combining tradition with his own fantasies. He can also be overly present in his dining room (one of the criticisms one hears of him recently), and this may account for the unevenness of some of the dishes. Nevertheless, even in the lesser dishes there is a glimpse of what Angelo is capable of producing when he's back in the kitchen thinking about *this* establishment—he's also the owner of a restaurant in Paris, which seems to have distracted him a bit. The waiters here do not seem to have been cut from the same professional cloth as those in other top-ranked restaurants. And I wish his wine list better represented Liguria.

The modern, farmlike *locanda* is Angelo's creation. Although it doesn't have a typical Italian look, the rooms are comfortable and pleasant for an overnight stay.

A side trip to the enchanting Cinque Terre (or Cinque-terre) is absolutely worth your while. The "Five Lands"—villages really: Monterosso al Mare, Vernazza, Corniglia, Manarola, and Riomaggiore—are situated on the magnificent cliffs overlooking the Tyrrhenian Sea, between Levanto and Portoveneré, near La Spezia. Monterosso and Vernazza can be reached by car, while the only way to reach the other three villages is by boat or train or on foot, although a road is now under construction. The scenic but at times rugged walking trail that takes you from town to town offers stunning views of the sea, high terraced vineyards, and even medieval remains.

Directions. If you're on the *autostrada* from Florence, exit at Carrara and take the coast road until you see a sign for Sarzana, do not go all the way to Ameglia. Turn right; Paracucchi is about half a mile away on your left.

SUGGESTED DISHES

*insalata ái scampi   A salad consisting of light, delicate scampi, tomatoes, and zucchini slices, dressed with a little balsamic vinegar.

carpaccio alle lattughe   Paper-thin slices of raw beef topped with oil and black truffle (from Umbria), served on a bed of various types of lettuce.

scaloppa di cernia al pomodoro e timo   A slice of Mediterranean grouper, served with tomatoes, thyme, oil, and lemon.

triglia croccante alla semola   Crispy red mullet.

branzino al vapore con caviale   Sea bass with caviar.

piccione in agrodolce con fichi freschi   Pigeon in a sweet-and-sour sauce with figs—an unusual preparation.

frutta flambée   Fruit flambé.

SUGGESTED WINES

White

Müller Thurgau, Mario Schiopetto   A white with serious finesse. Grassy, excellent fruit-acid balance, and a long, engaging finish.

Red

Cabernet, Colli Berici, Le Rive Rosse, Villa Dal Ferro A pleasant wine from the Veneto that won't offend. Quietly herbal it is, to be sure, a modest wine, but it's priced fairly on a list of overpriced wines.

Dessert

Picolit Although of Friulian origin, this locally made Picolit is interesting and unusual, worth trying while in Liguria.

Aosta

Milan 184 km	Novara 139
Saint-Vincent 29	Turin 113

Aosta, named after the emperor Augustus, is the bilingual (French and Italian) capital of Valle d'Aosta, Italy's smallest region. *Picturesque* best describes this walled city of Roman origin, placed in a valley surrounded by some of the most serious Alpine mountains—in the north Mont Blanc, the Matterhorn, and Monte Rosa; and Gran Paradiso to the south. The Swiss and French borders are only an hour from Aosta, and it's a wonderful drive into Switzerland through the Great St. Bernard Pass and Tunnel, or into France via the Mont Blanc tunnel. Valle d'Aosta contains Europe's highest vineyards, at Morgex. The inhabitants of this region are a mountain people who require a hearty fare, and so you will find offerings of thick soups, stews made with local wines and various meats. If you're lucky you will have the opportunity to sample one of Valle d'Aosta's rare meats: *camoscio,* chamois, which is served marinated and stewed, or *mocetta,* dried and salted chamois or goat. And you won't want to miss the chance to sample two world-famous cheeses, *fontina* and *toma.* There's a gambling casino in nearby Saint-Vincent, for those of that mind.

REGION	Valle d'Aosta
ADDRESS	via Aubert, 15
PHONE	(0165) 362-214
CREDIT CARDS	AmX, Visa, Diners
CLOSED	Sun dinner, Mon except July and Aug

CLASS	ATMOSPHERE	SERVICE	WINE	PRICE
4	3.5	4	4	E

This sixteenth-century inn, set inside a charming cobbled courtyard, has Swiss-German decor and atmosphere: dark wood wainscotting, white stucco walls, red curtains with brocaded borders, an impressive fireplace, handsome crockery adorning the tables, and plenty of pewter, copper, and wood ornaments around the room. It's not overly festive, but it feels sturdy and old-world; you are aware of heavy-handed but welcoming elegance as you sit firmly, comfortably at the table here. Get the "traditional" tasting menu—"Il Menú della Tradizione"—the cheaper and more interesting of the two tasting menus. Dishes from Valle d'Aosta are the specialty, and the food is presented as artfully as anywhere in Italy. Paolo Vai, the chef and co-owner with his brother Franco, who runs the dining room, will tell you that the presentation of his food and the colors he employs have been inspired by Matisse. Trust brother Franco's suggestions.

SUGGESTED DISHES

crêpe parmentière ai sanguinacci valdostani Pork-blood sausage in a crêpe served with a sauce over the top and a purée of potatoes and leeks, all highlighted with cinnamon and nutmeg.

tortino di robiola e rape rosse A croquette of *robiola,* a soft rich white cheese vaguely reminiscent of our cream cheese, and chopped beets.

tortelli di cavolo con fonduta Large green *ravioli*-like pasta filled with cabbage, potato, and eggs, served with a *fonduta* sauce.

filetto alla carbonade Beef fillet with a red wine sauce, served with sliced polenta on the side.

assortimento di formaggi valdostani A sampling of the regional cheeses—a must at this restaurant. Ask for aged *fontina* and *toma,* and some of the tastier goat cheeses.

bavarese al limone A lemon Bavarian cream.

piccola pasticceria Little pastries and cookies that come with the meal.

SUGGESTED WINES

White

Chardonnay de Moncenis, Montfleury Only 300 bottles of this wine are produced annually, all for the proprietor of Cavallo Bianco, by the priests at the Institut Agricole Régional Aosta. The wine has an unusual taste, but is soft, rich, even buttery. The wood in which the wine is aged—French *limousin*—may account for the odd taste. Start out with a bottle of this white.

Red

Pinot Noir, Sang des Salasses ("blood of the Salasses," the ancient people of the region). Six hundred bottles of this wine are produced annually for Cavallo Bianco, by the same priests who make the white mentioned above. It is reminiscent of Oregon Pinot Noirs: a slightly odd nose, but rich, well balanced, with a good show of fruit. The color is just a shade from brown.

HOTELS

Valle d'Aosta
corso Ivrea, 146
(0165) 41-845
AmX, Visa, Diners
Moderate ($100–$143)
   A basic, not very cheerful place, but the best in Aosta, and just outside the center of town. If you are looking for better accommodations, you might opt to stay in Saint-Vincent, 29 kilometers away, at the Grand Hotel Billia, viale Piemonte, 18; tel. (0166) 3446.

Wine

Enoteca La Cave
via de Tillier, 50
  This is the place to find the obscure and interesting wines
of Valle d'Aosta.

L'Aquila

Perugia 171 km   *Pescara* 105   *Rome* 119   *Terni* 94

L'Aquila, capital of the Abruzzi, owes its name, which means
"The Eagle," to Emperor Frederick II, who founded the city
in the thirteenth century. Abruzzi is Italy's primary saffron-
growing area. Milan (*risotto alla milanese!*) is its major consumer. Among the important native sons of the Abruzzi:
Ovid, born in Sulmona in 43 B.C., and D'Annunzio, born
near Pescara in 1863. Abruzzi is home of the *panarda*—an
all-day feast with at least twenty different dishes. If that seems
too great an undertaking, settle for a bowl of the famous
Abruzzi minestrone called *le virtù* or, if this sounds too elaborate, a dish of *maccheroni alla chitarra*, a pasta cut into thin
noodles with a *chitarra*, an instrument with strings like a guitar's (*chitarra* means "guitar"), and served with a lamb and/
or tomato sauce. For some reason this city has decided to
celebrate the number 99: L'Aquila has 99 neighborhoods, 99
squares, 99 churches, and 99 fountains (the largest of which
has 99 jets of water), and the clock on the tower of the Palace
of Justice rings 99 times—unfortunately, at two in the morning.

TRE MARIE
★ ★ ★

REGION	Abruzzi
ADDRESS	via Tre Marie, 3
PHONE	(0862) 20-191
CREDIT CARDS	Cash only
CLOSED	Sun dinner, Mon, Dec 25, Dec 31

CLASS	ATMOSPHERE	SERVICE	WINE	PRICE
3	3.5	3	3	M

Located on what was the site of a shrine honoring three Marys (Mary Cleophas, Mary Magdalen, and Mary mother of Christ), this restaurant now honors these women with its name. A modest but attractive place, reminiscent of a Greek *taverna*, with mock brick walls, a variety of ceramics from the Abruzzi, plants, and a working fireplace. Warm, rustic, and inviting.

SUGGESTED DISHES

antipasto abruzzese An assortment of local sausages, ham, salami, and cheese.

le scrippelle "m'busse" Thin cheese-filled crêpes served in a broth.

maccheroni alla chitarra Thin square noodles. Served with a hearty lamb and/or tomato sauce.

lo scrigno delle Tre Marie A crêpe filled with cheese, chicken, ham, artichoke hearts, and various seasonings, and baked.

SUGGESTED WINES

White

Trebbiano d'Abruzzo, Illuminati Pleasant, light and spicy. Not a major wine but a good representative Trebbiano.

Red

Montepulciano d'Abruzzo, Cantina Zaccagnini A strong, rich, purple wine, slightly rough but well made, with some friendly fruit. Good, earnest, earthy flavors. A rustic.

In Pescara, 105 km
Guerino
viale della Riviera, 4
(085) 421-2065
AmX, Visa, Diners
Closed Tues (except in July and Aug)

HOTELS

Duca degli Abruzzi
viale Giovanni XXIII, 10
(0862) 28-341
AmX, Visa, Diners
Moderate

Argenta

Bologna 50 km *Ferrara* 34
Ravenna 40 *Venice* 146

IL TRIGABOLO
★ ★ ★ ★

REGION	Emilia-Romagna
ADDRESS	piazza Garibaldi, 4
PHONE	(0532) 804-121
CREDIT CARDS	AmX, Visa, Diners
CLOSED	Sun dinner, Mon, July

CLASS	ATMOSPHERE	SERVICE	WINE	PRICE
3.5	3	4	4	E

You don't go to Il Trigabolo for its decor—which, by the way,
is sort of fifties modern with its attendant bland-wood appointments and nondescript atmosphere. Nevertheless, when
all is said and done, it's really pleasant enough. I'll point out—
and not gratuitously, because this is a crucial measure for me
after driving or walking long distances—that care has been

taken in selecting the chairs; these are, happily, more than adequate for a comfortable meal in this superb restaurant. Argenta is located in such a way that if you leave Venice by mid-morning, you can stop at Il Trigabolo for lunch, on your way to Ravenna. Life could be worse! Everything at Il Trigabolo is low-key, but when it comes to the actual laying on of hands—the presenting of the food—the acknowledgment of excellence becomes palpable, and ultimately digestible.

SUGGESTED DISHES

insalata tiepida di agnello all'olio di rosmarino   A warm salad of sliced lamb with oil and rosemary.

insalata tiepida di pesci all'olio di scalogno   A salad of green and red lettuce with shrimp, crayfish, clams, sole, salmon, baby artichokes, and scallions, served just slightly warm.

medaglie di faraona allo zabaione di parmigiano   Round ravioli stuffed with guinea fowl in a Parmesan cream sauce.

gnocchi di patate e ricotta stagionata in salsa di verdure   Thin potato-and-ricotta *gnocchi* presented in a star shape on a sauce of puréed greens.

garganelli piccanti in salsa all'aglio   Fresh *penne*-like pasta in a cream sauce with parsley, garlic, hot pepper, and shredded *prosciutto*.

fagiano alla crema con prezzemolo fritto   Sliced pheasant with a light sauce of red wine, game stock, and cream, garnished with fried mushrooms, tiny carrot balls, and fried parsley. One of the most delicate pheasant dishes I've tasted anywhere.

SUGGESTED WINES

White

Riesling Italico, Colli Bolognesi, Monte San Pietro, Terre Rosse, Vallania   Soft in texture, off-dry with subtle but undeniable fruit—pears are just notice-able in this delicate hay-colored wine that drinks like a mid-summer day: warm and gentle, everything at a standstill. A little butter in the mouth, firm body, and then a long relaxing finish.

Chardonnay, Terre Rosse, Vallania Apples and herbs mixed with some floral notes and a dash of vanilla in the first rush of the bouquet, then more fresh fruit filling the mouth. A terrific white, alive in its fruit-to-acid balance; delicate and elegant, it has a beautiful gold color with a slight green cast to it.

Red

Ronco delle Ginestre, Baldi, Castelluccio A big, rich, bright red with a good deal of complexity. "From Sangiovese Grosso grown at Casale near Modigliana in Romagna's hills. Aged in small barrels of new French oak, [it develops] elegant tone in deep ruby color, flowery bouquet in dry but rich and complex flavor" (Burton Anderson).

Assisi

| *Arezzo* 99 km | *Gubbio* 54 | *Orvieto* 110 | *Perugia* 26 |
| *Rome* 177 | *Siena* 131 | *Terni* 76 | *Torgiano* 27 |

A beautiful hill town on Mount Subasio, Assisi is probably best known as the home of St. Francis. In the Basilica of San Francesco you will find the Cloisters of the Dead, the Treasury, and work by Giotto (the fresco cycle of the Life of St. Francis, a Nativity, and a Crucifixion) and Cimabue (*Madonna and Child with Four Angels and St. Francis,* a Crucifixion). Assisi is also the birthplace of the Latin poet Propertius. The town has a magical atmosphere, especially in the late afternoon and early evening, the time to take a casual stroll through the narrow streets.

UMBRA
★ ★ ★

REGION	Umbria
ADDRESS	vicolo degli Archi, 6
PHONE ·	(075) 812-240
CREDIT CARDS	AmX, Diners
CLOSED	Tues, Jan 10–March 15, Nov 15–Dec 15
25 ROOMS	Basic but serviceable rooms. Inexpensive.

CLASS	ATMOSPHERE	SERVICE	WINE	PRICE
3.5	3.5	4	3.5	M

Of the two nicely created dining rooms here, the front room is the more elegant and polished; the other is homier, warmer, with slate blue walls that complement bright yellow curtains and cheerfully colored tile floors. The front room has a modern wooden floor that matches the light wood of the furniture—country, but fine. The wine list, although modest, offers a decent regional selection. An upbeat, comfortable place, well thought-out and executed.

SUGGESTED DISHES

prosciutto di cinghiale Prosciutto of wild boar—dark in color, with an intense flavor. Add a little of the house olive oil.

insalata di rucola con salmone affumicato Slices of excellent-quality home-smoked salmon, accompanied by a salad of arugula and capers, dressed with lemon and a touch of oil.

pappardelle con la lepre Wide, flat noodles with a rich but subtle rabbit sauce.

risotto con olive verdi, pecorino dolce e salsicce di maiale Perfectly cooked *risotto* with cream, sausage, green olives, and a trace of fried egg. Quite a salty dish.

piccione alla ghiotta Pigeon, roasted and served on the bone—not a great deal of meat but what's there is tasty. Served with toasted bread topped with chopped pigeon meat.

SUGGESTED WINES

White

Chardonnay, Colle Carduccio, Sportoletti A lulling, hazy yellow color; a soft, velvety texture on the tongue. Gentle nose, fruity, and round in the mouth. Full Chardonnay flavor, but light and buoyant, even expansive, with a good lift of acidity. Surprisingly good.

Red

Sacrantino di Montefalco, Val di Maggio (Arnaldo Caprai) A good, tight nose with the fruit held back at first, then delivered slowly. Something nearly off in the nose, with a tingle of cherries in the distance. In the mouth there's ample tannin, good depth with another signal of cherry in the finish.

Asti

Alba 30 km   *Alessandria* 37   *Boves* 95
Carmagnola 58   *Costigliole d'Asti* 16   *Genoa* 116
Milan 127   *Novara* 103   *Turin* 55

Asti, located near the heart of the Piedmont wine-growing district, is home of the world-famous sparkler Asti Spumante. On Saturday (in season) in piazza San Secondo, you'll find the little truck owned by Guido Prunotto, from which he sells white truffles and related items, such as truffle oil and cream.

GENER NEUV
★ ★ ★ ½

REGION	Piedmont
ADDRESS	lungo Tanaro, 4
PHONE	(0141) 57-270
CREDIT CARDS	AmX, Visa, Diners
CLOSED	Sun dinner, Mon, Jan or Dec, Aug

CLASS	ATMOSPHERE	SERVICE	WINE	PRICE
4	3.5	4	3.5	E

Germanic, perhaps Bavarian, is the first impression this place gives. Actually, it's just Piemontese. The main dining room, to your right as you enter, is preferable. It has pale salmon walls and warm red terra-cotta tiles and is adorned with a collection of rather clumsy paintings, blue floral curtains, and a cheerful fireplace. The heavy dark wooden beams are hung with copper pots and feature inscribed aphorisms in Piedmontese dialect. This room is bright, promoting among diners a happy camaraderie. The other dining room, with its high-gloss light wood and mirrors, is even brighter than the main room. You'll find Gener Neuv just along the Tanaro River, on the town side.

Gener Neuv has its own method of serving truffles: you select a truffle after a great deal of looking and smelling, and it's yours for the meal, to use as you wish. Italians slice a little on everything—even ice cream, for the avid. A medium-sized truffle weighs between 20 and 30 grams and costs around 75,000 lire (over $50).

SUGGESTED DISHES

insalata di carne cruda con tartufi   A light dish: raw veal chopped with raw vegetables and slices of the truffle you've selected.

fegato d'anatra all'aceto balsamico   Sautéed duck liver served with chopped onion, oil, parsley, and balsamic vinegar.

polenta con formaggio e tuorlo d'uovo   Polenta served in a bowl with a bright-orange egg yolk and a chunk of *fontina,* which you mix together at the table.

ricca finanziera all'astigiana   Various cuts of chicken—including cocks' combs, sweetbreads, and giblets—sautéed with veal marrow and mushrooms in a sauce of Marsala and lemon.

SUGGESTED WINES

White

Arneis, Blangè, Ceretto   A refined and subtle white, a natural opener. It has been described gracefully by Victor Hazan: "Its rich straw yellow color with flashes of brilliant gold signal from the first Arneis's notable character. The aroma is subtly fruited, possibly recalling that of pears, and the bouquet is fine and forthright. The succulent taste flows with velvety smoothness toward a buoyant aftertaste wherein for long moments a rich succession of flavors continues to develop and expand. Alcohol is substantial, between 12% and 13%, but in elegant balance with acidity and fruit."

Red

Barbaresco, Maria di Brun, Ca' Rome' A warm, seductive, complicated nose, followed by real clarity in the mouth. Fruit and tannin go hand in hand, with a distant glimpse of the Piedmont landscape: earth and flower.

Dessert

Brachetto d'Acqui, G. Carnevale A sweet red sparkling wine. You must try one glass while you're in the Piedmont, for tradition's sake.

See Costigliole d'Asti, Monforte d'Alba, and Neive.

HOTELS

Just outside Isola d'Asti, 9 km
Il Cascinalenuovo
strada statale 231 (Asti–Alba)
(0141) 958-166
AmX, Visa, Diners
Closed Aug 1–20 (Restaurant closed Sun D., and Mon)
Inexpensive

The most convenient hotel in the winegrowing area of Piedmont, Il Cascinalenuovo is a short drive from many of Piedmont's fine restaurants, such as Guido, ten minutes away, and La Contea, about fifteen minutes away. The hotel is nothing fancy, to be sure, but it is very serviceable, if at times a little noisy. Modern rooms with showers (no bathtubs, no terry-cloth towels, no porters) go with the do-it-yourself attitude. In the summer there's tennis and swimming. This is the perfect place to stay while investigating the unspoiled Piedmont wine country, Barolo and Barbaresco. Be sure to try the restaurant; it offers a serious *menú degustazione,* which might contain such specialties as *tajarin fatti in casa con tartufo,* thin homemade noodles served with butter and truffles.

In Cioccaro di Penango (outside Moncalvo), 18 km
Locanda del Sant'Uffizio
(0141) 91-271
AmX, Visa, Diners
Closed Jan 3–25, Aug 10–20
Moderate

The *locanda,* in a sixteenth-century monastery, is spectacularly located; you'll feel very far from anything, although you're only twenty minutes from Asti. The rooms are not deluxe but they have a charm, and the grounds are beautiful. In the summer you can swim in the hotel pool, walk in the gardens, work out in the gym, or ride one of the hotel bikes on country lanes. Da Beppe, the restaurant here, takes its cuisine very seriously; it's worth a trip to sample the fare. The restaurant is dark on Tuesday.

Bergamo

Bologna 239 km	*Brescia* 52	*Como* 95	*Goito* 102
Milan 47	*Piacenza* 108	*Verona* 116	

Bergamo, at the base of the Bergamese Alps, is a town divided: there is the modern lower town, Città Bassa, and the romantic old upper town, Città Alta. Bergamo has a number of claims to fame, not the least of which is the emergence of the *commedia dell'arte* in the sixteenth century; in that famous improvisational comedy, haughty masked characters, many of them Venetians, make fun of the local folk, whose representative star is Harlequin, the deceivingly clever fool of the rustics. Because of their particular accent (and impenetrable dialect), the Bergamese are considered the "rustics" of Lombardy. Bergamo claims as one of its own Gaetano Donizetti; the composer was born there in 1797, in a house that can be seen at via Borgo Canale, 14. The city is also home of world-renowned *taleggio,* a smooth, creamy cheese made from cow's milk. The Bergamese have a lesser-known gastronomical specialty, *polenta e osei,* which employs tiny songbirds wrapped in *pancetta* (bacon) and roasted on a spit, accompanied by the ubiquitous slice of grilled *polenta.* As Waverley Root notes, the sight of the "little birds skewered together . . . their beady eyes fixed reproachfully on the diner . . . has been known to indispose Anglo-Saxons. The birds are too small for successful shooting. They are taken in Italy by luring them into large circular wire enclosures, where later boards are shied at them; they dash themselves in panic against the wire, in which they become enmeshed by the hundreds, like fish in a gill net."

Bergamo can be a magical place, especially if you leave time to wander aimlessly in the Città Alta, through the winding stone-paved streets and the tiny guarded piazzas with their towers, archways, and medieval building façades. Spend an hour in the Galleria dell'Accademia Carrara (closed Tuesdays), which houses work by Mantegna, Giovanni Bellini, Carpaccio, Botticelli, Dürer, Lotto, Raphael, and Tiepolo. The beautiful church of Santa Maria Maggiore is a favorite for its Florentine and Flemish tapestries, fourteenth-century frescoes, and a choir with sixteenth-century panels; here too is the tomb of Donizetti. "Bergamo is a most beautiful place, and must on no account be unvisited," wrote the great travel writer Augustus Hare at the turn of this century.

DA VITTORIO
★ ★ ★ ★

REGION	Lombardy
ADDRESS	viale Papa Giovanni XXIII, 21
PHONE	(035) 218-060
CREDIT CARDS	AmX, Visa, Diners
CLOSED	Wed, Aug 8–25

CLASS	ATMOSPHERE	SERVICE	WINE	PRICE
4	4	4	3.5	VE

You'll note, as you enter this upper-class *trattoria,* a fine display of the day's catch. The decor is fresh and clean—stone floors, pale green walls, light wood, plants, and frosted, etched windows. It's pretty, expansive, open and airy. Ask for Gianni, one of the great waiters. All in all, a very refined (not luxurious) and comfortable place in which to eat superb food.

SUGGESTED   DISHES

tempura di scampi, brunoise di zucchine alle noci Scampi lightly coated with batter and quickly deep-fried—exceptionally light—served on a bed of salad greens, *radicchio,* cubed beets, zucchini, tomato, raisins, and nuts, garnished with fried leeks.

insalata di pesce calda al vapore   A salad of poached fish, served with a refreshing mayonnaise.

sfogliatine con punte d'asparagi e capesante   A puff pastry with asparagus and scallops set atop an asparagus sauce, garnished with sliced asparagus.

lasagnette al ragù di frutta di mare   Lasagne with a seafood sauce: cuttlefish, mussels, shrimp, and other fish.

zuppa di porcini freschi con sfoglia   A very thick and rich mushroom soup containing whole mushrooms, covered with a puff pastry.

*rombo con patate e carciofi   Delicately broiled turbot served with artichokes and roasted potatoes.

dessert dal carrello   A selection from the dessert cart; I had a spectacular *crème brulée*, a great chocolate *millefoglie*, and a dish of mixed fruit with two sorbets.

*piccola pasticceria della casa   The best pastry in Italy; the trip here is worthwhile if only for these after-dinner treats. The white chocolate and banana creams were my favorites.

SUGGESTED WINES

White

Arneis delle Langhe, Bricco Cappellina, Gianni Voerzio   *Frizzante* on first spill, strong fresh pears in the nose. Youthful and bright in the mouth, with a long, long finish. An excellent Piedmont white.

Red

Valcalepio, Colle Calvario, Tenuta Castello   Cabernet and Merlot combine to create an explosive perfume for the nose, and then a little tomato in the mouth. Warm, nutty, closing with a nice mellow finish. A wine from the Bergamo area.

Gourmet
via San Vigilio, 1 (Città Alta)
(035) 256-110
AmX, Visa, Diners
Closed Tues
10 rooms
Inexpensive

La Fontana
piazza Vecchia, 2 (Città Alta)
(035) 220-648
AmX
Closed Wed, Jan

In Iseo, 23 km
Osteria il Volto
via Mirolte, 33
(030) 981-462
Cash only
Closed Wed, Thurs lunch, July (3 weeks)

If you decide to make a side trip to picturesque Lake Iseo, you'll want to know about this small *osteria*. It is very close to one of the best vineyards in Italy, Ca' del Bosco and is fully stocked with its wines, which are a must here. If you have a little extra spending money, try the Ca' del Bosco Pinero, a truly memorable wine. Some of the fine, carefully produced dishes here are: *trota salmonata con aceto balsamico e arancia* (salmon trout prepared with balsamic vinegar and orange); *mousse di prosciutto tartufata* (a strange *prosciutto* and truffle dish); *insalata di trota al vapore* (a salad of steamed trout); *filetti dorati di pesce persico* (pan-fried perch); *tagliolini al pesce di lago e zafferano* (thin pasta with a lake fish and saffron sauce); *ravioli di carne con ragù di brasato* (meat *ravioli* with a meat sauce, a specialty of this region); *faraona di sossata ripiena al forno* (baked stuffed guinea fowl); *noce di vitello alle erbe aromatiche* (veal cooked with herbs); and an important white chocolate mousse, *mousse di cioccolato bianco*. The young owners of Il Volto have opened up a new restaurant also worth trying: Le Maschere; vicolo della Pergola, 7; [030] 982-1542; AmX, Visa; closed Sun dinner.

Excelsior San Marco
piazza della Repubblica, 6 (Città Bassa)
(035) 232.132
AmX, Visa, Diners
Moderate

A serviceable hotel with no noticeable charm, but it's the most comfortable hotel in Bergamo. Centrally located and not too far from the Città Alta.

Bologna

Bergamo 239 km	*Florence* 105	*Goito* 122
Imola 42	*Lucca* 170	*Maleo* 173	*Milan* 210
Modena 39	*Padua* 115	*Parma* 96	*Ravenna* 74
Treviso 170	*Urbino* 186	*Venice* 152	*Verona* 141
	Viareggio 180	

The capital of Emilia-Romagna, Bologna—"the Fat," it's sometimes called—is a city well known for its fine cuisine and its university, the oldest in Europe, founded in the eleventh century. It's also called the City of Arches—Città dei Portici; word has it that twenty miles of Bologna's sidewalks are covered with arches. Because the city hasn't yet been overwhelmed by tourists, it's a wonderful place to visit. One of the great pleasures of being in Bologna, aside from having the good fortune of sampling its fine cuisine, is wandering through the center of town—the area around piazza Maggiore, piazza del Nettuno with its Fountain of Neptune, and piazza di Porta Ravegnana with its signature leaning towers.

Bologna takes its intellectual, political, and gastronomic life quite seriously. There's a story of a thirteenth-century woman, Novella d'Andrea, who taught in the university here. She was so beautiful that she was forced to lecture behind a curtain, so her serious-minded students would keep their thoughts engaged on the higher subjects at hand. Seriousness of her sort is one of the impressive qualities in evidence here—and travelers interested in eating will certainly encounter it in the Bolognese attitude toward the preparation and presentation of food. Among the specialties, be sure to try *mortadella,* large round peppered pork sausage, and *tortellini,* Bologna's most important pasta. Waverley Root quotes a Bolognese poet: "If the first father of the human race was lost for an apple, what would he not have done for a plate of *tortellini?*"

SILVERIO				
★ ★ ★ ½				
REGION	Emilia-Romagna			
ADDRESS	via Nosadella, 37a			
PHONE	(051) 330-604			
CREDIT CARDS	AmX, Visa, Diners			
CLOSED	Mon, Aug			
CLASS	ATMOSPHERE	SERVICE	WINE	PRICE
3	2.5	3	3	M

Be prepared not to judge Silverio too quickly. This restaurant, just outside the center of town, is probably unlike any other you've been to. You enter a bar area and are then escorted into a room with a gray carpet, green-speckled walls, a modest set of furniture, and various decorations. Paintings on the walls are by Zanetti, a friend of chef-owner Silverio. It's a little odd, to be sure, but don't be put off by the strangeness. Silverio's place is more like a living room than a restaurant; everything has been seen to with a very personal hand, including the room and the conception and presentation of the food. People tend to eat on the late side here; a very hip Bolognese crowd will begin to arrive about nine. Silverio, who worked at the well-respected La Frasca in Castrocaro Terme before opening what is now the best—and most unusual—restaurant in Bologna, considers himself an artist; he is very sensitive to color and texture in the presentation of his cuisine. His restaurant reminds me a little of Cibreo in Florence.

SUGGESTED   DISHES

teneri verdi cuori addolciti d'arancio   Artichoke hearts served in a very red blood-orange sauce.

stagionato Parma gratificato dal balsamico *Prosciutto* and arugula with a Parmesan cream sauce.

gialli passatelli in verde crema di spinaci   A creamy spinach soup with threads of Parmesan and short pasta.

pasticcio di carciofi   A baked crêpe stuffed with artichokes and cheese, covered with béchamel sauce.

colorate caramelle al viola trevisano   Red, white, and green bow-tie–shaped *ravioli*, stuffed with cheese and nuts and covered with chopped *radicchio* and slices of Parmesan.

*filetto di Silverio all'agresto   A steak served with a vinegar and meat sauce.

fior fior di latte in salsa   Silverio's surprise.

SUGGESTED   WINES

White

Pinot Grigio, Terre Rosse, Vallania   Big fruit from the start, off-dry, full-bodied, large, and generous. Finely made, balanced, and very appealing, like all the Terre Rosse wines.

Red

Bricco dell'Uccellone, G. Bologna   Here is Barbera at its very best and most graceful, a wine Burton Anderson says is "filled with fantasy and humor." Powerful color, nose, and flavor; big and rich, alcoholic, fruity and earthy, this is a wine of the earth with a moment of cherry in the finish. It comes on like Mike Tyson.

NOTAI
★ ★ ★ ½

REGION	Emilia-Romagna
ADDRESS	via de' Pignattari, 1
PHONE	(051) 228-694
CREDIT CARDS	AmX, Visa, Diners
CLOSED	Sun, Aug 15–30

CLASS	ATMOSPHERE	SERVICE	WINE	PRICE
3.5	3.5	3.5	2.5	E

There's a little of the Upper East Side bar about Notai: red plush carpet, wicker chairs, hanging lamps with hanging beads, wood-and-brass overhead fans, and so on. Definitely uptown. Notai remains one of the best restaurants in town because the owner, Nino Castorina, has managed to maintain the level of quality while many other important Bolognese restaurants have fallen by the way. Don't be put off by the piano-bar aspect; Nino is a charming restauranteur who likes to sing. Come here for the finest pasta in town, especially the *tagliatelle alla Notai (al profumo di cedro e prosciutto crudo)*, noodles prepared with pieces of *prosciutto* and the "perfume" of citron, which is considerably more interesting than our lemon.

SUGGESTED DISHES

*tagliatelle alla Notai See above.

tortelloni di ricotta ai funghi porcini Large *ravioli*-like pasta stuffed with ricotta and served with a sauce of *porcini* mushrooms.

ravioli di cervo al burro e tartufo *Ravioli* stuffed with venison and served with a butter and truffle sauce.

agnolotti al ripieno di radicchio trevigiano in crema di pomodoro e basilico Pasta envelopes stuffed with *radicchio* and presented with a thick basil and tomato sauce.

*rosette di agnello e patate al rosmarino Medallions of lamb cooked rare, in a sauce of reduced meat juices and rosemary. Served with roasted potatoes and string beans.

bavarese alla menta e cioccolato A two-tone chocolate and mint pudding—yellow for the mint, brown for the chocolate—decorated with a *zabaglione* sauce.

SUGGESTED WINES

White

Sauvignon, Colli Bolognesi, Monte San Pietro, Terre Rosse, Vallania A simple Sauvignon. Light grass, pale and fresh, a good fruit/acidity balance. Light

and most agreeable at lunch, or with a simple first course
at dinner.

Red

Sangiovese di Romagna (Selezione Particolare),
Braschi A secretive, dark wine—tough fruit that softens
with a little time in the air. There's a note of amber in the
nose of this wine, nearly opaque and devoted to its tannin.

PAPPAGALLO				
★ ★ ★ ½				
REGION	Emilia-Romagna			
ADDRESS	piazza della Mercanzia, 3c			
PHONE	(051) 232-807			
CREDIT CARDS	AmX, Visa			
CLOSED	Sun, Jan 12–18, Aug 1–22			
CLASS	ATMOSPHERE	SERVICE	WINE	PRICE
4	3.5	4	3.5	E

Pappagallo has been changing owners with considerable reg-
ularity. It's now owned by Ezio Salsini, owner of the popular
restaurant Tre Frecce, around the corner. The space has a
touch of the grand to it—orange walls, orange tablecloths,
mirrors, and generally a lot of show. It does seem that under
Mr. Salsini the restaurant is more in control than under his
predecessors—who include Gianluigi Morini, of San Domenico in Imola, and Dante Cesari of the now defunct restaurant
Dante. If I had one request, it would be to turn in the garish
orange tablecloths for good old-fashioned white ones, to tone
the place down a bit.

galantina di pollo con gelatina A galantine of chicken.

affettati misti regionali A fine assortment of local cured meats—*prosciutto,* sausage, salami.

insalata di funghi porcini con parmigiano Sliced *porcini* mushrooms, served with Parmesan shaved over the top, and a little olive oil and balsamic vinegar.

tortellini del Pappagallo in brodo di carne A meat broth with little doughnut-shaped pasta stuffed with chopped meat.

*lasagne gialle del Pappagallo "Yellow" lasagne, made with a meat sauce, béchamel, and Parmesan.

costola di vitello alla bolognese A veal chop breaded and fried with *prosciutto* and cheese.

*budino di patate al caramello An unusual custard, made with potatoes and caramel.

SUGGESTED WINES

White

Albana di Romagna, Vigna dell'Olivo, Fattoria Paradiso A good rich wine; thick, very yellow, very herbal with amusing hints of rosemary in the nose, it shows very little fruit. Made from the Albana grape, this is an unusual, memorable, important white from the region. Let it grow on you. Italy's only white DOCG.

Red

Ronco delle Ginestre, Baldi, Castelluccio Burton Anderson says of this wine: "From Sangiovese Grosso grown at Casale near Modigliana in Romagna's hills. Aged in small barrels of new French oak, [it develops] elegant tone in deep ruby color, flowery bouquet in dry but rich and complex flavor."

Ronco del Casone, Modigliana, Castelluccio
Made with the Brunello grape, this wine displays an inviting, almost Bordeaux-like nose. Orange-red in color, with an orange rim. Elegant, but frail of body and flavor, and light. Even so, there's a richness and a nice cherry fruitiness.

OTHER RECOMMENDED RESTAURANTS

Diana
via dell'Indipendenza, 24
(051) 231-302
Cash only
Closed Mon, Jan 1–10, Aug
  A brightly lit, lighthearted, cheerful eating spot, popular with the younger crowd. Good tasty food, simply prepared. Terrific for a quick and pleasing lunch. Select from the list of Bolognese specialties, "I Piatti della Tradizione Bolognese."

Franco Rossi
via Goito, 3
(051) 238-818
AmX, Visa, Diners
Closed Sun May–Aug; Tues Sept–April; July
  A nicely put together restaurant, a good backup to the reviewed restaurants, if you have extra nights in Bologna. Right across from the Grand Hotel Baglioni, if you're tired and want a quick meal.

See Imola, Castrocaro Terme, Modena, and Tossignano.

FOOD AND WINE SHOPS, MARKETS

Food

A. F. Tamburini
via Caprarie, 1
  Located in the food center of Bologna, Tamburini is stocked with traditional foodstuffs of Emilia-Romagna and the rest of Italy.

Paolo Atti & Figli
via Caprarie, 7
   Just down the street from A. F. Tamburini you'll find this
engaging shop that sells Emilia-Romagna's traditional pastas
and breads.

Wine

Enoteca Italiana
via Marsala, 2
   A handsome store, where you'll find many wines from this
region, as well as a great selection of the best olive oils.

HOTELS

Grand Hotel Baglioni
via dell'Indipendenza, 8
(051) 225-445
AmX, Visa, Diners
Expensive/Luxury
   The newly renovated Grand Hotel Baglioni with its 130
luxury rooms, by far the best hotel in Bologna, is beautifully
and intelligently arranged, excellently run, and perfectly located near the top of via dell'Indipendenza, close to the best
shopping areas and the center of town. Double windows
make all the rooms *absolutely* quiet, and the rooms are
adorned with reproductions of frescoes by the Carracci family
and others. The grand and festive lobby sees quite a bit of
activity, which is modulated by the warm pastel colors—a vi-
sual theme throughout the hotel. For my money, one of the
most consistently comfortable and elegant hotels in Italy, due
to the vigilance of its enlightened manager, Pier Luigi Magrini.

Milano Excelsior
viale Pietramellara, 51
(051) 246-178
AmX, Visa, Diners
Moderate
   A straightforward and reliable hotel, across from the train
station. It's a pleasant fifteen-minute walk to central piazza

Maggiore and piazza del Nettuno, and to any of the restaurants reviewed above.

Borgo Pace

Ancona 134 km   Arezzo 69   Florence 150
Perugia 99   Pesaro 74   Siena 158   Urbino 38

DA RODOLFO–LA DILIGENZA	
★ ★ ½	
REGION	The Marches
ADDRESS	piazzetta del Paese
PHONE	(0722) 89-124
CREDIT CARDS	AmX, Visa
CLOSED	Wed, Sept 1–15
7 ROOMS	Very basic. Inexpensive.

CLASS	ATMOSPHERE	SERVICE	WINE	PRICE
2.5	3	3	2	M

A basic restaurant, but one that takes its cooking seriously. There's not too much to say about the decor but that it's functional. A scheduled stop here for lunch on your way to or from the art treasures of Urbino, a city without a notable restaurant, would be a wise and prudent decision.

Directions. On the road between San Giustino (Sansepolcro) and Urbino, about 45 minutes from Urbino.

SUGGESTED DISHES

tagliatelle al tartufo   Flat noodles served with white truffles.

gnocchi verdi alla ghiottona   Green *gnocchi*. The chef decides among various ways of preparation.

caccia assortita allo spiedo   Assorted pieces of spit-roasted game.

tordi, fagiano, beccacce   Spit-roasted birds: thrushes, pheasant, woodcocks.

agnello delle nostre montagne allo spiedo Spit-roasted lamb from local ("our") mountains.

crema al cucchiaio A rich cream dessert—"cream with a spoon."

SUGGESTED   WINES

White

Verdicchio di Matelica A white from this region. As you're unlikely to come across many wines from The Marches, it's definitely worth sampling a glass or two while you're here.

Red

Chianti This restaurant specializes in wines from the Chianti region of Tuscany. For the best results, ask the proprietor, Rodolfo, to advise. If you'd like to try a red from The Marches, ask for Rosso Piceno or Rosso Cònero.

Boves

AL RODODENDRO
★ ★ ★ ★ ½

REGION	Piedmont
ADDRESS	in San Giacomo
PHONE	(0171) 680-372
CREDIT CARDS	AmX, Visa, Diners
CLOSED	Sun dinner, Mon, Tues lunch, Jan 8–22, Aug 15–31
	Reservations necessary
3 ROOMS	They don't advertise the fact that these three rooms exist, but staying here is a fine way to manage dinner in this out-of-the-way restaurant—worth the drive from wherever you're coming. The road *ends* in San Giacomo, and the restaurant is on the hill with plenty of lovely places to walk and view the Alps in the distance. Breakfast is worth the price of admission.

CLASS	ATMOSPHERE	SERVICE	WINE	PRICE
5	4.5	4	3.5	VE

When you *finally* arrive, through territory unlike anything you're used to seeing in Italy, you are greeted as if a guest long awaited. The elegant and elaborate dining room has walls of pastel green going to turquoise, rust suede chairs, a soft green and rust carpet, and warm yellow drapes with green tassels. The feeling here is somewhere between Swiss and French, graceful and well thought-out, old-world high style and very comfortable. Everything has been selected with care, from the colors and fabrics to the glassware, silverware (Christofle), china (Limoges), cutting knives (Henckel), and cut-glass knife holders. Fine antiques, fine atmosphere, everything anticipated by Maria Barale, the gifted owner-chef.

Directions. From Turin take the *autostrada* toward Savona and exit at Fossano. Go in the direction of Cuneo, and at Cuneo go toward Boves and then on to San Giacomo, to the restaurant. It's a drive of just about 1½ hours.

terrina di gamberi A subtle block of shrimp pâté with an herb sauce on the side.

*animelle brasate Sweetbreads and mushrooms braised in wine and then baked. Presented on a bed of lettuce and dressed with oil, vinegar, and a little of the braising liquid.

ramequin di porri An airlike crêpe stuffed with spinach, leeks, and ricotta, tied at either end with a leek string and coated with thyme-laced butter sauce.

*zuppa di porri An intense leek soup—enriched with eggs and butter. The essence of leeks!

branzino al caviale A slice of sea bass served with a cream sauce, dotted with caviar, and garnished with carrot roses and asparagus.

bianco d'anatra con salsa di soia Duck breast, sliced and served with soy sauce.

bianco di piccione al porto Pigeon breast with a port sauce, garnished with vegetables.

formaggi A mix of cheeses: *bra, castelmagno,* and *raschera.*

cassata con frutta candita, e salse di fragole, pesche, e kiwi An ice cream cake with candied fruit and three sauces: strawberry, peach, and kiwi.

SUGGESTED WINES

White

Gavi, Riserva dei Gavi, La Scolca For many years *the* chic Italian white; called *Gavi dei Gavi* before the DOC board forced the makers to give up that name. A severe but finely made wine, reminiscent of a Chablis in its dry flintiness, complexity, and integrity.

Red

1979 Gattinara, Monsecco, Le Colline Rich inviting nose, good velvet texture, and serious depth. With a touch of bitter almonds, this wine closes in a gentle, lingering sort of way.

Canneto sull'Oglio

Brescia 51 km   *Cremona* 32   *Mantua* 38
Milan 123   *Parma* 43   *Piacenza* 161   *Verona* 77

DAL PESCATORE
★ ★ ★ ½

REGION	Lombardy
ADDRESS	via Runate, 13 (near Carzaghetto)
PHONE	(0376) 70-304
CREDIT CARDS	AmX
CLOSED	Mon, Tues, Jan 2–14, Aug 7–25

CLASS	ATMOSPHERE	SERVICE	WINE	PRICE
5	5	4	4	VE

One of the most inviting and beautiful of the country restaurants. Fine marble floors, Chinese carpets, an exotic tree planted in the middle of the main room, brick archways, burning fireplaces, dark-beamed ceilings, elegant wood appointments—decorated *alla nuova cucina*. It's not a large restaurant: six tables in the main room, a room with a table for six to eight, and a banquet room. In many ways, a perfect restaurant in terms of decor and atmosphere.

Directions. From Mantua take the road toward Cremona to Piadina. Turn right at the sign for Canneto sull'Oglio ("S/O"). Go about 3 kilometers (do not go into the town itself) to the circle and follow the sign at eleven o'clock for Dal Pescatore, placed under a tree. Go another kilometer and turn left at the yellow sign for the restaurant.

SUGGESTED   DISHES

salame, culatello, gras pistà e polenta   Salami and "heart" of *prosciutto*, served with *polenta* filled with cheese.

tortelli di zucca   Large *ravioli*-like pasta stuffed with pumpkin, preserved fruit (*mostarda*), crumbled *amaretti*, and nutmeg, and sauced with a little butter and Parmesan.

tortelli di pecorino dolce e parmigiano *Ravioli*-like pasta stuffed with fresh, sweet pecorino and Parmesan.

stracotto di cavallo al Barbera con polenta Horse meat stewed like a pot roast, in Barbera wine; the meat is somewhat sweeter than beef and does not have beef's good texture. Served with *polenta*, this traditional dish is more interesting than "to die from."

*gorgonzola A. Croce con mostarda di anguria Gorgonzola topped with watermelon preserved in a honey, white wine, and mustard sauce.

fantasia di sorbetti di frutta Fruit sorbets: peach, kiwi, and raspberry are among the flavors.

SUGGESTED WINES

White

Lugana di Lugana, Visconti Pale in color with assertive flowers and fruit in the nose. With its engaging complexity behind a spritely personality, this is a white both graceful and delicate.

Red

Barbacarlo, Oltrepò Pavese, Maga Lino Barbera appears to be in dominance, although the mixture includes only 5 percent Barbera. It has the deep ruby color of Barbera, an earthy taste, good spritz (it's *frizzante*), and a lot of raw fruit in the nose. There is some bitterness of almonds in evidence, but overall this is a good, earthy and rich drink.

Dessert

Recioto di Soave, dei Capitelli, Anselmi Gold, Sauterne-like, more rich than sweet—but a wine that remains on the surface, showing little depth; a good closing wine nevertheless.

Carmagnola

Aosta 140 km   *Asti* 75   *Boves* 80   *Cuneo* 71

Genoa 164   *Milan* 184   *Savona* 118   *Turin* 27

LA CARMAGNOLE
★ ★ ★ ½

REGION	Piedmont
ADDRESS	via Sottotenente Chiffi, 31
PHONE	(011) 971-2673
CREDIT CARDS	Cash only
CLOSED	Sun dinner, Mon, Aug 10–20
	Reservations necessary

CLASS	ATMOSPHERE	SERVICE	WINE	PRICE
4	3	3.5	3.5	E

Once you *find* this well-hidden restaurant, you'll feel you've been invited to dine with an old friend of the family who lives on the second floor of what looks like an apartment building. When you enter there's a waiting room to your right and two dining rooms to your left. The floors are arresting: natural, multicolored wood. The decor in general is old-world. Rather a strange place, on the sober side, but the food is serious and the owner is deeply committed to presenting it well to you. Even though this restaurant is minutes from the center of town, it's almost impossible to find it on your own—the façade is simply two large old wooden doors with a lantern and a small brass plaque. Your best bet is to ask a friendly soul in the street for directions.

SUGGESTED DISHES

avocado farcito con insalata di crostacei An avocado stuffed with shellfish.

galantina di coniglio in gelatina al Sauternes e aceto di mele A galantine of rabbit, with a sauce of Sauternes and apple vinegar.

gnocchetti al profumo di pesto in guazzetto di moscardini e seppie Small dumplings "perfumed" with a little pesto, in a sauce of tiny octopuses and cuttlefish cooked in butter, wine, and herbs.

zigotto d'agnellino alla menta e aceto balsamico con sformato di carciofi e fagiolini Leg of baby lamb with mint and balsamic vinegar, served with a timbale of artichokes and green beans.

SUGGESTED WINES

White

Arneis delle Langhe, Bricco Cappellina, Gianni Voerzio Frizzante on first spill, strong fresh pears in the nose. Youthful and bright in the mouth, with a long, long finish. An excellent Piedmont white.

Red

Barbaresco, Bruno Rocca, Cascina Rabaja One of the newer-style Barbarescos, fresh, open, rich, and very well made. Spicy and fruity nose. A good fruit/acidity balance; soft but with spine, body, and subtle flavor, the full rich Nebbiolo character.

Cassinetta di Lugagnano

Alessandria 74 km   *Milan* 23   *Novara* 26   *Pavia* 33
Ranco 77   *Stresa* 82   *Turin* 121

Cassinetta di Lugagnano is a tiny village just outside Abbiategrasso, which is a charming agricultural market town. The drive from Milan is a pleasant one, and if you arrive here a bit early for your meal at Antica Osteria del Ponte, it's more than agreeable to walk the short length of the main street. Make sure to look in the window of the local butcher shop, where you'll witness an amazing display of game birds, stuffed as well as ready for cooking.

ANTICA OSTERIA DEL PONTE
★ ★ ★ ★ ★

REGION	Lombardy
ADDRESS	Cassinetta di Lugagnano (near Abbiategrasso)
PHONE	(02) 942-0034
CREDIT CARDS	AmX, Diners
CLOSED	Sun, Mon, Jan 1–15, Aug

CLASS	ATMOSPHERE	SERVICE	WINE	PRICE
5	5	5	3.5	VE

You'll feel as if you're entering another century when you approach this beautifully preserved stone farmhouse; the village of Cassinetta feels very much out of the way but is in fact just 45 minutes from Milan. The restaurant announces its excellence the moment you step through the door, in the attention paid to every detail. A dark, heavy beamed ceiling plays off the white stucco walls; exposed brick archways, cane chairs, and dark-wood window frames participate in a beautifully appointed interior. The atmosphere is friendly, warm, compatible. And then there's the serious and amazingly well-trained staff.

Certainly there is the unmistakable feeling in the air informing you that something wonderful is about to happen. As the evening progresses, it becomes clear in what ways this feeling is accurate. If it's your first visit, ask one of the owners, Renata or Ezio Santin, to prepare a tasting menu for you. The wine list is a beautiful piece of work, with a solid sampling of Italian wines; regrettably, it has almost no Lombard representation: only two whites, both from Ca' del Bosco, and one red (two vintages), also from Ca' del Bosco—hence the low wine rating.

Directions. From piazza Napoli in Milan, take the road toward Vigevano. Near the Abbiategrasso bridge, before the slope, turn left, then right, following the Naviglio River. Cross into Cassinetta di Lugagnano at the bridge; the restaurant is immediately on your right.

SUGGESTED   DISHES

insalata di aragosta e avocado in salsa al curry
A salad of lobster medallions in a curried cream sauce with tomato, avocado balls, and black pepper.

salmone scozzese marinato all'aneto in vinaigrette di agrumi Scottish salmon marinated in dill and dressed with a vinaigrette of blood oranges, served with sweet mustard and garnished with blood oranges and zucchini.

*foie gras fresco di anitra al naturale Fresh foie gras, the way it's served in heaven.

foie gras caldo di anitra su insalata di rucola Sautéed foie gras on a bed of arugula.

ravioli al tartufo nero fresco di Norcia Ravioli filled with black (Norcia) truffles in a brown sauce of truffles and foie gras.

fagottino di pasta fresca di frutti di mare A "pasta bundle" filled with seafood, tied with green-vegetable string, dressed with a light court boullion—and topped with Beluga caviar.

moscardini con patate e funghi Small octopi cooked with potatoes and mushrooms.

filettini di triglia di scoglio alle prime fave fresche e basilico Fillets of red mullet cooked in a bag and served with a touch of *pesto,* and *fava* beans, tomatoes, and a butter sauce.

*scaloppine di dentice alla julienne di carciofi Fillets of *dentice* (dentex, a Mediterranean fish similar to a sea bass) with a subtle note of curry, served with sliced raw artichokes, which give a slightly bitter but interesting twist.

*filetto di agnello di latte al profumo di aglio e timo Milk-fed lamb done perfectly, scented with garlic and thyme and served with a single leek and a Brussels sprout.

*formaggi The cheese plate: a local *gorgonzola, toma* from neighboring Piedmont, *pannerone* from Lodi in Lombardy, *aostino* from Valle d'Aosta, and *capra,* a goat cheese also from the Piedmont.

cassata all'italiana in salsa di pistacchio Nougat cake with pistachios and other nuts suspended in it, topped with an orange, pistachio, and chocolate sauce.

SUGGESTED WINES

White

Chardonnay, Ca' del Bosco This one rivals any white in Italy—a spectacular Chardonnay, hay-colored and handsome in the glass, with a complicated nose that's immediately rich, full, and airy, with a hint of mild wood and herbs in the background. In the mouth the wine is a delight—herbal, spicy, achieving great structure and a terrific balance of fruit and acidity. As in the nose, the wood remains modestly present in the mouth; the wine finishes with a show of fruit and flowers.

Red

Maurizio Zanella, Ca' del Bosco In my opinion one of the best wines to come out of this important vineyard, and therefore one of the most important in Italy. A youthful wine composed of Cabernet, Cabernet Franc, and Merlot, it has a beautiful, intense garnet color, a perfumed nose, and a rich taste—graceful even, long and smooth on the finish, with impressive depth. A surprisingly sophisticated creation, especially if many of the Milanese restaurant owners are right in their pessimistic appraisal of Lombard wines—a view I don't share, and one that this wine disputes convincingly by the very fact of itself.

Dessert

Malvasia delle Lipari, Hauner One of Italy's most distinguished and luscious dessert wines, from the tiny island of Lipari, off the coast of Sicily.

Bologna 74 km   *Florence* 98   *Forlì* 11   *Imola* 41
Milan 293   *Ravenna* 38   *Rimini* 60

LA FRASCA				
★ ★ ★ ★				
REGION	Emilia-Romagna			
ADDRESS	via Matteotti, 34			
PHONE	(0543) 767-471			
CREDIT CARDS	AmX, Diners			
CLOSED	Tues, Jan 2–20, Aug 1–15			
CLASS	ATMOSPHERE	SERVICE	WINE	PRICE
4	4	4	4.5	VE

La Frasca, in the heart of Romagna, was opened by Gianfranco Bolognesi in 1971. It has three dining rooms, each well thought-out and elegant. Choose the back room—"the stable," as it's referred to—to the left by way of the bar as you enter; it has stone walls and lovely ceramics from nearby Faenza. The floor of the room is carpeted, for necessary warmth, and its ceiling is covered with a striped canvas, which adds a certain degree of festiveness to the room's austerity. The other rooms are lighter, more conventional for dining, especially if stone walls are not your thing. Bottles of wine are in evidence, inside and outside the restaurant; this is because Bolognesi is actively involved in the wine production of this region.

The restaurant cares much about the bread it serves: rosemary and sage bread, and *piadina alla romagnola,* the flat pitalike bread, typical of the region. The restaurant name derives from an old Italian tradition, which is to hang a branch (*frasca*) on the door or sign of a restaurant, inn, or shop to announce that a new wine is ready to be consumed. Ask to be served by Bruno.

Directions. Take Highway 67 southwest from Forlì to Castrocaro. Continue past the thermal baths and the bridge, then turn right. The restaurant is 11 kilometers from Forlì.

insalata di piccione, fagiolini e nocciole A salad of tender breast of pigeon, string beans, and hazelnuts.

garganelli al vino rosso, scalogno e zucchine Homemade *penne*-like pasta with a Sangiovese wine sauce and strips of zucchini and scallion.

noci di capriolo con polenta concia Medallions of venison in a red wine and game stock, with *polenta*, enriched with *gorgonzola*, and celery purée.

*coniglio farcito agli aromi Rabbit stuffed with veal, pork, cheese, bacon, mortadella, and olives.

*semifreddo alla nocciola, zabaione al miele e salsa profiteroles A rich, soft hazelnut ice cream with chocolate on one side, *zabaione* on the other, and chocolate scrapings over the top.

SUGGESTED WINES

Sparkling

Ferrari Brut de Brut, Lunelli A fine wine from one of the best producers of sparkling wines in Italy.

White

Albana di Romagna, Fattoria Paradiso An important white wine from this region, made from the Albana grape. It's unusual, even odd, and memorable—herbal with a little well-focused fruit, and quite unlike other Italian whites you've tasted—but it's a wine that will grow on you.

Red

Sangiovese di Romagna, Carla Foschi A soft, fruity, youthful red. Very pretty and, given its youth, oddly gentle, rich, and intense.

Dessert

Ramandolo, Giovanni Dri, Colli Orientali del Friuli An interesting and by no means ordinary or predictable dessert wine. Commanding it's not, and it seems to lack proper structure, but the taste is engaging, one you're not likely to come across elsewhere.

Mantua 75 km   *Milan* 145
Parma 23   *Reggio nell'Emilia* 9

PICCI				
★ ★ ★ ★				
REGION	Emilia-Romagna			
ADDRESS	via XX Settembre, 4			
PHONE	(0522) 57-201			
CREDIT CARDS	AmX, Visa, Diners			
CLOSED	Mon dinner, Tues, Aug 5–25, Dec 26–Jan 20			
CLASS	ATMOSPHERE	SERVICE	WINE	PRICE
3	3	3	3.5	M

A dark, family-style *trattoria*. The entryway is laden with bottles of wine, which create a first impression of warmth and coziness. Pink tablecloths, dark red floors, and a piano in the middle room add to this impression—and also indicate the restaurant's serious intent. Picci is an accommodating eating establishment, absolutely intent on pleasing its patrons. It's run by Raffaele Piccirilli, a rather shy and retiring man who has nonetheless managed to create a first-rate and even important restaurant.

The truffles served here in the months excluding October, November, December, and perhaps the beginning of January—when you get the true white truffle—are what might be called "gray" truffles; the Italian term differs according to city or region. In Cavriago the term is *bianchetti* ("little whites"). Although often listed as black truffles, these "grays" are clearly relatives of the white truffle (which bears no resemblance at all to the black) and have the same unmistakable and inimitable aroma; only the intensity and depth are different.

Directions. If you are coming from Milan, take the *autostrada* toward Bologna and get off at Reggio nell'Emilia. From the *autostrada* go right, following signs toward Parma, and then the signs for Montecchio as soon as they appear; you don't want the main road to Parma. Continue until you see the signs for Cavriago. On the far side of that town make a right at the sign for the restaurant, which is about 10 minutes from the *autostrada*.

balsamiche sensazioni (insalata di filetto con esotica, uvetta, pinoli ecc. al balsamico Thinly sliced raw beef over salad greens, with sultanas, pine nuts, pomegranate seeds, and a dampening of balsamic vinegar.

*misto di funghi Mushrooms in various guises, some served hot, some cold: in an omelette, puréed, fried, *en croûte,* in crêpes, and so on.

crêpes di mela con cipolle novelle al balsamico Crêpes stuffed with apple purée, onions, a touch of béchamel, and a splash of balsamic vinegar. Garnished with apple slices.

bottoni ai funghi su fonduta di tartufo Ravioli-like pasta stuffed with mushrooms and served with a light butter, cheese, and truffle sauce, and topped with truffle.

*scaloppe di foie gras al tartufo nero Generous slices of goose liver with truffle over the top and a light sauce of balsamic vinegar, raisins, pine nuts, and pomegranate seeds. Garnished with mashed potato spiked with truffle. A magical dish—foie gras and truffle!

*filetto di coniglio al finocchio selvatico Fillet of roasted rabbit served with wild fennel and carrots in an intense sauce of reduced rabbit broth flavored with fennel. One of the best rabbit dishes in Italy.

torta casareccia al gusto di limone A delicious lemon tart.

crema all'antica con fragole calde Zabaione served with hot strawberries.

SUGGESTED WINES

White

Chardonnay, Terre Rosse, Vallania Apples and herbs mixed with some floral notes and a dash of vanilla in the first rush of the bouquet, then more fresh fruit filling the mouth. A terrific white, alive in its fruit-to-acid balance; delicate and elegant, it has a beautiful gold color with a slight green cast to it.

Red

Lambrusco Reggiano, Baldini (Selezione Picci)
A sparkling red, showing all the characteristics of well-made Lambrusco: a deep ruby red color, cherry notes, and a pleasing fresh taste. The nose is oddly cast, and the finish contains the slightest suggestion of vinegar. Lambrusco certainly doesn't appeal to everyone—it's a regional favorite but definitely an acquired taste. It ought to be sampled at least once while you're in Emilia-Romagna.

Dessert

Acini Nobili della Breganze, Maculan (Selezione Picci)   Like Sauterne but sweeter and thicker in texture, and without the depth and complexity of Sauterne. From the Veneto and very good.

Digestivo

Nocino   A green walnut liqueur.

Costigliole d'Asti

Alba 15 km   *Alessandria* 51   *Asti* 15   *Cuneo* 77
Genoa 108   *Milan* 141   *Turin* 75

GUIDO				
★ ★ ★ ★ ★				
REGION	Piedmont			
ADDRESS	piazza Umberto I, 27			
PHONE	(0141) 966-012			
CREDIT CARDS	Cash only			
CLOSED	Every day at lunch, Sun			
	Reservations necessary.			

CLASS	ATMOSPHERE	SERVICE	WINE	PRICE
3.5	3	5	5	VE

A squarish, unambitious room, which you enter by walking down a flight of stairs: the restaurant has a little of the feel of a finished basement or recreation room, with mostly wood paneling and a tile floor. But it's tastefully appointed with dark wood armoires, Italian antiques, and Oriental carpets, which give an odd formality without the grace of many better restaurants. It's quite clear that the restaurant's sole concern is the food and wine. In any case, it is comfortable, with a sort of general *simpatico* permeating the place. The hand-embroidered linens and large urns filled with plants are cheering, and most important, with Mamma manning the flames in the kitchen, you're not likely to find better food in Italy. A loose assortment of long breadsticks are the table decorations, and the light and dark breads kept on your plate will steal your appetite if you aren't aware of the way they are replaced. The service is impeccable—in fact, only family works in this restaurant. The father is Guido Alciati, and Lidia, the mother, is the chef. Have Piero, the eldest son, wait on your table.

Seventy percent of the clientele comes from outside Piedmont—the restaurant is especially favored by French, Swiss, and Germans—and Italians from Genoa and Milan don't think twice about jumping in a car to partake of a dinner here. Driving in the Piedmont would make the trip worthwhile even if Guido didn't exist—but then, it does. Reservations are absolutely necessary.

If you have time, visit some of the important vineyards that produce Barolo and Barbaresco, between the towns of Asti and Alba. There's also a very special school in Roddi, where dogs are trained to hunt for the famous white truffles. It's worth investigating this notable establishment, especially if you're a truffle hound yourself. (See page 135 for a hotel.)

Directions. Take the *autostrada* from Torino toward Asti, getting off at "Asti Est." Follow the signs for Alba until you see signs for Costigliole, which is 15 kilometers southwest of Asti, off Highway 231.

SUGGESTED DISHES

*zuppa di funghi   Mushroom soup as the gods intended it.

*mousse tartufata   Duck pâté with truffle, garnished with sliced carrots.

*peperoni farciti   Peppers stuffed with capers, anchovies, tuna, and parsley.

*cardi con fonduta e tartufi   Cardoons with a fondue of *fontina* cheese and truffles.

sformato di parmigiano con creme di verdure   Parmesan flan atop swirls of puréed spinach, carrots, and truffles. A pretty dish: green, yellow-orange, and white.

agnolotti   Green *ravioli*-like pasta stuffed with vegetables, rabbit, pork, and veal, served with a sauce made from Parmesan and the juices from the roasted meats.

*tacchino e funghi   Turkey with mushrooms and hearts of palm, perked up with a little olive oil and lemon. Tender and excellent in every way.

vitello con crema e tartufi   Veal with a cream sauce and truffles.

*formaggi piemontesi   A selection of cheeses from this region. A must.

crostata di pera   A delicious pear tart with a little cream.

mousse di castagne con crema   A fine chestnut mousse with rich homemade cream.

SUGGESTED   WINES

White

Chardonnay, Piodilei, Pio Cesare   Pale yellow and engagingly buttery. The initial hit of apples and vanilla is followed by a lot of earth and some wood. Long, mellow finish.

Red

Bricco dell'Uccellone, G. Bologna   Here is Barbera at its very best and most graceful, a wine Burton Anderson says is "filled with fantasy and humor." Powerful color, nose, and flavor; big and rich, alcoholic, fruity and earthy, this is a wine of the earth with a moment of cherry in the finish. It comes on like Mike Tyson.

1979 Barolo, Bussia di Monforte, Bruno Giacosa, Riserva Speciale   A powerful Barolo with plenty of alcohol and tannin, the fruit a little under wraps, but it's a big, big luscious wine—a wine that demonstrates convincingly why Barolo has the reputation it does.

1967 Barolo, Francesco Rinaldi   Still youthful, deep garnet to mahogany brown in color. Dense, alert, complex, and avid: there are serious depths to be plumbed in this wine. The fruit is a little shy, but all in all a wonderful Barolo. Young though it is, it's drinkable nonetheless.

Dessert

Barolo Chinato, Castello di Canelli   An extremely unusual red dessert wine; clove highlights, very spicy. The flavor is created by soaking *chinino* (quinine, from the bark of the cinchona tree) in Barolo. It's unlike anything you've tasted before, a very appealing specialty from this region, rarely found outside of it—or even in it!

Cremona

Bergamo 98 km	*Brescia* 52	*Crema* 38	*Genoa* 180
Mantua 66	*Milan* 95	*Pavia* 86	*Piacenza* 34
	Turin 214	*Verona* 118	

Among the famous sons of Cremona are Claudio Monteverdi, father of Italian opera, and Antonio Stradivari and his sons, whose violins are the most famous in the world. The Museo Stradivariano is worth a visit if you have a little time before your meal, as is the Torrazzo, the thirteenth-century campanile reputed to be the highest medieval tower in Italy, in beautiful piazza del Comune. Cremona is known for its *mostarda di Cremona,* a chutney-like sauce composed of a variety of fruits (cherries, grapes, figs, plums, pears, apricots, melon) preserved in a spicy, sweet syrup flavored with mustard and various other seasonings; this *mostarda* is often served with boiled meats. Another specialty of Cremona is *marubini,* a stuffed pasta.

High-tech Italian contemporary, modulated by Italian good taste. The walls, made of a tan plastic material, have a lacquered look. The tile floors feature oriental carpets and there are marble archways. The brightly colored glass lamps and blue tablecloths are stylish, but there is something slightly dour about the atmosphere, perhaps because of the lighting. The owner is, apparently, uncomfortable in his front-room role and has done little to cheer the space.

CERESOLE				
★ ★ ★ ½				

REGION	Lombardy
ADDRESS	via Ceresole, 4
PHONE	(0372) 23-322
CREDIT CARDS	AmX, Visa, Diners
CLOSED	Sun dinner, Mon, Jan 22–30, Aug 6–28

CLASS	ATMOSPHERE	SERVICE	WINE	PRICE
3.5	3	3	3	E

SUGGESTED DISHES

cotechino, fagioli freschi e salsa di noci Pork sausage with brown beans, served with a nut and mustard sauce and a traditional *mostarda di Cremona.*

marubini ai tre brodi Little round ravioli-like pasta stuffed with meat, served in a rich broth. This pasta originated in Cremona.

carretto di vitello con funghi porcini Veal with *porcini* mushrooms, served with a reduced veal stock and garnished with half-moons of *polenta.*

spuma di torrone in salsa di nocciole Cold nougat mousse with a hazelnut sauce.

SUGGESTED WINES

White

Chardonnay, Ca' del Bosco This one rivals any white in Italy—a spectacular Chardonnay, hay-colored and handsome in the glass, with a complicated nose that's immediately rich, full, and airy, and a hint of mild wood and herbs in the background. In the mouth the wine is a delight: herbal, spicy, achieving great structure and a terrific balance of fruit and acidity. Wood remains modestly present; the wine finishes with a show of fruit and flowers.

Red

Il Felicino, La Muiraghina di Montu Beccaria
A mix of Barbera, Croatina, and Uva Rara. Deep red, almost purple. Rustic and rough, with notes of grace and elegance. A slightly bitter finish, but not unpleasant. Shows some interesting fruit after an hour. A country wine with city aspirations.

OTHER RECOMMENDED RESTAURANTS

In Crema, 38 km
Guada'l Canal
via Crocicchio, 46 (near Santo Stefano)
(0373) 200-133
AmX, Visa, Diners
Closed Sun dinner, Mon, Aug

In Roncole Verdi, 30 km
Guareschi
via Processione, 13 (near Busseto)
(0524) 92-495
Cash only
Serves lunch only. Closed Fri, Feb, July, Dec

Florence/Firenze

Arezzo 81 km	*Bologna* 105	*Lucca* 74	*Milan* 298
	Parma 184	*Perugia* 154	*Pisa* 92
Ravenna 136	*Rome* 277	*Siena* 68	*Urbino* 188
	Venice 254	*Verona* 229	

Florence has so many things to recommend it that even a selective list would take up more space than this volume allows. One of the most important artistic and intellectual centers during the Renaissance, Florence produced some very significant figures—among them, Giotto, Masaccio, Donatello, Uccello, Botticelli, Michelangelo, Leonardo, Dante, Boccaccio, Machiavelli—and of course the Medici, who so put their stamp on this town.

The Galleria degli Uffizi (closed Sunday afternoons and Mondays), some say the most important art museum in the world, has Botticelli's *Primavera* and *Birth of Venus*, Leonardo's *Adoration of the Magi* and *Annunciation*, Giotto's *Maestà*, Uccello's *The Battle of San Romano*, and important works by Fra Angelico, Piero della Francesca, Filippo Lippi, Antonio Pollaiuolo, Giovanni Bellini, Michelangelo, Raphael, and Titian. And across the Arno is the Pitti Palace, or Palazzo Pitti (closed Mondays and afternoons), with works by Titian, Raphael, and Caravaggio, among others. Michelangelo's famous *David* and various statues of slaves are housed in the Galleria dell'Accademia (closed Mondays and afternoons). The outdoor Loggia dei Lanzi, near Palazzo Vecchio (the old city hall, closed Sunday afternoons and Saturdays), has one of my favorite statues, a Perseus with the head of Medusa by Benvenuto Cellini. The Bargello (closed Mondays and afternoons) has a David by Donatello, a drunken Bacchus by Michelangelo, and *Hercules and Antaeus* by Pollaiuolo.

The cathedral of Florence, Santa Maria del Fiore, one of the largest churches in the world, was built between 1296 and 1434. The original façade was destroyed in 1588 and replaced in the late nineteenth century. But it's the entire piazza del Duomo, with cathedral, campanile, and baptistry together, that is breathtaking. Brunelleschi's beautiful Church of San Lorenzo should not be overlooked. The Old Sacristy he designed is equaled only by the two pulpits decorated by Donatello.

Spend some time on the Ponte Vecchio, the world-famous bridge built in the fourteenth century, now lined with jewelers' shops on either side. From it you can gaze out and imagine the colors and tones of the old city exactly as they were 500 years ago. This, the oldest bridge in Florence, is for pedestrians only, and it crosses the Arno River at its narrowest point.

The region of Florence, Tuscany, produces some of the most important food and wine of Italy. A quick list would have to include Tuscany's three DOCG wines: Brunello di Montalcino, Chianti, and Vino Nobile di Montepulciano. Of the regional food specialties, one thinks immediately of the inimitable Florentine steak, *bistecca alla fiorentina;* the hearty bread and cabbage soup called *ribollita; fagioli all'uccelletto,* a dish of white beans cooked with oil, garlic, tomatoes, and sage; and *crostini,* slices of toasted bread with various toppings.

ENOTECA PINCHIORRI

★ ★ ★ ★ ★

REGION	Tuscany
ADDRESS	via Ghibellina, 87
PHONE	(055) 242-777
CREDIT CARDS	AmX, Visa
CLOSED	Sun, Mon lunch, Aug, Dec 24–28

CLASS	ATMOSPHERE	SERVICE	WINE	PRICE
5	4.5	5	5	VE

One of the most sumptuous restaurants in Italy, full of old-world grace and elegance, certainly near the top of any responsible list. It began as the wine cellar and bar of Giorgio Pinchiorri; later, under the ever-watchful gastronomical eye of Annie Feolde, originally from France, the two started this impressive haven for *alta cucina*. The walls display contemporary Italian paintings, exhibited in conjunction with a Florentine art gallery. Wooden floors, soft colors, salmon-colored tablecloths, pastel-colored chairs—this restaurant in a beautiful Florentine *palazzo* is, to be sure, what eating at the top is all about! Ask to sit downstairs, in the larger of the two dining rooms.

Gianni Fortunati, the *cantiniere,* or wine steward, is brilliant; allow him to select your wine. Pinchiorri is said to have one of the finest wine cellars in the world, and it has even received awards stating as much. In any case, here's a chance to taste something you won't likely find anywhere else, as well as important vintages of wines already familiar to you; Gianni will be tremendously helpful in this regard.

The waiters are very young, very serious—and best of all, very well trained. It's advisable to select one of the tasting menus; the restaurant is set up to present its food in this manner. Select a *menú degustazione,* loosen your belt, and bite the golden bullet, for it's dear.

SUGGESTED   DISHES

insalata di funghi porcini con tartufo di Alba   A salad of *porcini* mushrooms, lettuce, truffle, pomegranate seeds, and tarragon, with a touch of balsamic vinegar and oil.

zucchini farciti con melanzane e gamberi   Zucchini stuffed with eggplant, shrimp, and lobster in a light sauce of butter, cream, and stock made with crustaceans.

lasagne con salsa di granchio e besciamella   An ethereal lasagne made with crab meat, fennel, and béchamel.

ravioli farciti con olive nere e profumati alla salvia   Large, oval orange *ravioli* colored with carrot, stuffed with black olives and perfumed with fresh sage.

*piccione con salsa del suo fegato, vino rosso e lamponi, con guarnizione di patate arrosto e prugne farcite di cipolle   Pigeon in a sauce made with its liver, red wine, and raspberries, served with roasted potatoes and prunes stuffed with onions.

*petto di faraona al cartoccio in salsa di rosmarino   Breast of guinea fowl stuffed with vegetables and cooked in a paper bag, served with a rosemary sauce.

parfait alla cannella con ventaglio di pere e vainiglia   Cinnamon ice cream served with pear slices arranged in a fan shape, and a vanilla cream.

biscotto con mousse di banane e salsa di fragole   Banana mousse cake with strawberry sauce.

SUGGESTED WINES

White

Le Ragne, Poggio alla Sala   A wine from the area that produces Vino Nobile di Montepulciano, made from Malvasia grapes. Intensely yellow in color, with an incredible floral bouquet. A little residual sugar adds some caramel to the delicate nose of this wine. Dense, almost resinous, deep and interesting. One year in a *barrique* gives it an extremely winning woodiness.

Fontanelle Chardonnay, Fontanelle, Villa Banfi   A white in the Burgundian tradition, showing serious butter, wood, color, and grace, with something reminiscent of Sauterne in the finish. Rich, very deep—a wine engaging in a supreme fiction of its own.

Red

Capannelle Rosso, Raffaele Rossetti, Capannelle A blend of Sangioveto and Cabernet, but almost Burgundian in style, off-red, tarnished just slightly toward brown around the edges. This finely rich wine gives up some fullness and warmth in favor of a willed complexity and a moment of harshness as it closes.

Solaia, Antinori One of the great, distinctive wines of Italy—smooth, rich, complex, and always unforgettable. A big Cabernet, with all the classical characteristics of this varietal.

Dessert

Malvasia delle Lipari, Hauner One of Italy's most distinguished and luscious dessert wines, from the tiny island of Lipari, off the coast of Sicily.

CIBREO				
★ ★ ★ ½				
REGION	Tuscany			
ADDRESS	via dei Macci, 118			
PHONE	(055) 234-1100			
CREDIT CARDS	AmX, Diners, Visa			
CLOSED	Sun, Mon, Jan 1–7, Apr 4–10, Aug 1–Sept 5			
CLASS	ATMOSPHERE	SERVICE	WINE	PRICE
2.5	3	4	2.5	M

This lively, festive restaurant near the Sant'Ambrogio market, owned by a serious and charming couple—Benedetta Vitali and Fabio Picchi—is at first glance a simple eating establishment, but it soon becomes apparent how the gastronomical ambition works here. A carpet adds warmth in a room that is not overly concerned with comfort or elegance. If you are a couple, you're placed at a table with another couple, probably Italian, because Cibreo is frequented by Italians who care about the food they eat. And it's a mixed crowd—old and young, blue-jeaned and suited. (Note how Florentine males admire checkered sport coats.) The fare is simple, but accomplished with a flair that raises this restaurant into the ranks of the very best of Italy's "avant-garde," by which I do not mean *nouvelle cuisine.* There's no menu here, and you won't be offered a wine list—you pick your wine from the shelf, or take the advice of your waiter. The offering is limited, but each of the wines is first-rate and has been selected with obvious loving care—and they're not necessarily wines you'll find elsewhere.

Your meal will begin with a little sampler; for example, I was recently served a slice of cheese soufflé, *bresaola* (cured dried beef), tripe, liver pâté, and a piece of goat cheese. The dishes are inventive, thoughtful, and respectful of the Tuscan tradition. I haven't found anything quite like it anywhere in Italy, except at Silverio, in Bologna, and, to a lesser extent, at Da Noi, the restaurant around the corner. At Cibreo all the categories seem to break down as the evening advances, and fine dishes, one after another, emerge from the kitchen in the hands of one of the well-informed waiters. You'll be guided through the meal by one of the owners. Be sure to pace yourself, or you'll find the meal over before you wish to consider the remainder of the evening.

SUGGESTED DISHES

minestra di peperoni   Bell pepper soup with a trickle of olive oil over the top, served with Parmesan.

*minestra di pane e cavolo   Bread and cabbage soup, the very finest *ribollita* I've tasted.

anatra ripiena   Stuffed duck.

quaglia con salsa di fegatini e marroni   Quail served with a sauce of chicken livers and chestnuts.

crostata di limone   Lemon pie.

dolce di formaggio con pere   Cheesecake with pears.

torta al cioccolato amaro   A bitter chocolate tart with pears.

SUGGESTED WINES

White

Grattamacco, Piermario Meletti Cavallari   A wonderful Tuscan white: pears in the nose, delicate and seductive, and a beautiful lemon color. A good explosion of fruit in the mouth, with a noticeable kick of acidity to tighten the focus. A smart wine, ready to go and very with it. More *there* than most Italian whites.

Red

Bruno di Rocca, Vecchie Terre di Montefili Half
Cabernet, half Sangioveto. Inviting, open nose with a deep
beautiful garnet color. The Cabernet adds a wonderful rich
softness, with good fruit and oak immediately available in
the mouth. A graceful and important red, one of Tuscany's
best.

Dessert

Malvasia delle Lipari, Hauner One of Italy's most
distinguished and luscious dessert wines, from the tiny island of Lipari, off the coast of Sicily.

LA TAVERNA DEL BRONZINO
★ ★ ★

REGION	Tuscany
ADDRESS	via delle Ruote, 25
PHONE	(055) 495-220
CREDIT CARDS	AmX, Diners
CLOSED	Sun, Aug 1–21

CLASS	ATMOSPHERE	SERVICE	WINE	PRICE
3	3	3	2.5	M

An old-fashioned *trattoria* a little out of the way but worth
the short trip by cab—or the longer walk, if that suits you.
It's a pleasing space; old prints of birds, plants, and spices
cover the walls, and it's surprisingly comfortable for this type
of restaurant. Ask for Piero, who will take care of everything
for you; he's full of information about the food of Tuscany,
so save your questions for him, his English is excellent.

SUGGESTED DISHES

prosciutto rosso di montagna A slice of prosciutto on
toast, with chopped tomatoes and chopped arugula. Spicy
and good, unusual.

*tortellini neri al tartufo Black tortellini colored
with the skin of nuts (*mallo di noci*), stuffed with meat and
truffle, topped with pieces of Parmesan and a butter sauce,
and garnished with sage leaves. Available September
through November—a must.

storione in gremolada Sturgeon served in a sauce of butter, lemon, and parsley. You can have the fish nicely grilled without the sauce, served with deep-fried artichokes as a side dish.

*involtini di vitella al gorgonzola Veal rolled around a piece of celery and cooked in a stock impregnated with *gorgonzola*. The chunks of cheese disappear in the cooking but leave behind a subtle flavor.

albicocche The apricots are served here in a delicate sauce made from their own cooking liquid.

SUGGESTED WINES

White

Chardonnay, Colline di Ama, Fattoria di Ama A wine gentle in its approach: its subtle nose discloses modest fruit, it is soft on the palate, it has some wood and perhaps too little acidity. Well made if not the most exciting Italian white.

Red

Flaccianello della Pieve, Fontodi A hundred percent Sangiovese—a wine with all the varietal characteristics. Ruby to brick-red in color, with a nose that doesn't give too much away, but does suggest definite fruit and oak. The first taste is big, full-bodied, tannic with good fruit coming behind; then subtlety, a little spice; and then a long, tasty finish. Beautifully balanced, rich but not soft, sturdy and powerful. An intelligent if cool wine.

DA NOI				
★ ★ ★				

REGION	Tuscany
ADDRESS	via Fiesolana, 46
PHONE	(055) 242-917
CREDIT CARDS	Cash only
CLOSED	Sun, Mon, Aug

CLASS	ATMOSPHERE	SERVICE	WINE	PRICE
2	2	3	3.5	M

There's no menu in this *trattoria,* but the pleasant Scandinavian woman who works alone in the dining room speaks at least five languages and will repeat the names of the dishes for you if your memory is feeling strained by the riches of Italian menus. The wines available represent small regional vineyards, and she will suggest one—there is no written wine list—according to your food selection. It's worth trying something from a small and local vineyard here to accompany the thoughtfully prepared cuisine. It should be added that this establishment is not without pretension, although it's clear the woman is extremely informed—with a vengeance, one might be tempted to say; she knows and is proud of Tuscan cuisine and has a great deal to share with you if she's not too busy.

The food is good if not inspired, but Da Noi is definitely worth a visit. Because the space is simply put together, nearly stark and, unhappily, not overly comfortable with its stiff chairs, I'd save this place for lunch. It's not unlike its neighbor, Cibreo (see above), which is the more accomplished of the two when it comes to the execution of simple regional food and which is, finally, a little less precious.

SUGGESTED DISHES

bevette con radicchio e lardo Thin pasta with *radicchio* and very tasty bacon.

piccione con funghi Pigeon served on a bed of mushrooms, with a sauce made of stock and pigeon liver.

Red

Cepparrello, Isole e Olena   A new-wave Tuscan red, made only with Sangiovese and aged in chestnut; good and clean with extremely attractive body and richness. The wood balances nicely with the fruit and tannin. A very well-made wine.

SABATINI
★ ★ ★

REGION	Tuscany
ADDRESS	via de' Panzani 9a
PHONE	(055) 282-802
CREDIT CARDS	AmX
CLOSED	Mon

CLASS	ATMOSPHERE	SERVICE	WINE	PRICE
3.5	3	3	3.5	E

This restaurant is better than its general reputation might suggest—that of a tourist trap. Really, it's quite agreeable, friendly and warm, with dark wood and comfortable tables. The clientele may be more touristy than you'd wish, but if you take my recommendations you'll be pleased you came. I've suggested dishes that are particularly good if you've had a number of big, complicated meals and want something simple and straightforward. All the suggested red wines are trustworthy companions to the Florentine steak. This is the time to have one of the great Tuscan reds, price be damned.

SUGGESTED DISHES

crostini alla fiorentina   Toasted bread with various toppings—cheese, liver, truffle, and so on.

*bistecca alla fiorentina   The famous Florentine steak: a large T-bone, grilled rare over coals.

insalata mista   An excellent mixed salad.

arancia sbucciata   An orange that will be peeled for you at the table by your waiter if you can pronounce the *s* word—don't be shy. It's the best way to eat an orange.

White

Grattamacco, Piermario Meletti Cavallari A wonderful Tuscan white: pears in the nose, delicate and seductive, and a beautiful lemon color. A good explosion of fruit in the mouth, with a noticeable kick of acidity to tighten the focus. A smart wine, ready to go and very with it. More *there* than most Italian whites.

Red

Tignanello, Antinori A blend of Sangiovese and Cabernet (usually around 20 percent), this wine is, as Burton Anderson points out, "the inspiration for a whole new breed of Tuscan winemakers." A lovely rich garnet that hits you with a subtle, unaggressive nose. Complex, deep, but not overbearing. Beautifully balanced with fine highlights of fruit and tannin.

Digestivo

Centerbe A powerfully alcoholic after-dinner drink— beautiful pale green in color, lightly scented with a hundred herbs, as its name indicates, and dangerous after three sips. Get the 70 *gradi* (70 percent alcohol).

OTHER RECOMMENDED RESTAURANTS

Trattoria Le Quattro Stagioni
via Maggio, 61
(055) 218-906
AmX, Visa, Diners
Closed Sun, Aug 9–31, Dec 21–Jan 4

An excellent "model" *trattoria* around the corner from the Pitti Palace, and the obvious place for lunch after a journey through that wonderful collection. You might want to begin with a plate of the local salami—*salame toscano*. Another good choice is *insalata Caterina Medici*—capers, cheese, anchovies, and pine nuts along with green and red lettuce. Then head for the *ravioli* of the day or the *pasticcio della casa,* oven-baked noodles with a meat and cream sauce. Consider also *tagliatelle Quattro Stagioni,* pasta with mushrooms, tomatoes, and cream. If you're still hungry, a little *filetto* of fine Tuscan beef would not be harmful. Save room for a few spoonfuls of their *tiramisù,* that important dessert of ladyfingers, *mascarpone, espresso,* chocolate and various liquors.

Ottorino
via delle Oche, 12–16
(055) 218-747
AmX, Visa, Diners
Closed Sun, Aug

A crisp, lively restaurant that gets a pretty good-size lunch crowd from the business sector. The food is prepared carefully and the feeling is fresh; the contemporary decor is a nice change of pace. I generally order the *malfatti all'aurora* to begin, which are very light spinach and ricotta dumplings— sometimes described as *ravioli* without the pasta. Also recommended are the *fagioli*, Tuscan beans that are cooked *all'uccelletto*, in oil with tomatoes; *cotechino di Modena con rapini*, a large pork sausage served with broccoli rabe; and wild boar with mushrooms, *cinghiale alla maremmana con funghi*. Perfect for an informal but fine lunch or dinner.

Relais Le Jardin
piazza Massimo d'Azeglio, 3 (in the Hotel Regency)
(055) 245-247
AmX, Visa, Diners
Closed Sun

Al Campidoglio
via del Campidoglio, 8
(055) 287-770
AmX, Visa, Diners
Closed Thurs

Al Campidoglio is a solid Florentine *ristorante* where a good and uncomplicated meal can be had for a moderate price. The pastas are generally well made, as are the grilled dishes—for example, the chicken, *mezzo pollastro nostrale alla Campidoglio,* or the veal, *costola or lombatina di vitella.* Or select from the "Piatti del Giorno." A pleasant restaurant in which to enjoy a casual meal. And it's conveniently located, just off piazza della Repubblica.

Antico Fattore
via Lambertesca, 1
(055) 261-215
AmX
Closed Sun, Mon

This an old, working-man's *trattoria,* serving good, basic, inexpensive food. The specialties include a country-style vegetable soup called *zuppa alla contadina.* Start with the mixed appetizers, *antipasti misti della casa,* and continue with *rigatoni strascicati,* an unusual sautéed rigatoni; *trippa alla fioren-*

tina, tripe with tomatoes, herbs, and Parmesan; *stracotto,* a Tuscan beef stew; or grilled sausages, *salsicce alla griglia.* Of three restaurants in Florence that seem to me cut from the same cloth—all simple *trattorie* serving basic, traditional Florentine cuisine—Il Latini, Coco Lezzone, and Antico Fattore, I prefer the last. A little more care is taken with the preparation and presentation of food, and it seems, generally, a more rewarding place to eat—hearty fare and fun. The restaurant is located on the Uffizi side of the Ponte Vecchio, near the bridge.

Mamma Gina
borgo San Jacopo, 37
(055) 296-009
AmX, Visa, Diners
Closed Sun, Aug 7–21

Good food is served here and the wine cellar is surprisingly fine. Over the past few years it's been overrun with tourists and the quality of the food has suffered, although it is a trustworthy restaurant if you're in the mood for something low-key but tasty.

Sostanza detto Il Troia
via della Porcellana, 25
(055) 212-691
Cash only
Closed Sun, Sat dinner, Aug

An inexpensive *trattoria* where decent Florentine food is served simply, to an eager and lively clientele.

Coco Lezzone
via del Parioncino, 26
(055) 287-178
Cash only
Closed Sun, Tues dinner; summer: closed Sun, Sat, but open weekdays lunch and dinner

Coco Lezzone is a tiny, rustic, and rather uncomfortable *trattoria,* but it does have an avid local crowd and consequently there's a great deal of camaraderie and good cheer at the tables, which are, by the way, communal. The dishes to order: *pappa al pomodoro,* the famous bread soup cooked with tomatoes, local olive oil, basil, and garlic; and *ribollita,* the Tuscan soup made with cabbage, beans, and bread, reheated—or literally, "reboiled." Also try *braciola col carciofo,* a meat and artichoke dish.

Cammillo
borgo San Jacopo, 57
(055) 212-427
AmX, Visa, Diners
Closed Wed, Thurs, Aug 1–21, Dec 20–Jan 15

A simple *trattoria* on the Pitti Palace side of the Arno. It has lost some of its luster over the past few years—in fact, it recently lost its Michelin star. It serves decent *antipasti* and pastas, and is quite handy if you're staying at the Hotel Lungarno, just down the street.

Il Latini
via dei Palchetti, 6
(055) 210-916
Cash only
Closed Mon, Tues lunch, July 20–Aug 10

This is an extremely popular *trattoria*—especially on Sundays, when customers line up in the street. It's communal, rustic, loud, and sloppy, but if you're in the right mood, it can be fun. The food is mediocre, with more attention being paid to the giving over of food. I suggest you keep it simple: *ribollita,* the "reboiled" Tuscan bread, cabbage, and bean soup, which is very good here, and *fagioli,* excellent Tuscan beans. Also trustworthy are the roasted pigeon, *piccione arrosto intero,* and the roasted rabbit, *coniglio arrosto*—or, if you feel undecided, try the mixed roast meats, called *arrosto misto,* a specialty of the house.

H O T E L S

Savoy
piazza della Repubblica, 7
(055) 283-313
AmX, Visa, Diners
Very expensive/Luxury

The Savoy was built in 1893 on the site of the old Jewish ghetto, now piazza della Repubblica. Located in the center of Florence, this is one of the finest-run hotels in Italy, thanks to the constant attention of its general manager, Vittorio Spicciani, who came to the Savoy in 1974. The rooms are beautifully and comfortably designed. The main concierge, Giuseppe Azzerboni—call him Joseph—has the answer to any question that may occur to you during your stay in Florence; and he's *interested,* or at least while you're in his care you will believe he is, which is not always the case with the staff of deluxe hotels in Italy. The Savoy is a member of the Leading Hotels of the World chain.

Lungarno
borgo Sant'Jacopo, 14
(055) 264-211
AmX, Visa, Diners
Moderate

This is a hotel in which I love to stay if I can arrange for one of the rooms with a terrace facing the Arno, which is no more expensive than the other large double rooms that don't; unfortunately, the hotel does not commit to one of these rooms, so you're forced to take your chances when you arrive. It's very well located—it's a two-minute walk to the Ponte Vecchio on the Pitti side of the Arno, which makes the journey back and forth to your room an easy affair. This is an important consideration if you enjoy going in and out at all hours. A very pleasant bar area overlooks the Arno; this is the perfect place to take your continental breakfast, which, by the way, does not come with the room. Book well in advance. There is easy hotel parking.

Tornabuoni Beacci
via Tornabuoni, 3
(055) 268-377
AmX, Visa, Diners
Moderate

Housed in a wonderful fourteenth-century *palazzo* in the center of one of the main shopping areas, a stone's throw from the Arno on the Uffizi side, this can be a magical *pensione* if you get one of the two large rooms, which can be requested. Part of the charm is the elevator that takes you to the *pensione,* which occupies the top floors. A favorite among literati.

FOOD AND WINE SHOPS, MARKETS

Food

Salsamentaria Paolo e Massimo
via De Sanctis, 12
A full display of the foods of Tuscany and the other regions of Italy.

Alessi
via delle Oche, 27–29
One of the finest wine stores in Italy, featuring an impressive selection of wines from every region of the country.

Markets

Mercato di San Lorenzo
piazza del Mercato Centrale
An indoor market with stalls filled with various foodstuffs—meat and poultry, game birds, fish, cheese, vegetables, mushrooms, herbs, and on and on. Go early, have a coffee, and take in the atmosphere of this impressive market. It's open mornings only.

Genoa/Genova

Alessandria 81 km	*Asti* 116	*Boves* 153	*Milan* 142
Parma 198	*Piacenza* 148	*La Spezia* 103	
Turin 170	*Viareggio* 155		

Genoa is Italy's most important seaport, and one of the largest ports in the Mediterranean. Be sure to wander in and around the *centro storico,* the historic center, which is well worth investigating for its atmosphere of old Genoa. This is the city whose name is nearly synonymous with *pesto,* the internationally famous sauce prepared with basil, garlic, olive oil, *pecorino* and/or Parmesan, and pine nuts. In purer days, basil (*basilico;* the word derives from the Greek for "king") grew everywhere in Genoa and loaded the air with its scent. A rather less known gastronomical fact is that this city also fathered—or mothered, given the omnipresence of *la mamma* in the kitchen—the pasta we know as *ravioli*; the word derives from a term meaning "things of little value" or "leftovers." On Genovese sailing boats, leftovers were chopped up together, stuffed into pasta, and cooked. A somewhat surprising fact about Liguria, of which Genoa is the capital, is that 25 percent of all tourism in Italy takes place here.

GRAN GOTTO
★ ★ ★

REGION	Liguria
ADDRESS	via Fiume, 11
PHONE	(010) 564-344
CREDIT CARDS	AmX, Visa
CLOSED	Sun, Aug 10–31

CLASS	ATMOSPHERE	SERVICE	WINE	PRICE
3	3	3	2.5	M

Gran Gotto, more than welcome in a town without a notable eating spot, is a lively and cheerful place; the stuccoed walls of the rooms are lined with bottles and the colorful collection of Piatti del buon Ricordo ("Good Memory Plates"). These are distributed by the Unione Ristoranti del Buon Ricordo, an organization set up to promote traditional Italian cuisine and supported by the Touring Club Italiano. Participating restaurants feature a regional dish; if you order it, you become the proud owner of a colorfully illustrated plate with the name of that dish along with the restaurant's name and location.

Naturally, Gran Gotto is equipped with a center table laden with flowers and good things to come: vegetables, fruits, cheeses, desserts, and liqueurs. A back room is announced with a pink neon sign created by the artist Joseph Kossout that reads, "Five words in pink neon." Plain white tablecloths, blue wainscotting, comfortable and elegant chairs each do their part to elevate the class here. All in all, a very popular, very hip restaurant. A ten-minute walk from the Hotel Bristol, the only place to stay in downtown Genoa.

SUGGESTED DISHES

antipasto caldo di mare A mix of seafood, served warm: fried sole; chopped octopus with a potato and leek sauce; and *bianchetti,* a specialty of this region; these newly hatched (nearly fetal) red mullets, sardines, or anchovies appear on menus in February and March; small and young, they look more like interconnected pieces of shredded fish without skin than fish. They are boiled for a fast second and served with a little lemon and oil.

gnocchetti di branzino al "pesto corto" Little dumplings, *gnocchi,* made with puréed sea bass and egg whites, boiled and served with a pesto sauce (*corto* means "short," by which the owner means "subtle") and fresh tomatoes. Before the final presentation a little cheese is grated over the top and the dish is placed under the broiler for a minute.

tagliolini ai bianchetti Long, thin, flat noodles served in a sauce of *bianchetti* (see above), oil, tomatoes, and herbs.

scaloppe di branzino al rossese Perfectly cooked fillets of sea bass in a sauce of red wine, shallots, and *fumetto* (fish stock). Basic good fish.

SUGGESTED WINES

White

Pigato dei Massaretti, Pippo Parodi A generous and unusual white, well matched to the fish and seafood served here. The Pigato wines have been described as mouth-filling, strong, amply structured, and smooth in flavor.

Red

Ormeasco di Pornassio, Eno Val d'Arroscia, Lupi Deep red to purple, in color, with a surprisingly mild nose for such intense color. Not an overly elaborate wine, it's composed of Dolcetto, and part of its charm is its simplicity, making it easy to drink. Honest fruit, moderate body, and unobtrusive tannin. It's worth sampling this regional wine, as it's not something you'll find often.

OTHER RECOMMENDED RESTAURANTS

In Leivi, 44 km
Cà Peo
strada Panoramica
(0185) 319-090
Visa
Closed Mon, Tues lunch, Jan 4–18, Nov

FOOD AND WINE SHOPS, MARKETS

Markets

Mercato Orientale
via XX Settembre

A pleasant circular indoor affair, packed with very attractive local foodstuffs.

HOTELS

Bristol
via XX Settembre, 35
(010) 592-541
AmX, Visa, Diners
Moderate
A comfortable old-world hotel in the center of town.

The Hotel Baglioni, part of the COGETA/Palacehotels chain and scheduled to open this year, promises to make a contribution to the Genovese hotel life in the same way other hotels in the chain have contributed to their cities.

Goito

Bergamo 102 km	*Bologna* 122	*Brescia* 50
Mantua 16	*Milan* 141	*Modena* 83
	Venice 149	*Verona* 35

AL BERSAGLIERE
★ ★ ★ ½

REGION	Lombardy
ADDRESS	via statale Goitese, 258
PHONE	(0376) 60-007
CREDIT CARDS	AmX, Visa, Diners
CLOSED	Mon, Tues lunch, Jan 2–12, Aug 7–27

CLASS	ATMOSPHERE	SERVICE	WINE	PRICE
3.5	3	3	4	E

This restaurant is located near the Mincio River just outside Mantua. The dining room walls have been painted in brown tones, to achieve a marbleized effect, and the restaurant is comfortable but not, in terms of atmosphere, memorable: it's difficult to visualize the day after you've eaten there. Nevertheless, the service is good if casual, the cuisine is taken seriously, and at times the chef rises to definite heights. If you come here for lunch, its an easy and quite pleasant drive into Verona for the night. You're also just 16 kilometers from Mantua, but the drive isn't as pretty in that direction.

Directions. Take the Milan–Venezia *autostrada* and exit at Desenzano. Go toward Castiglione delle Stiviere–Mantova. Goito is the town after Guidizzolo.

SUGGESTED DISHES

salumi della casa   Various cured meats, including *prosciutto* and an assortment of sausages.

zuppa di carciofi   An intensely flavored artichoke soup, prepared with pomegranates and mushrooms.

tagliatelle al sugo d'anitra   Flat noodles tossed with a rich and tasty duck sauce.

*risotto con lumache   Snail *risotto* with garlic and chives; an unusual dish with serious rewards.

luccio in salsa alla mantovana   Pike with a basil, anchovy, and caper sauce, served at room temperature. The taste of pike is not unlike that of skate.

persico trota con porri   Black bass with leeks.

petto d'anitra al rosmarino e ginepro   Duck breast prepared with rosemary and juniper berries.

sbrisolona mantovana   A "crumbly" almond cake-cookie. A typical Mantuan sweet.

SUGGESTED WINES

White

Franciacorta Pinot, Ca' del Bosco   One of Italy's fine whites. Spicy and well-defined, pale yellow with a slight green tinge. Beautifully balanced, just sharp enough to keep itself on your mind, the fruit mellow behind the acid. Generally, a pleasing, subtle experience. It's produced by one of the newer and more innovative vineyards in Italy and is widely available.

Red

Maurizio Zanella, Ca' del Bosco   In my opinion one of the best wines to come out of this important vineyard, and therefore one of the most important in Italy. A youthful wine composed of Cabernet, Cabernet Franc, and Merlot, it has a beautiful, intense, garnet color, a perfumed nose, and a rich taste—graceful even, long and smooth on the finish, with impressive depth. A surprisingly sophisticated creation, especially if many of the Milanese restaurant owners are right in their pessimistic appraisal of Lombard wines—a view I don't share, and one that this wine disputes convincingly by the very fact of itself.

Gubbio

Ancona 109 km	*Arezzo* 92	*Assisi* 54	*Orvieto* 125
Perugia 39	*Pesaro* 92	*Siena* 146	*Sinalunga* 104
	Todi 84	*Torgiano* 55	*Urbino* 72

Gubbio, known as the City of Silence, is said to be the most purely medieval town in Italy. Whether this is completely accurate or not, it is definitely an unusual place, dark and mysterious with ocher walls overshadowed by the town's towers and Mount Ingino. Many houses have what the Italians call *portoncini dei morti* "little doorways of the dead." Through these narrow doorways (sometimes plastered up), built next to the larger, operating doorways, the dead were taken from the house after they died.

In *Cento Città*, Paul Hofmann writes: "One Gubbio theme recurs in religious art throughout Italy, the legend of St. Francis and the wolf. The huge and greedy animal . . . had long been terrorizing the countryside when the ascetic from Assisi (1182–1226) came to town. St. Francis sought out the wolf of Gubbio in its lair, gently upbraided it for its ferocity, and soon had the brute at his feet. The wolf promised in tears never again to harm anyone, and proffered its paw to the saint to seal its vow, a scene on which painters would later feast. According to the edifying story, the people of Gubbio grew fond of their former tormentor, fed the reformed wolf until it died of old age, and gave it a Christian burial."

It will become immediately obvious from a quick look in the town's shops that ceramics is one of Gubbio's notable industries, as it has been since medieval times, when a master potter known as Mastro Giorgio developed a method that gave his ceramics an enviable reddish metallic sheen.

Even though Gubbio is definitely off the beaten path, the trip here is well worth the handful of "extra" kilometers—if only for the landscape that accompanies your drive in and out of town, and the fine meal that awaits you at Taverna del Lupo. A walk through the Città Vecchia, the Old Town, around piazza della Signoria, before or after your meal will be time well spent.

TAVERNA DEL LUPO
★ ★ ★ ½

REGION	Umbria
ADDRESS	via Ansidei, 21
PHONE	(075) 927-1269
CREDIT CARDS	AmX, Visa, Diners
CLOSED	Mon, Jan 7–Feb 6

CLASS	ATMOSPHERE	SERVICE	WINE	PRICE
2.5	2.5	2	2	M

This is a rustic restaurant, housed in a building that dates to the fourteenth century, a utilitarian place with all the energy going into the preparation of the food. The decor too is straightforward: white plaster walls trimmed with brick, and tile floors and wrought-iron chandeliers. Basic but easily one of the very best *trattorie* in Umbria.

Directions. From Perugia, take the back road via Mengara to Gubbio. When you leave, take the road to Umbertide, which has some breathtaking landscape to partake of.

S U G G E S T E D   D I S H E S

bruschetta con pomodoro Garlic-rubbed bread, spread with olive oil and tomatoes.

*lasagne del lupo Lasagne with mushrooms, prosciutto, truffle, and béchamel sauce.

risotto della casa *Risotto* with peas, corn (*sic!*), mushrooms, and parsley.

imbrecciata A soup made with chickpeas, lentils, and beans.

*coniglio del Buon Ricordo Pieces of rabbit prepared "*porchetta* style"—roasted with fennel and wine.

frico A fricassee of lamb, chicken, and rabbit, prepared with vinegar.

White

Torgiano, Torre di Giano Riserva, Lungarotti
A clean, fruity wine, with some attractive perfume to it. It's more substantial and much more pleasant than the Lungarotti Chardonnay.

Red

Torgiano, Rubesco, Lungarotti A bright, deep, fruity, and finally simple wine—smooth, rich, and soft, with an inviting nose. This is one of the tastiest red wines Italy has to offer. The perfect mate for the rabbit.

OTHER RECOMMENDED RESTAURANTS

Alla Fornace di Mastro Giorgio
via Mastro Giorgio, 2
(075) 927-5740
AmX, Visa, Diners
Closed Mon, Feb 4–28

Imola

| Bologna 33 km | Ferrara 81 | Florence 98 | Forlì 30 |
| Milan 249 | Ravenna 44 | Tossignano 14 | |

SAN DOMENICO
★ ★ ★ ★

REGION	Emilia-Romagna
ADDRESS	via Sacchi, 1
PHONE	(0542) 29-000
CREDIT CARDS	AmX, Visa, Diners
CLOSED	Mon, Jan 1–16, July 24–Aug 16

CLASS	ATMOSPHERE	SERVICE	WINE	PRICE
4	3.5	4	4.5	VE

For all the grace and design of this space, San Domenico is not the most comfortable restaurant in Italy—the tables are stationary, which can prove a disadvantage if you do not fit into the size category "Italian normal." Nevertheless, the dark pink tablecloths cast a nice glow, which is toned down by beige burlap-covered walls, brown leather banquettes, and cane chairs. The paintings on the walls change periodically. The ceiling has been covered in a cheerful fabric with a floral design in autumn colors, and hanging lamps are covered with the same material. The lovely dark paneled entryway opens onto one room followed by another, the two rooms separated by an archway adorned with elegant flower arrangements in tall silver vases. It's a decidedly un-Italian look, but you still get the impression the food and your involvement with it is taken seriously here.

There's a new menu prepared every day in Italian; the Italian-English menu does not change daily. If this is your first trip, I recommend the latter; if you've been here before, go for the daily menu. I'd advise lunch over dinner at this tasteful if not luxurious establishment, which is on your way from Bologna to Ravenna, or vice versa.

SUGGESTED DISHES

terrina di fegato con tartufi bianchi A pâté of liver and white truffles, served in a lovely little handmade terrine shaped like an egg (which you can purchase). This comes with the meal, included in the *coperto*.

riso mantecato con burro e parmigiano Rice cooked in a rich beef stock, with a little reduced beef stock used as a sauce, which turns the rice a rich shade of brown.

branzino al basilico e vino bianco Fillet of sea bass covered with cooked julienned onions and basil, with a touch of fresh tomato, fish stock, and white wine. A "pastry shark" makes a cute garnish.

carré d'agnello arrostito al rosmarino con verdure di stagione Rack of lamb roasted with rosemary and served with its own juices. Garnished with seasonal vegetables.

*fantasia del pasticciere Lemon ice cream, poached pear, and nougat layered in that order in a pastry shell, with chocolate sauce over the whole construction. Thigh food, but brilliant nonetheless.

White

Riesling Italico, Colli Bolognesi, Monte San Pietro, Terre Rosse, Vallania Soft in texture, off-dry with subtle but undeniable fruit—pears are just noticeable in this delicate hay-colored wine that drinks like a midsummer day: warm and gentle, everything at a standstill. A little butter in the mouth, firm body, and then a long relaxing finish.

Red

Barbarossa di Bertinoro, Fattoria Paradiso, Pezzi Impressively deep garnet color—a full, energetic wine with good depth. There's an interesting first hit of chocolate, followed by a richness moving toward something almost sweet that reminds me of Spanna from Piedmont. Not often found on a wine list.

Lucca

Bologna 157 km	*Florence* 74	*Genoa* 155
Livorno 46	*Massa* 45	*Milan* 274	*Parma* 189
Perugia 228	*Pisa* 22	*Pistoia* 43
Ponte a Moriano 9	*Siena* 142	
La Spezia 74	*Viareggio* 27	

Lucca, an exemplary walled town, invites the visitor merely to walk, to take in the sights, sounds, and smells of its beautiful streets and squares, ancient towers, mysterious alleyways. Be sure to experience the wonderful Passeggio delle Mura, or Wall Promenade, on the wall that encircles central Lucca; lined with beech and chestnut trees, the sixteenth-century ramparts make for one of the more memorable walks you're likely to take in Italy.

There's something magical in the atmosphere here, especially in the off-season, when tourists are at a minimum. Piazza del Mercato (Anfiteatro Romano) is a beautiful old square, the site of a Roman amphitheater. It feels like a sub-city here, with life taking place in the apartments that surround the square as it might have hundreds of years ago. When I'm in Lucca, I'm drawn first, however, to the Cathedral of San Martino, begun in the sixth century. The exterior is Romanesque and the interior Gothic. But it is Jacopo della Quercia's beautiful tomb of the young Ilaria del Carretto, who is shown lying on her sarcophagus with a little dog at her feet, that's so moving. There's also a beautiful Last Supper by Tintoretto.

Some would say Lucca's most illustrious citizen was Giacomo Puccini, who was born here in 1858. Lovers of opera will want to visit Villa Puccini in the town of Torre del Lago, where Puccini is buried—just 25 kilometers away. It was here the composer wrote *La Bohème, Tosca,* and *Madama Butterfly*. Lucca's also known for its silk factories and olive oil. This exquisite little town is only 9 kilometers from the five-star restaurant La Mora, in Ponte a Moriano, where either lunch or dinner is a possibility.

SOLFERINO
★ ★ ★

REGION	Tuscany
ADDRESS	near San Macario in Piano
PHONE	(0583) 59-118
CREDIT CARDS	AmX, Visa, Diners
CLOSED	Wed, Thurs lunch, Jan 12–19, Aug 10–24

CLASS	ATMOSPHERE	SERVICE	WINE	PRICE
3	3	2.5	2.5	M

Although Solferino isn't the easiest restaurant to find, and the provincial crossroads near it could be in a New England village, or just as easily in the south of France, the drive here is transporting. You enter through a rather shabby but charmingly local bar that serves as a *pasticceria,* meat market, and general store—an inauspicious beginning, to be sure; but the restaurant, up a few stairs, is composed of a number of neatly put-together rooms, including a large one, two stories high, surrounded by rather private balcony rooms. The walls are covered in gold-to-rust burlap with a tile strip running around the restaurant. The ceiling, curtains, and hanging lamps, all with the same floral pattern, create a certain country charm: simple, honest, sturdy, and sweet. This good, solid *trattoria* is best for lunch, given its out-of-the-way location.

Directions. From Lucca, follow the *blue* signs for Viareggio. You will eventually cross Ponte San Pietro into San Macario.

On the right you'll see a sign for Solferino. Turn right; at the fork go left and proceed until you see the restaurant.

SUGGESTED DISHES

prosciutto di cervo   Venison *prosciutto*—strong, rich, excellent.

risotto sul colombaccio   *Risotto* with a wild pigeon sauce, made with a few finely chopped herbs, vegetables, and pigeon stock.

anatra ripiena alla Giacomo Puccini   Duck stuffed with *prosciutto* and chopped veal, in a sauce of duck juices and cream.

SUGGESTED WINES

White

Montecarlo, Cercatoia, Teso   Fine for lunch, a brightly cheerful-looking wine that shows shy and floral with backup fruit. Refreshing, spritely, altogether a happy white.

Red

Castelrapiti, Montellori   A Cabernet and Sangiovese blend from the Chianti Colli Fiorentini zone. Distinct Cabernet in the nose; good fruit-tannin balance, for a deep, complex, and satisfying wine. Perhaps a touch of metal in the finish.

BUCA DI SANT'ANTONIO
★ ★

REGION	Tuscany
ADDRESS	via della Cervia, 1/5
PHONE	(0583) 55-881
CREDIT CARDS	AmX, Visa, Diners
CLOSED	Sun dinner, Mon, July 9–24

CLASS	ATMOSPHERE	SERVICE	WINE	PRICE
2.5	3	2.5	2	M

A festive restaurant in the center of town. Decorated with a variety of copper objects, tubas, and miscellaneous pieces of kitchen equipment hung on the beams, the atmosphere here plays a bit to tourists, but it's certainly cheerful enough. Quite busy, even in the off-season. *Buca* in Tuscan dialect means *taverna* or *osteria*, "tavern."

SUGGESTED DISHES

farro alla garfagnana A rich soup made with emmer (a kind of wheat), a specialty of this area worth sampling.

pappardelle alla lepre Wide noodles with a sauce of wild rabbit and wine.

capretto nostrano allo spiedo Goat from this region, roasted on the bone until tender.

braciola di maiale al carbone A charcoal-grilled pork chop.

torta di verdura Swiss chard pie, unusual and interesting (not a dessert).

mousse di cioccolata Chocolate mousse.

SUGGESTED WINES

White

Montecarlo, Cercatoia, Teso Fine for lunch, a brightly cheerful-looking wine that shows shy and floral with backup fruit. Refreshing, spritely, altogether a *happy* white.

Red

Rosso delle Colline Lucchesi, Maria Teresa Just a pleasant local Chianti-style wine worth sampling.

HOTELS

In Massa Pisana, 4.5 km
Villa La Principessa
(0583) 370-037
AmX, Visa, Diners
Closed Jan 7–Feb 18
Expensive
   A lovely villa of a hotel—one of the Relais & Châteaux chain—set in a lush park right outside the walls of Lucca. The rooms are comfortable but just so; they overlook the rich veg-

etation of the park. There's a swimming pool, and large airy drawing rooms. Pleasant for a stay in Lucca, especially as there is no place in the town itself. From Lucca, follow the blue signs toward Pisa; the hotel is on your right just beyond Lucca.

Lugana di Sirmione

Bergamo 91 km	Bologna 164	Brescia 39
Mantua 48	Milan 126	Sirmione 5
	Venice 148	Verona 34

VECCHIA LUGANA
★ ★ ★ ½

REGION	Lombardy
ADDRESS	piazzale Vecchia Lugana, 1 (strada statale Milano-Venezia)
PHONE	(030) 919-012
CREDIT CARDS	AmX, Visa, Diners
CLOSED	Mon dinner, Tues

CLASS	ATMOSPHERE	SERVICE	WINE	PRICE
3.5	3.5	3.5	3	E

Lake Garda casts a languid light into the various rooms of this excellent, even beguiling restaurant, which overlooks well-kept gardens leading to the lake. In the summer months terrace dining is the right decision. Inside, the ceiling is done up with various colored woods, creating an unusual but pleasing look; white stucco walls, exposed antique brick around the rooms, beautifully designed dark-wood–framed windows, and modern terra-cotta floors add to the Mediterranean feeling here. And then there's a bird that sings on cue, providing just the right touch for a casual lakeside lunch. Note the large, friendly, and seductive *antipasto* tableau surrounding the grill to your right as you enter: this is where you'll assemble your appetizers, and where your fish will be grilled. The rest of your food will be served by well-trained women servers in little black tuxedo dresses. The gifted owner, Pierantonio Ambrosi, also owns the magical Villa Flordaliso in Gardone Riviera, once the hangout of Clara Petacci, a girlfriend of Mussolini.

Directions. From Sirmione, make a left at the light where you meet the road to Verona. The restaurant is just east of Sirmione. From the *autostrada,* go toward Sirmione and then to Lugana via the road to Verona. Vecchia Lugana is about 3 kilometers from Sirmione.

SUGGESTED DISHES

*self-service The *antipasti,* which you put together yourself: anchovies, seafood salad, salmon with a green sauce, squid, octopus, beet salad, goat cheese and *prosciutto* roll, tomatoes and *mozzarella,* among others. If you select eggplant, endive, zucchini, peppers, or *radicchio,* you can have it grilled on the spot. One of the best selections of *antipasti* in Italy.

anguilla e carpa gardesane marinate agli aromi di timo e alloro Eel stuffed with a purée of carp marinated with thyme and bay leaves, set on a bed of arugula.

*tortelloni di carne al burro fuso e parmigiano *Ravioli*-like pasta stuffed with meat and sage, with a clarified butter and cheese sauce. A light dish.

pasticcio di carciofi Crêpes stuffed with cheese and artichokes, and baked.

filetto di luccio in salsa di rafano con barbabietole Perch fillet with a horseradish and beet sauce. Garnished with sliced beets.

zuppa inglese A pudding of sponge cake, chocolate, vanilla cream custard, and Alchermes liqueur.

semifreddo al torroncino con salsa di cioccolato A rich mousse of nougat, served up with a chocolate sauce.

SUGGESTED WINES

White

Lugana, Trattoria Vecchia Lugana, Zenato A pale yellow-green wine with pleasingly aggressive fruit, not overly dry. A nice level of acid gives spine to this considerable white.

Rosé

Bardolino Chiaretto, Le Vigne di San Pietro A subtle rosé, light, refreshing, and very pretty to look at.

Although from the Veneto, this wine is so nearly local and so perfectly suited to the cuisine of Vecchia Lugana that I've taken the liberty of listing it here.

Dessert

Moscato Passito di Pantelleria, Tanit, Agricoltori Associati di Pantelleria   A rich, dark muscat that comes from Zibibbo (large Moscato) grapes grown in the volcanic soil of Sicily. Tanit is the *passito extra* put out by the Agricoltori Associati Cooperative.

Maleo

Brescia 75 km   *Bologna* 173   *Cremona* 23   *Milan* 60
Parma 77   *Pavia* 51   *Piacenza* 19   *Verona* 141

A quiet little town, it is one among quite a few in this area that boast of excellent restaurants—Busseto (Roncole Verdi), Guareschi; Canneto sull'Oglio, Dal Pescatore; Crema, Guada'l Canal; Cremona, Ceresole; Goito, Al Bersagliere; Piacenza, Antica Osteria del Teatro; Santa Franca, Da Colombo; and Trescore Cremasco, Trattoria del Fulmine. The landscape itself is flat and rather unremarkable, but the very remarkable geographical cluster of accomplished chefs and their restaurants makes this an appealing area to spend a day or two in pursuit of the simple but refined glories of Italian country cooking.

ALBERGO DEL SOLE

★ ★ ★ ½

REGION	Lombardy
ADDRESS	via Trabattoni, 22
PHONE	(0377) 58-142
CREDIT CARDS	AmX
CLOSED	Sun dinner, Mon, Jan, Aug
7 ROOMS	Fresh, welcoming, and clean contemporary rooms, in a beautiful fifteenth-century brick inn. A nice place to stop if you need a place to sleep in this area. Expensive.

CLASS	ATMOSPHERE	SERVICE	WINE	PRICE
3.5	4	4	2.5	E

Albergo del Sole is a restored fifteenth-century farmhouse with tile floors and high beamed ceilings; the main room of its restaurant contains a long central communal dining table and a charming special service kitchen backed by red, blue, and white tiles next to a huge open hearth. This is a country restaurant at its most luxuriant. Kitchen equipment placed around the room—copper molds and pans, espresso makers—adds to the ambience here. And during the lunch hours a beautiful light drifts through the restaurant, igniting the copper utensils and the fine collection of Renaissance paintings that honor the walls.

The proprietors, Franco and Silvana Colombani, are proud of the tradition they've inherited and warm to any discussion of the building's history. It isn't surprising that with this sense of the past, many of the recipes served here date from the seventeenth century. In fact, Franco often prepares dishes directly from the cookbooks of that century, one being the dish of large prawns and small white beans described below. The house wines, made from grapes grown in this area, are recommended; they're good, solid country wines, appropriate to the restaurant's fare.

Directions. Take the Milan–Parma–Bologna *autostrada* to Casalpusterlengo. Go in the direction of Codogno, then toward Cremona, and on to Maleo.

SUGGESTED DISHES

insalata di cappone Light and dark pieces of capon and cubed beets on a bed of lettuce greens, with chopped cooked zucchini and cauliflower on the side.

**gamberoni con fagioli cannellini* Large prawns and small white beans with a touch of chopped tomato and oil, served slightly warm, *tiepido*.

zuppa di chiocciole Snail soup—an odd dish, perhaps not for everyone. . .

minestrone alla genovese An intense green soup made with basil and peas.

pasticcio di radicchio A baked pasta dish with *radicchio*.

salmone in salsa di rucola Salmon served with a green sauce of arugula.

germano arrosto Roasted mallard duck.

formaggi Assorted cheeses: *aostina, gorgonzola, taleggio,* among others.

SUGGESTED WINES

White

Sauvignon, Albarola The fresh, light house white, with just enough fizz to give it some pleasing zip.

Red

Barbera, Oltrepò The house red, a young, powerful country wine from this area. Rich, fruity, tannic; rough but in a playful way.

Dessert

Vin Santo Trentino, Pedrotti A really beautiful dessert wine from Trentino–Alto Adige, dark amber in color. In complete balance with regard to sweetness, acid, and structure. A deeply pleasing taste.

In Trescore Cremasco, 26 km
Trattoria del Fulmine
(0373) 70–203
AmX, Diners
Closed Sun dinner, Mon, Jan 1–10, Aug

Malgrate

Bellagio 20 km   *Bergamo* 35   *Como* 27
Lecco 2   *Milan* 54

IL GRISO				
★ ★ ★ ½				
REGION	Lombardy			
ADDRESS	via Provinciale, 51 (in the Hotel Il Griso)			
PHONE	(0341) 283-217			
CREDIT CARDS	AmX, Visa, Diners			
CLOSED	Dec 20–Jan 6			
CLASS	ATMOSPHERE	SERVICE	WINE	PRICE
4	4	3	3.5	VE

The square dining room is relatively unattractive, modern and functional, with its marble tile floors and light wood appointments circa 1950. But the view of Lake Como and the attending mountains is spectacular, thus the 4 for atmosphere. Very much a utilitarian hotel dining room, with some attempt made to raise the ante.

Directions. If you're on your way from Milan, Malgrate is the little town you pass through on your way to Lecco, at the base of Lake Como. The hotel is on your left as you enter town.

SUGGESTED DISHES

*sinfonia d'insalata di gamberi Incredibly sweet shrimp served in a ring around green and red lettuce, with

avocado slices and a sauce of butter, olive oil, and a touch of vinegar.

stufato di scampi con fonduta di porri Braised scampi as delicate and sweet as the shrimp described above, topped with finely sliced fried leeks and garnished with chopped parsley and fresh tomato.

escaloppe di fegato grasso con mele renette Three very large pieces of rich duck liver with a good amount of butter to make it that much richer; garnished with apples.

formaggi della regione A selection of local cheeses, including *asiago, robiola, taleggio, gorgonzola,* and *cacioreale.*

SUGGESTED WINES

White

Franciacorta Pinot, Ca' del Bosco A spicy, well-defined white, pale yellow with a slight green tinge. Beautifully balanced and just sharp enough to keep itself on your mind, the fruit mellow behind the acid. Generally, a pleasing, subtle experience. One of Italy's fine whites, it's widely available, produced by one of the newer and more innovative winemakers in Italy.

Red

Inferno Riserva, Valtellina Superiore, Casa Enologica Valtellinese The distinctive Valtellina nose, which can seem a little tired and dour, is energized by good fruit coming up behind, and even a little spice. Well put together, the wine finishes long and intense.

Mantua/Mantova

Bergamo 118 km   Bologna 106
Brescia 66   Canneto sull'Oglio 4   Cremona 66
Ferrara 89   Lugana di Sirmione 48   Milan 158
Modena 67   Padua 130   Parma 62   Piacenza 199
Quistello 27   Venice 153   Verona 39

> *Mantua me genuit.*
> (Mantua gave me birth.)
>
> —Virgil

A city of Etruscan origin, Mantua is visually pleasing and peaceful. Its countryside has been evoked by Virgil, who was born just outside the modern city, in what was once Andes, which Napoleon destroyed, now the town of Pietolo. In his *Aeneid*, Virgil recounts the founding of Mantua by the Etruscans.

During the Renaissance, Mantua thrived as an important artistic and cultural center under the patronage of the Gonzaga family. Andrea Mantegna, who is buried in the church of Sant'Andrea, was brought here on a commission to create, among other things, the frescoes in the Palazzo Ducale (closed Mondays and afternoons). His frescoes in the Camera degli Sposi, the Room of the Spouses, are spectacular— worth even the rather tedious tour of the entire ducal palace, which is mandatory if you want to see any of it. Other rooms (apartments) of the palace are also worth seeing, especially the Sala del Pisanello, with Pisanello's frescoes and recently discovered *sinopie*, or underdrawings for frescoes. The tour is guided, like it or not, and will take you over an hour.

★ ★ ★ ½

REGION	Lombardy
ADDRESS	piazza d'Arco, 1
PHONE	(0376) 327-101
CREDIT CARDS	AmX, Visa, Diners
CLOSED	Mon, Tues, Aug 7–20

CLASS	ATMOSPHERE	SERVICE	WINE	PRICE
3.5	3.5	3.5	3	E

Il Cigno, "The Swan," housed in a sixteenth-century palazzo, immediately makes a good impression: a paned glass door leads into the dining area, where there are marble tile floors and Oriental carpets; the large square room has modern paintings on the walls, and a dark-beamed ceiling. Red half-globe hanging lamps produce a nice effect, as do the Mantuan antiques that act as serving tables. The seating is comfortable, with booths done up in richly embroidered woven fabrics and dark wood. There's something reminiscent of an elegant old-world café. The restaurant attracts an intelligent and hip crowd; clearly it is the most serious eating spot in town. Ligurian olive oil is used here; the owner, Tano Martini, claims it's the best there is. Enlist his services when ordering.

SUGGESTED DISHES

insalata tiepida di coniglio alle noci A just-warm salad of chunks of rabbit on lettuce, with chopped walnuts over the top.

filetti di anguilla all'aceto balsamico Fillets of marinated eel served in a coil and dressed with balsamic vinegar, white wine, and oil, and garnished with cubed beet and carrot. The eel tastes something like pickled herring.

tortino di polenta robiola e tartufo bianchetto A soft *polenta* with *robiola* cheese in the center and *bianchetto*—an out-of-season white truffle—on top.

tortelli di zucca al burro e parmigiano An important regional dish: delicate *ravioli*-like pasta stuffed with pumpkin, preserved fruit (*mostarda*), crumbled *amaretti,* and nutmeg, sauced with a little butter and Parmesan.

maltagliati con fagioli A soup of thick, irregularly shaped pasta and beans; the pasta is called *maltaja* in Lombardy.

**piccione alle olive nere* A whole pigeon, butterflied, roasted, and placed on a bed of savoy cabbage and bacon. Garnished with black olives.

*formaggi A sampling of cheeses: *robiola:* a soft, sour cream–like cheese; *crescenza:* a soft white cheese, served with *mostarda,* a condiment of various preserved fruits in a thick syrup of honey, white wine, and mustard; *quartirolo:* a rich, soft cheese; sweet *parmigiano;* and a tasty, fresh young *pecorino* softened with white wine.

dolce al cioccolato fuso A thick vanilla mousse with chocolate over the top.

SUGGESTED   WINES

White

Pinot Grigio, dell'Alto Mincio A simple local product. Nothing complicated but a nice zesty little taste to begin your meal with.

Red

Maurizio Zanella, Ca' del Bosco In my opinion one of the best wines to come out of this important vineyard, and therefore one of the most important in Italy. A youthful wine composed of Cabernet, Cabernet Franc and Merlot, it has a beautiful intense garnet color, a perfumed nose, and a rich taste—graceful even, long and smooth on the finish, with impressive depth. A seriously sophisticated creation.

Dessert

Vin Santo, Avignonesi A wine that has managed the perfect negotiation between sweet and spine. One of the best Vin Santos I've tasted.

OTHER RECOMMENDED
RESTAURANTS

Aquila Nigra
vicolo Bonacolsi, 4
(0376) 350-651
AmX, Visa
Closed Sun dinner, Mon

If you're running late or you're too tired to walk more than a few meters after your visit to the Palazzo Ducale, this restaurant is just across the way, at the end of a small *vicolo,* or alleyway. But if you have another ten minutes and a little more energy, head for Il Cigno, which is considerably better, and avoid the rather unpleasant arrogance of the owner of Aquila Nigra, which is serviceable but caters to tourists. The place has the feel of the Renaissance, which in a way makes up for the basically indifferent cuisine. Stick with a sampling of the local salami, *salame nostrano,* then try the *maccheroni al ducale,* pasta with beans and ground pork and a touch of tomatoes and herbs. The veal kidney with mushrooms, *rognone di vitello trifolato con funghi chiodini,* is passable.

See Canneto sull'Oglio, Goito, and Quistello.

HOTELS

San Lorenzo
piazza Concordia, 14
(0376) 327-194
AmX, Visa, Diners
Moderate

An elegant little hotel—well run, friendly, and perfectly located just behind the Rotonda di San Lorenzo. The rooms are simple but comfortable, with decent heating in the cold season! Good views of Mantua from some rooms.

Milan / Milano

Bologna 210 km		Florence 298		Genoa 142
Padua 234	Parma 122		Perugia 449	Modena 170
Rome 572	Turin 140		Venice 267	Verona 157

Milan is Italy's second largest city, but economically the most important; it has been said that if Rome is famous for its churches, then Milan's churches are its banks. Milan is a northern city in many ways, especially in terms of its fast pace. It's a city that *works* in ways quite different from cities farther south: Milan is a city more in sync with Paris and London, while Rome belongs very much to the Mediterranean world.

Milan's charm is entirely different from that of Rome with its antiquities or the walled hill towns. Although it may take time to know, there's plenty you *will* want to know about Milan. Here you'll find La Scala, Italy's greatest opera house—and perhaps the most famous anywhere. Opened in 1778, it draws opera aficionados from all over the world. Its auditorium, which holds more than 2,000 people, is said to have perfect acoustics. Tickets are as difficult to get as box seats for the World Series, and more expensive. If you haven't discovered a way to purchase tickets at home, your best bet is through the *portiere* at your hotel, who will have a relative or some other connection. Failing the successful purchase of tickets, you can at least arrange to visit the opera house by calling 805-9535 in Milan; dial (02) first, if calling from out of the city.

Between La Scala and the Duomo is Galleria Vittorio Emanuele II, which dates back over a hundred years. It's an extended arcade that contains a variety of shops, bookstores, the restaurant Savini, and places where those of the leisure class—which you're now a part of—take tea or late afternoon coffee. Or you may stop in for ice cream at one of the side-walk cafés. The Galleria is a political and social center of the city. At the La Scala end is a monitor over which news from the Milanese daily *Corriere della sera* is shown. Of the Galleria, Augustus Hare wrote: "The handsomest and loftiest arcade of shops in the world—eighty feet high—erected by the architect Mengoni for an English company. When lighted up in the evening and filled with people, walking or sitting in the Cafés, it has the effect of a great ball-room."

The Duomo is a monumental structure of white marble that holds to itself over 2,000 statues and endless pinnacles and spires. The cathedral was begun in 1386, but it wasn't finished until the beginning of the nineteenth century, its

> O Milan, O the chanting quires,
> The giant windows' blazon'd fires,
>   The height, the space, the gloom, the glory!
> A mount of marble, a hundred spires.
>
>   —TENNYSON, "The Daisy"
>
> The lords of Milan did not monopolize their luxury but per-
> mitted the people to participate whenever they gave a feast. . . .
> While the guests were wolfing down eel, lamprey, sole, trout,
> pullet, capon, quail, partridge, pheasant, peacock, boiled and
> roasted pork and veal, lamb, kid, rabbit, hare, venison, deer,
> meat tart with cooked pears, and marzipan (most of it gilded
> to assure 24-karat indigestion), there stood untouched in the
> middle of the floor an impressive display of gilded sturgeons,
> pigs, calves, deer, and bears, all in their natural pelts, though
> they had been seasoned, stuffed and cooked. They were de-
> signed for distribution to the people.
>
>   —WAVERLEY ROOT

completion ordered by Napoleon. Santa Maria delle Grazie
(closed Sunday afternoons and Mondays) is a fifteenth-
century church that contains in its refectory Leonardo da
Vinci's awesome *Last Supper,* now in the process of being restored, but nevertheless requiring a stop.

The important museums include the Pinacoteca di Brera
(closed Mondays and afternoons) with works by Mantegna
(*The Dead Christ*), Giovanni Bellini (a Pietà and various Ma-
donnas), Tintoretto (*The Finding of the Body of St. Mark*),
Piero della Francesca (*Madonna with Saints and Angels*), Raphael (*The Betrothal of the Virgin*), and Caravaggio (*The Supper at Emmaus*). In the Castello Sforzesco (closed Mondays)
are works by Mantegna, Giovanni Bellini, Tiepolo, and
Guardi, and Michelangelo's last work, the unfinished *Ron-
danini Pietà.* Caravaggio's *Basket of Fruit* as well as Leonardo's *Portrait of a Musician* are in the Pinacoteca Ambrosiana
(closed Saturdays and Sundays). And there are works by Raphael, Ghirlandaio, Ambrogio da Predis, Piero della Francesca, Giovanni Bellini, Botticelli, and Antonio Pollaiuolo in
the Museo Poldi-Pezzoli (closed Sunday afternoons from
April to October and Mondays).

Milan has lent its name to a number of world-famous
dishes, such as *risotto alla milanese,* sometimes referred to as
"the national dish of Lombardy"; *costoletta alla milanese,* the

undeniable Milanese veal cutlet; and *minestrone alla milanese*. It's also the home of Campari, where that slightly bitter red *aperitivo* has been made since 1867.

The city has a German ancestry—the Longobards inhabited Milan in the sixth century, preceded by, among others, the Etruscans—and thus many Milanese dishes have strong ties to German cooking. *Ossobuco*, for example, is related to *Pfefferpotthast; panettone* to *Kugelhof;* and of course, *costoletta alla milanese* to the familiar *Wiener Schnitzel*—although the Italians claim it was the Austrians who copied their dishes! As with other cities in Lombardy, Milanese cooking utilizes local products, sometimes in ways that may seem atypical of Italian cooking—butter in place of olive oil, rice predominating over pasta, and so on. Restaurant menus here reflect these predilections, offering plenty of dishes with butter and rice, as well as sage, cheese, parsley, nutmeg, beef, *polenta*—a favorite of the Veneto as well—and tripe, or *busecca*. In fact, tripe is so popular among the Milanese that they are sometimes affectionately called *busecconi,* or tripe eaters.

The cultivation of rice was introduced into Italy in the fifteenth century by the infamous Gian Galeazzo Visconti, who was eventually murdered for one bad deed or another. According to Waverley Root, it's likely that saffron was first brought to Italy by Philip, a Spanish duke of Milan, during his rule here. This would make *risotto alla milanese,* with its reliance on saffron, a relative of Spanish *paella*. Most of Italy's saffron now comes from the Abruzzi, and much of it still goes to Milan. And it's in Lombardy that Julius Caesar tried his first asparagus—cooked in butter, naturally.

AIMO E NADIA				
★ ★ ★ ★ ½				
REGION	Lombardy			
ADDRESS	via Montecuccoli, 6			
PHONE	(02) 416-886			
CREDIT CARDS	AmX, Visa, Diners			
CLOSED	Sun, Sat lunch, Aug			
CLASS	ATMOSPHERE	SERVICE	WINE	PRICE
4.5	4	4	3.5	VE

Somewhat out of the way, it can be a thirty-minute cab ride to Aimo e Nadia in traffic, but it will be among the most rewarding cab rides you'll take. This is simply one of the finest restaurants in the country, serving traditional food with grace, elegance, and finesse—not to mention a little of what Aimo calls *fantasia*. The restaurant has been renovated recently, and the ambience improved considerably. The warm brick floors are clothed with Oriental rugs, and the lighting is now modern; in fact, the new lines give the place a contemporary feel, despite the fine antique furniture employed here and there. Handsome paintings adorn the walls and colorful arrangements of flowers enliven the two dining rooms, making this a very pleasant place to consume some of the best food to be had in Italy.

I have only one complaint, and that's the lack of wines from Lombardy. There's only one red on the list—a Bonarda from the Oltrepò Pavese, which I passed over for a Tuscan wine, to accompany a meal too elegant for the rustic Bonarda.

Aimo and Nadia, his wife and co-chef, are two of the loveliest people you'll meet in the restaurant business—gentle, soft-spoken, and very keen on their cuisine. You won't go wrong if you enlist their advice.

SUGGESTED DISHES

pâté di fegatini al tartufo bianco d'Alba   Liver pâté with white truffle, served on toast.

*zuppa di mazzancolle e calamaretti al pepe rosa
Fish soup with large prawns, squid, and a sprinkling of red peppercorns.

melanzane con formaggi freschi e aromi   Eggplant stuffed with ricotta and mozzarella, and herbs.

fagioli, cavolo nero, cavolo verza e verdure al finocchietto selvatico   White and red beans, black cabbage, savoy cabbage, other vegetables, and wild fennel.

tagliolini con ragù di scampi e frutti di mare
Seafood pasta—with plenty of seafood.

branzino nostrano alla crema di scampi   Sea bass with a scampi cream sauce.

*lingua di vitello stufata con carciofi   Slices of veal tongue braised with artichokes in a natural sauce of meat juices and herbs.

agnello al fegato grasso d'oca   Roast lamb with goose liver.

*sorbetto di agrumi   Sorbet, including one of blood oranges.

S U G G E S T E D   W I N E S

Sparkling

Ca' del Bosco, Cremant, Franciacorta   A finely modulated wine, with acid and fruit in control. A well-formed carbonation bead.

White

Pinot, Querciolo, Oltrepò Pavese, Doria   A light, pale wine, with a faint floral nose. Well-balanced, finishing with a hint of spice. A wine with modest ambition.

Red

Vino Nobile di Montepulciano, Avignonesi   A sturdy, powerful, garnet-colored wine; earthy, with a considerably stylish and subtle nose and a strong grapey presence in the mouth. A wine willing to commit itself—big, austere, tannic, but with good fruit on the finish.

SCALETTA
★　★　★　★　½

REGION	Lombardy
ADDRESS	piazzale Stazione Genova, 3
PHONE	(02) 835-0290
CREDIT CARDS	Cash only
CLOSED	Sun, Mon, April 1–11, Aug, Dec 24–Jan 6

CLASS	ATMOSPHERE	SERVICE	WINE	PRICE
4	4	4	3.5	VE

Immediately upon entering Scaletta you are aware of an unusual and very personal sensibility at work; you feel as if you've walked into the living room or salon of someone with a sure sense of what a room ought to look like. There are cookbooks on shelves, colorful Venetian glass in different parts of the room, brown walls and wood paneling, cane chairs, and black tile floors. The crockery fits the decor perfectly, and wherever the eye rests, there are signs of a very personal touch. There's an intensity here, with Albinoni often on the tape deck and tropical flowers filling the air with their lulling, dreamy scent, the light subdued.

The sensibility and food are the result of the collaborative efforts of Pina and Aldo, mother and son, who own the restaurant. Pina, a well-known and respected chef in Italy, is the resident genius in the kitchen; there are only two waiters, one of whom is Aldo. There *is* a menu but you won't see it; put yourself in Aldo's hands and you'll have nothing to worry about—he'll arrange the meal for you, suggesting a personalized tasting menu that suits *your* individual taste. Because the written menu is not offered, I've rendered in generic Italian all the dishes I sampled.

SUGGESTED DISHES

insalatina di carciofi crudi Sliced raw artichokes dressed with olive oil.

trota salmonata affumicata alla tartara Smoked salmon trout tartare, on a crêpe with a salmon-mayonnaise sauce.

lasagne Lasagne with meat, peas, vegetables. Very light.

ravioli con verdure tritate *Ravioli* topped with minced vegetables. The pasta dough is made with truffles, which play a prominent role in this dish.

*coniglio con peperoni Small medallions of loin of rabbit stained with a little of its own juice, placed on a bed of finely diced red and yellow peppers.

*gelato alle infusioni di erbe odorose fresche Mixed sorbets: rosemary, mint, and sage.

SUGGESTED WINES

As there's no wine list, you'll have to depend on Aldo for suggestions; let him make several before you make your selection. I've discovered many fine and unusual Italian wines in this way. You might ask for a wine from the region, although Aldo's quite fond of his Tuscan wines.

GUALTIERO MARCHESI
★ ★ ★ ★

REGION	Lombardy
ADDRESS	via Bonvesin de la Riva, 9
PHONE	(02) 741-246
CREDIT CARDS	AmX, Visa, Diners
CLOSED	Sun, Mon lunch, Sat in July, July 29–Aug 29, Dec 23–Jan 9

CLASS	ATMOSPHERE	SERVICE	WINE	PRICE
4.5	4	4	4	VE

The feeling here is that of a very elegant restaurant caught in late middle age. There's something tired, worn-out about the decor. Brown carpet, contemporary arching lamps, precious sculptures hoping to adorn each table. . . . And there's something in the atmosphere that suggests the expensive without achieving elegance. The brown earth tones, instead of providing a gentle, relaxed air, seem dead—autumnal; and the numerous lamps, aside from light, merely provide a lot of distracting curving metal. But the problems go beyond the decor; the last time I was here at least one waiter had a terribly difficult time simply carving a roasted chicken. At these prices, one isn't looking for a ticket to amateur night.

The ingredients that go into the dishes at Gualtiero Marchesi are clearly of the highest quality, but the cooking is willed where it ought to be inspired. To put this description in proper context, I must say that a great deal has been written about Gualtiero, this very visible owner, and his much-regarded restaurant, which is usually given the very highest marks—Michelin makes it the only three-star restaurant in Italy. I have eaten here on a number of occasions in the past two years and do not agree with the general acceptance of Gualtiero Marchesi as the best restaurant in Italy. It may have been the brightest star at one time—and there's no question that Gualtiero himself has been the seminal (and colorful) figure in the development of Italian *nouvelle cuisine*—but now there's more show than good cooking. What started a new wave of Italian cooking is in need of a little rejuvenation of its own. Indicative of how this restaurant has gone astray is a dish I've listed for its oddity—*riso oro e zafferano*. Aside from the garish display of gold leaf, the rice was far too rich and too heavily dosed with saffron. But Gualtiero is certainly one of the most enterprising men in the Italian food world, and I have no doubt that he will again rise to the gastronomical heights he once achieved, if that turns out to be his ambition.

SUGGESTED DISHES

stuzzichini Eggs scrambled with a little parsley and whitefish.

insalata di carne cruda con tartufi e sedano Finely sliced marinated raw beef with black truffles and celery, placed on various salad greens.

riso oro e zafferano Basically a *risotto alla milanese*, rice prepared with saffron, marrow, and beef stock, with a large square of gold leaf on top. It's an extremely gaudy presentation, what one might even call "high tack."

*piccione al Torcolato con spinaci, pinoli e uvetta Roasted pigeon served with a light sauce of juices and a reduced sweet wine on a bed of spinach with raisins and pine nuts.

formaggio Get a selection from the cheese tray here.

crescenza con mostarda A soft, creamy cheese served with pears cured in a mustard sauce.

ricotta con miele amaro Ricotta served with a bitter honey.

fondente al cioccolato A very dense, rich chocolate cake.

SUGGESTED WINES

White

Franciacorta Pinot, Ca' del Bosco Straw-colored and powerful. Good acid, good fruit, good balance. The steady intensity of this wine makes it a good choice in any restaurant; it comes from one of the newer and more innovative vineyards in Italy and is widely available.

Red

Maurizio Zanella, Ca' del Bosco In my opinion one of the best wines to come out of this important vineyard, and therefore one of the most important in Italy. A youthful wine composed of Cabernet, Cabernet Franc and

Merlot, it has a beautiful intense garnet color, a perfumed nose, and a rich taste—graceful even, long and smooth on the finish, with impressive depth. A surprisingly sophisticated creation, especially if many of the Milanese restaurant owners are right in their pessimistic appraisal of Lombard wines—a view I don't share, and one that this wine disputes convincingly.

ALFREDO–GRAN SAN BERNARDO
★ ★ ★ ½

REGION	Lombardy
ADDRESS	via Borgese, 14
PHONE	(02) 331-9000
CREDIT CARDS	Cash only
CLOSED	Sun, Aug, Dec 21–Jan 19

CLASS	ATMOSPHERE	SERVICE	WINE	PRICE
3	3	2.5	2	M

Don't be disappointed when you arrive here and enter through what looks like an uninteresting bar. The dining room is a brightly lit rectangular affair with a cut-stone floor and laminated-wood paneling with the mandatory gold stripping, and the clientele seems local. Remember, however, that "local" here can mean very sophisticated. Alfredo is a traditional restaurant, like a *trattoria,* and very much a Milanese scene, serving many of Milan's typical dishes—often with an unusual twist by the somewhat eccentric but winning proprietor-chef, Alfredo Valli. Sit opposite the kitchen so you can watch him perform in his busy arena, and be sure to get a good sampling of his specialties, as it will please the waiters and the boss—and most importantly you.

SUGGESTED DISHES

* *risotto all'onda alla Valli*   This typical Milanese *risotto,* made with marrow and saffron, is an exemplary version of the classic *risotto alla milanese. All'onda,* which means "wavelike" or "wavy," is meant to describe the texture: wavy in its creamy smoothness, not dry.
* *risotto alla milanese al salto*   A pancake of leftover rice, fried in butter. Another typical Milanese dish and a must here.

soufflé di formaggio   Cheese soufflé.

ossobuco di vitello alla Valli   Braised shin of veal cooked in wine, herbs, and various secret ingredients, and finished off with the traditional lemon peel, garlic and parsley.

cazzoeula o bottaggio di maiale alla pavese   A hearty, filling, very tasty stew of various pork parts and sauerkraut.

involtini di verza   Sauerkraut, stuffed and rolled up.

*gorgonzola di Romentino   Perhaps the best *gorgonzola* I've tasted.

SUGGESTED   WINES

White

Riesling, Bertoglio   A simple but pleasing table wine, with a slight nod toward sweetness.

Red

Oltrepò Pavese Montebuono, Maga Lino   A wine with some bite—rustic, powerful, fun to drink.

SAVINI
★ ★ ★

REGION	Lombardy
ADDRESS	Galleria Vittorio Emanuele II
PHONE	(02) 805-8343
CREDIT CARDS	AmX, Visa, Diners
CLOSED	Sun, August 10–19, Dec 23–Jan 3

CLASS	ATMOSPHERE	SERVICE	WINE	PRICE
4	3.5	3	3	VE

A well-heeled, well-appointed restaurant, with service that's crisp if uninspired. Savini's reputation of being touristy is earned, but care is taken here and it has retained some element of seriousness. It's not a bad place to begin your Italian journey, trying the obvious city specialties to drive out the webbing of jet lag.

It has a relatively youthful wine list for so fancy a restaurant, few wines going back further than 1979. Many of them are overpriced, but Lombardy is well represented and its wines are priced quite reasonably. Overall, the list lacks depth, risk, and ambition, and you won't feel you can make a real discovery.

SUGGESTED DISHES

antipasti dal carrello   A selection from the appetizer cart.

tortelloni di ricotta al burro e salvia   Large *ravioli* stuffed with ricotta and served in a butter and sage sauce.

taglierini alla Savini   Thin noodles with a seafood sauce.

*risotto alla milanese   The traditional Milanese *risotto*, made with stock, marrow, and saffron. A fine example of this signature dish.

branzino glassato al forno   Baked sea bass.

gran misto di pesce alla griglia   A plate of mixed grilled fish.

costoletta di vitello alla milanese   Delicately executed: breaded veal cutlet, fried in butter with the bone left in, and finished with a splash of lemon—the way it's supposed to be done, in the Milanese tradition.

SUGGESTED WINES

White

Müller Thurgau, Oltrepò Pavese, Vigna La Giostra, Montelio   Wonderful herbal nose, fragrant and inviting. A clean, well-made wine with plenty of grip and body. Very entertaining all by itself.

Red

Franciacorta Rosso, Ca' del Bosco   Intensely bright in color, this wine is mellow, full, and easily pleasing.

Monsupello, Oltrepò Pavese, Boatti   You won't see this on many wine lists, so it's worth trying a bottle while you're here. Good ruby color and a good, solid, interesting nose. The balance of fruit and tannin is right, although overall it's an overtly fruity wine, with some cherry and a hint of bitterness on the finish. It's also slightly hot, in spite of a reasonable 12.5 percent alcohol, but it's exactly this quality that seems to keep the fruit honest. Very pleasing with modest complexity, if not a big wine.

Sassella, Valtellina Superiore, Negri   Good balance of fruit and tannin. This is a more sophisticated production than some of the other Valtellina wines, smoother and showing greater complexity and grace.

PECK
★ ★ ★

REGION	Lombardy
ADDRESS	via Victor Hugo, 4
PHONE	(02) 876-774
CREDIT CARDS	AmX, Visa, Diners
CLOSED	Sun, July 3–24

CLASS	ATMOSPHERE	SERVICE	WINE	PRICE
3.5	3.5	3.5	3	E

A clean, simple, modern restaurant in the primary food area of Milan; just around the corner is Gastronomia Peck, the affiliated specialty food store, which is one of the two best in the city (the other being Il Salumaio on via Monte Napoleone). The restaurant, while not in the top category, is serious, and everything here is done tastefully in the Italian way; it's a little crowded but all in all an extremely pleasant place to dine in Milan.

The wine list has some depth, and is fairly priced, to encourage experimentation. This is a good thing, as I wasn't impressed with the house wines—the white, Collio Pinot Bianco, Russolo, and the red, Borgo di Peuma, also from Russolo—both from Friuli-Venezia Giulia; any number of wines from this region would have been more thoughtful choices—and more important, better-tasting.

SUGGESTED   DISHES

affettati Peck   A sampling of Peck's sliced cold meats: *prosciutto,* sausage, cured beef (*bresaola*), and so on.

insalatina con funghi e cappone   A salad of porcini mushrooms and capon.

risotto con funghi misti A rich *risotto* using a variety of mushrooms, including fresh or dried *porcini*, depending on the season. The dish is perfectly executed—the rice cooked *al dente*, the consistency rich and creamy, the taste of mushrooms intense.

ravioli di branzino con vongole veraci e broccoli Ravioli stuffed with sea bass served with a sauce of clams and broccoli.

costoletta di vitello alla Milanese Breaded veal cutlet, sautéed in butter, in the Milanese tradition.

gratin di mele Apple gratin.

SUGGESTED WINES

Sparkling

Ca' del Bosco, Brut, Franciacorta The carbonation of the Brut is slightly more forceful, the wine a little more yeasty, than the Cremant. A beautifully made *spumante*—arguably one of the two or three best in Italy—balanced carefully, in harmony with the world.

White

Lugana di Lugana, Visconti Pale in color with assertive flowers and fruit in the nose. With its engaging complexity behind a spritely personality, this is a white both graceful and delicate.

Chardonnay, Ca' del Bosco This one rivals any white in Italy—a spectacular Chardonnay, hay-colored and handsome in the glass, with a complicated nose that's immediately rich, full, and airy, with a hint of mild wood and herbs in the background. In the mouth the wine is a delight—herbal, spicy, achieving great structure and a terrific balance of fruit and acidity. As in the nose, the wood remains modestly present in the mouth; the wine finishes with a show of fruit and flowers.

Red

Maurizio Zanella, Ca' del Bosco In my opinion one of the best wines to come out of this important vineyard, and therefore one of the most important in Italy. A youthful wine composed of Cabernet, Cabernet Franc and Merlot, it has a beautiful intense garnet color, a perfumed nose, and a rich taste—graceful even, long and smooth on the finish, with impressive depth. A surprisingly sophisticated creation, especially if many of the Milanese restaurant owners are right in their pessimistic appraisal of Lombard wines—a view I don't share, and one that this wine disputes convincingly by the very fact of itself.

Barbacarlo, Oltrepò Pavese, Maga Lino Barbera appears to be in dominance, although the mixture includes only 5 percent Barbera. It has the deep ruby color of Barbera, an earthy taste, good spritz (*frizzante*), and a lot of raw fruit in the nose. There is some bitterness of almonds, but overall a good, rich drink.

Dessert

Passito di Chambave, Voyat A dessert wine made from semidried Moscato grapes from Valle d'Aosta.

GRILL CASANOVA
★ ★ ★

REGION	Lombardy
ADDRESS	piazza della Repubblica, 20 (in the Palace Hotel)
PHONE	(02) 6336
CREDIT CARDS	AmX, Visa, Diners
CLOSED	Aug

CLASS	ATMOSPHERE	SERVICE	WINE	PRICE
4	4	3.5	2.5	VE

The dining room here is a long, rectangular affair, done up with great taste and grace. Elegantly sculpted wood chairs, white pillars, pale yellow tablecloths to match the yellow walls, and well-spaced tables make this a refined, quiet, and peaceful space in which to eat. The clientele is well-heeled Milanese.

SUGGESTED DISHES

insalata di mare con toscanelli A salad of mussels, shrimp, clams, bass, and beans, dressed with a little oil, pepper, and basil.

tagliolini bianchi con tartufi   Simple well-cooked noodles tossed with butter and topped with truffle slices.

entrecôte   Grilled sirloin steak.

**galletto croccante all'aceto*   Crispy spring chicken prepared with vinegar.

branzino alle melanzane   Excellent poached bass, served with sautéed eggplant.

tiramisù   A dessert made with *mascarpone, espresso,* liquor, ladyfingers, and chocolate.

mousse al cioccolato   Chocolate mousse.

SUGGESTED WINES

White

Pinot Guarnazzola, Oltrepò Pavese, Tenuta Mazzolino   A strong hit of pears in the nose and front taste. Slightly bitter in the finish—but pleasant and summery.

Red

Franciacorta Rosso, Cà del Bosco   Intensely bright in color, this wine is mellow, full and easily pleasing.

OTHER RECOMMENDED RESTAURANTS

Giannino
via Amatore Sciesa, 8
(02) 545-2948
AmX, Visa, Diners
Closed Sun, Aug
   A lively and festive place, with exposed kitchens and inviting food displays. In the back room sits a notably talkative caged bird. Giannino is on the tourist circuit, so be prepared for an abundance of foreign visitors. The food is good if not inspired, and it's fun to eat here.

Grattacielo
via Vittor Pisani, 6
(02) 659-2359
AmX, Visa, Diners
Closed Fri dinner, Sat, Aug, Dec 26–Jan 8

This restaurant was better a few years ago. Still, it's a pleasant, low-key place, plain but handsome in the ways that exhibit the Italians' innate good taste. It's always reassuring to find a center island loaded with the trademark Italian foodstuffs—fresh vegetables and fruits, cheeses and desserts, and so on. The art on the walls is certainly one of this restaurant's most attractive offerings. In the summer, the garden makes Grattacielo an even more appealing dining spot.

Try the *farfalle saltate in salsa di tonno*, butterfly pasta with tuna, tomato, and parsley; or *braciola di maiale con cime di rape*, a pork chop with turnip tops. And for dessert, ask for *colomba*, an excellent thigh food composed of egg whites, bread, and rum. The wine list leaves something to be desired, with a very poor selection of regional wines—not a single white from Lombardy!

Bagutta
via Bagutta, 14
(02) 702-767
AmX, Visa, Diners
Closed Sun, Aug 7–31, Dec 23–Jan 5

A fine place for lunch—lively, with contemporary art on the walls, and a hip, handsome clientele. Not high cuisine, but good for an amusing lunch on your way to the Brera. Begin with the mixed salad, *insalata mista*, followed by *salsiccia*, sausage, and *broccoletti di rape*—what we call broccoli rabe. The house red will do.

HOTELS

Principe di Savoia
piazza della Repubblica, 17
(02) 6230
AmX, Visa, Diners
Very expensive/Luxury

Arguably one of the two or three best hotels in Italy—or anywhere, for that matter. Ably run by veteran hotelier Giorgio Daina, master of five languages, this CIGA hotel is a model of elegance and excellence—what great hotels are all about. Everything here has been anticipated, nothing is left to chance, and at the same time the service is personal and thoughtful. The hotel itself is understated, subdued and elegant with nothing overly flashy, all in good taste and carefully executed. The concierges are among the most knowledgeable I've encountered and will help you with whatever you might need to know. And if something out of the ordinary is required, Sarah Jane Battersby, a charming Englishwoman who is head of guest relations, will take charge. The rooms, needless to say, are superb. It is for these reasons that the Principe is *the* place where *the* people stay while in Milan.

Grand Hotel Duomo
via San Raffaele, 1
(02) 8833
AmX, Visa
Expensive
   Located right next to the Duomo, this is a seriously run, comfortable hotel. Ask for a room overlooking the square.

Hotel de la Ville
via Hoepli, 6
(02) 867-061
AmX, Visa, Diners
Expensive
   Basic but serviceable. Located on a pleasant street, a short walk from Galleria Vittorio Emanuele.

FOOD AND WINE SHOPS, MARKETS

Food

Peck
   For those who have as much fun wandering through food shops as making purchases for an evening meal, Peck stores with their smiling-sun logo are a treat. The cheese store, La Casa del Formaggio, via Speronari, 3, was founded in 1893 by a Czech immigrant named Francesco Peck (all the Peck stores are now run by the four Stoppani brothers). Gastronomia Peck at via Spadari, 9, offers a full assortment of specialty foodstuffs as well as a small selection of wines; best of all is the little Parmesan stand at the front of the store, which is reported to sell nearly half a million pounds of this yellow gold every year. The Pecks also have a reputable restaurant (reviewed on page 218), as well as a shop that sells fresh and cured pork, La Bottega del Maiale on via Spadani, with an address of via Victor Hugo, 3.

Also on via Spadari, but not part of the Peck empire, you'll find an excellent fish store, Pescheria Spadari, and a first-rate vegetable market, L'Ortolano, which specializes in unusual seasonal vegetables and fruits, as well as herbs and standard produce.

Il Salumaio
via Monte Napoleone, 12
Il Salumaio, along with Gastronomia Peck, is Milan's answer to Paris's Fauchon. These are the Uffizi of Italian food stores; a trip to both is mandatory.

Wine

Enoteca Solci
via Morosini, 19
This store boasts one of the largest wine collections in Milan. The well-informed clerks are very helpful and more than willing to answer any questions you may have about Italian wines; they'll also be happy to help you make a selection, if you're in the market for such.

Enoteca Cotti
via Solferino, 42

An informal wine shop run by Luigi Cotti. Wine tasting by the glass is encouraged, and there are more formal presentations by various producers as well. A worthwhile visit.

Modena

Bologna 39 km   *Cremona* 142   *Ferrara* 84
Florence 130   *Milan* 170   *Parma* 56   *Piacenza* 118
Ravenna 113   *Verona* 101

Modena has a few gastronomical claims to fame—balsamic vinegar, *zampone* (sausage meat stuffed into pigs' trotters), and Lambrusco, a slightly carbonated red wine made nearby. The city, although friendly enough, is quite industrial; there's little need to spend a great deal of time here beyond experiencing Fini, its sterling restaurant.

FINI

★ ★ ★ ★ ½

REGION	Lombardy
ADDRESS	rua Frati Minori, 54
PHONE	(059) 223-314
CREDIT CARDS	AmX, Visa, Diners
CLOSED	Mon, Tues, July 24–Aug 22, Dec 24–31

CLASS	ATMOSPHERE	SERVICE	WINE	PRICE
4	4	5	3	VE

When you make your reservation, ask to be seated in the dining room to your left as you enter, the one with brightly colored booths. This appealing room is kept brightly lit, its olive-green walls, gold trim, and boldly colored cubist murals making for a refined cheerfulness. Handsome maroon lacquered chairs, a dark orange ceiling, enameled jade-green booths adorned with seasonal flowers and plants are offset by the soft carpeting and dark wood anterooms—a quantity of good taste went into creating this space.

The definition of the ultimate waiter could be written here: a sixth sense attuned to any gesture of the hand, eye, or head of each man at every table—very Italian in this. Italian too is the close association of the Fini family. Modena is home of the Fini company, perhaps best known for its production of balsamic vinegar and charcuterie, including *zampone* and *cotechino* available in the United States. The Fini family runs the entire operation, including the restaurant.

Directions. This is not the easiest restaurant to locate. It might be useful to ask for directions immediately upon entering Modena. I found a man on a bicycle who agreed to lead me there—maybe you'll be as lucky.

SUGGESTED DISHES

insalata al salmone   Pieces of raw marinated salmon on a bed of greens, with grated hard-boiled egg yolk and egg white arranged in the shape of a star.

*varietà di salumi nostrani   A selection of sausages, salamis, and *mortadella* from Modena, made by Fini—a must for lovers of cured meats.

pasticcio di tortellini in pasta dolce   A pie composed of *tortellini* with veal, cheese, and cream. A slightly sweet crust proves an imaginative and welcome touch.

*gran bollito misto dal carrello (salse e cipolline all'aceto balsamico   This is the place to have *bollito misto,* boiled meats: chicken, ham, sausage, zampone, tongue, beef, and so on. The *bollito* is served with a selection of five sauces: fresh *salsa verde*; or the same green sauce cooked with vinegar; a green tomato sauce; a perfect traditional *mostarda,* preserved fruits suspended in a syrup of mustard, honey, and white wine; and a sauce of baby onions cooked in balsamic vinegar. Ask for a side order of *purè di patate* (mashed potatoes).

insalata mista   The Fini mixed salad is wonderful—it's dressed with Fini balsamic vinegar. Ask for an accompaniment of Fini's salted breadsticks.

zuppa inglese   A pudding of sponge cake, chocolate, vanilla cream, and Alchermes liqueur. This dessert was first prepared by a chef in Modena for visiting English (*inglese*) royalty.

torta Barozzi   Something like a homemade brownie, made with chocolate and coffee.

SUGGESTED WINES

White

Albana di Romagna, Olivo di Capocolle, Fattoria Paradiso A very important white wine from this region, made with the Albana grape. Very yellow and herbal, with strong hints of rosemary in the nose and a smattering of up-front fruit. It's an odd wine, unusual and unlike most Italian whites. This wine grows on you, into something memorable.

Red

Sangiovese di Romagna, Vigneti delle Lepri, Fattoria Paradiso Deep red to purple, with a keen, appealing nose. A rich-tasting wine with depth and youthful spunk.

OTHER RECOMMENDED RESTAURANTS

Borso d'Este
piazza Roma, 5
(059) 214-114
AmX, Visa, Diners
Closed Sun, Aug

Montefollonico

Arezzo 53 km	*Florence* 112	*Lucca* 186
Montepulciano 11	*Orvieto* 93	*Perugia* 75
	Siena 60	*Sinalunga* 15

This beautiful hill town appears after a picturesque drive— from whichever direction you happen to be coming. Arrive for lunch so you have time to enjoy the landscape. Because Montefollonico is slightly out of the way, you could do worse than to spend the night in one of La Chiusa's pleasant rooms and use the day to drive around this important wine region. Perhaps a modest lunch at Pulcino (see below), a simple, rustic *fattoria* (farm) in Montepulciano: grilled chicken and the local product, Vino Nobile di Montepulciano. And then a grand dinner at La Chiusa.

LA CHIUSA
★ ★ ★ ½

REGION	Tuscany
ADDRESS	via della Madonnina, 88
PHONE	(0577) 669-668
CREDIT CARDS	AmX, Visa, Diners
CLOSED	Jan 6–March 15, Nov 5–Dec 5, lunch July and Aug
8 ROOMS	Clean and comfortable. Moderate.

CLASS	ATMOSPHERE	SERVICE	WINE	PRICE
3.5	4	3.5	3.5	E

A well-appointed country eatery placed high up in this handsome hill town. At the far end of the dining room is an imposing fireplace that immediately instills a sense of security—as do the brick arcades, vaulted ceilings of new brick, high beams, and the sensible brick floor. The centerpiece is a massive wooden island burdened happily with glasses and bottles of wine. If you're short on time, you'll want to order à la carte. The tasting menu is certainly worth trying but it goes on and on; you'll need a couple of hours, and it's important to be in the right spirit. All in all, it's one of the most striking and polished hill-town restaurants, with a notable kitchen. If you ask Umberto Lucherini, the proprietor, he will tell you with a smile that *fresh* white truffles are available on his land the year round—which is why so many of his dishes, whatever the season, include these precious darlings. This may go against the current literature on white truffles, but it is possible to enjoy fresh out-of-season white truffles at any time of the year in various restaurants in Italy (see page 36 for a note on truffles).

Directions. Take the *autostrada* from Florence to Rome, exiting at Valdichiana. Drive in the direction of Torrita di Siena for about 7 kilometers; then follow the fork to the left and proceed to Montefollonico.

SUGGESTED   DISHES

melanzane dorate in salsa di pomodoro   Slices of fried eggplant whose centers are filled with fresh tomato sauce.

collo di oca farcito, con salsa di pecorino   Goose neck stuffed with veal, pork, goose, and pistachios, with a sauce of eggs, oil, and sweet *pecorino*.

pâté di fegato d'oca ai tartufi   A pâté of goose liver with brioche bread.

ravioli di ricotta ai tartufi   *Ravioli* stuffed with ricotta, in a sauce of oil, Parmesan, and white truffles.

pappardelle Dania   Flat, wide, green pasta (it gets its color from green *radicchio* and spinach) with a spicy tomato sauce. (Dania is chef and co-proprietor.)

filetto di vitello marinato, con zucchini e pomodori   *Carpaccio* of veal marinated in oil and lemon and served with slices of zucchini and tomato, scented with chives.

*piccione al Vin Santo   Pigeon served with a sauce of Vin Santo, which imparts a slight sweetness to the dish.

*fagioli all'olio   Perfectly executed beans with very fine local olive oil.

sformato di cavolfiore   A timbale of cauliflower.

*insalata dell'orto   The house salad—exemplary.

SUGGESTED   WINES

White

Le Ragne, Poggio alla Sala   This comes from the nearby area that grows Vino Nobile di Montepulciano, and is made from Malvasia grapes. Intense yellow in color, with an incredible floral bouquet; a little residual sugar adds some caramel to its delicate nose. Deep, dense, almost resinous. One year in the *barrique* gives a woodiness that's extremely winning.

Vernaccia di San Gimignano, Pietrafitta   Floral notes in this crisp, clean white. A pleasing and easygoing wine.

Red

Vino Nobile di Montepulciano, Poderi Boscarelli
A hot wine, rich ruby red, bright, with good fruit and general good balance. Burton Anderson calls it the noblest of the recent Vino Nobile wines.

OTHER RECOMMENDED
RESTAURANTS

In Montepulciano, 11 km
Fattoria Pulcino
Strada Statale, 146—via Chianciano Terme
(0578) 716-905
Closed Mon in winter
Beautifully situated in the hill town of Montepulciano, home of the internationally famous Vino Nobile di Montepulciano, this is the place to stop for a casual lunch of *bruschetta con aglio e olio* (toasted bread with garlic and oil), a little grilled chicken, some *fagioli* (white beans)—and of course, a bottle of the house wine.

Neive

Asti 31 km   *Cuneo* 96   *Milan* 155   *Turin* 70

LA CONTEA
★ ★ ★ ½

REGION	Piedmont
ADDRESS	piazza Cocito, 8
PHONE	(0173) 67-126
CREDIT CARDS	AmX, Visa, Diners
CLOSED	Sun diner, Mon except Sept, Oct, Nov

CLASS	ATMOSPHERE	SERVICE	WINE	PRICE
3	3.5	1	4.5	M

What you'd call a charming little restaurant. There are three dining rooms, with antique marble fireplaces in the two main dining areas. Old terra-cotta floors, yellow plaster walls, and a decoratively painted ceiling give the place a country look. Bronze chandeliers, white tablecloths, and then a candle at each table add an elegant touch.

Directions. From Asti, take Route 231 toward Alba. Turn left at the sign for Neive/La Contea. Follow the signs to the restaurant.

SUGGESTED DISHES

*salumi della Contea   Mixed sausages—a top-rate assortment.

*tajarin su fonduta al tartufo bianco d'Alba   Thin egg noodles with a butter and *fontina* sauce and, of course, white truffle.

maltagliati al pomodoro, erbette e robiola   Irregularly shaped flat pasta served with a sauce of fresh tomatoes, herbs, and *robiola* cheese.

tenerone di spalla alle verdure   A slice of braised beef with a meat and wine gravy, surrounded by soft *polenta* and garnished with cardoons.

SUGGESTED WINES

White

Chardonnay, Gaia & Rey, Gaja   Clean, hay-colored, everything in perfect balance: wood, fruit, acid. Soft, gauzy, rich, and deep, with a long finish. Very elegant.

Red

1985 Barbaresco, Gaja   A deep garnet color, a touch of caramel and butterscotch in the nose, a straight translation of Nebbiolo to the mouth. Big and demanding, cherries and berries. This can satisfy even the most finicky.

Orvieto

Arezzo 110 km *Assisi* 99 *Florence* 188 *Perugia* 86
Rome 121 *Siena* 123 *Sinalunga* 78
Terni 75 *Todi* 39 *Viterbo* 45

Out of the flat Paglia River valley, Orvieto suddenly and dramatically appears, high on an outcropping of volcanic tufa. Of Etruscan origin, Orvieto is one of Umbria's finest hill towns; it is dominated by its famous Gothic cathedral, built of black and white marble and adorned with an imposing mosaic façade. Construction of the Duomo began in 1290, on the order of Pope Urban IV in honor of a miracle at Bolsena, and was completed in the seventeenth century. The façade is perhaps the brightest and most colorful of any Gothic church in Italy. Equally important is the Cappella della Madonna di San Brizio, which contains frescoes of the Apocalypse that were started by Fra Angelico and finished by Luca Signorelli. If time permits, a ride on the funicular from the train station below town to the town itself is memorable. Or take a walk during the hour of the *passeggio,* at sundown, to get a good sense of this medieval town: walk from the Duomo down via del Duomo to the main street in town, corso Cavour, with its notable ceramic shops and cafés. Everyone is out. Orvieto gave refuge to popes during the Middle Ages, and its name to one of Italy's noble white wines, grown in the valley of the Paglia River.

MAURIZIO
★

REGION	Umbria
ADDRESS	via del Duomo, 78
PHONE	(0763) 41-114
CREDIT CARDS	Cash only
CLOSED	Tues, Jan

CLASS	ATMOSPHERE	SERVICE	WINE	PRICE
2.5	2.5	2.5	2.5	M

A contemporary country-style restaurant just off the large cathedral piazza. The place has a kind of youthful zest: cheerful wooden clouds on the white walls cleverly shading the lighting; orange chairs, black appointments, marble floors; locally made wooden animal sculptures hanging here and there around the two rooms. There's something reminiscent of a children's playroom about the decor, but certainly it's a pleasant spot to lunch after a morning in the Duomo and walking around this beautiful hill town. A rather interesting list of Umbrian wines offers you the occasion to sample a number of hard-to-find regional wines.

SUGGESTED DISHES

antipasti di cinghiale   A plate of wild boar prepared in various ways: *prosciutto;* sausage; *crostini* of boar liver; boar air-cured in the manner of *bresaola;* and others.

bruschetta al tartufo nero   Black truffle on toasted bread.

lombata di vitello alla brace   A grilled veal chop.

SUGGESTED WINES

White

Castello della Sala, Antinori   Very fruity, open, even expansive. Something slightly odd in the nose, but an honest, earthy fruit with good structure and spine. Closes with a hint of bitter.

Red

Rosso di Allerona, Scambia   A good, solid Umbrian red from a vineyard near Orvieto. Plain, rustic, but a good taste. And you're not likely to find this wine on other lists.

OTHER RECOMMENDED RESTAURANTS

In Cetona, 62 km
La Frateria di Patre Eligio
In the Convento di San Francesco
(0578) 238-015
Cash only
Closed Tues, Jan

In Baschi (Civitella del Lago), 11 km

Vissani
Strada Statale 448
(0744) 950-206
AmX
Closed Wed, July

I'm making note of this extremely odd eating establishment because it receives some very high ratings in Italian guides—for example, the *Espresso* guide ranks it as one of the two best restaurants in *all* Italy. But I am not recommending it, I'm merely responding to it. On the occasions I have visited Vissani, it has been empty. In some restaurants this wouldn't necessarily make for an unpleasant experience, but it's not the case here. Everything is overdone, including the two waiters who stand at attention during your meal, returning to the kitchen from time to time to discuss the evidently humorous fact of two solitary diners. And then there's the wine thermometer dutifully immersed in your bottle of red, to illustrate the good cellaring practices of Gianfranco Vissani. More amusing is the music menu, from which you are allowed to make a selection. One wonders how this would work if the restaurant were full, one faction pulling for Mozart, another for Rossini, and so on. But more important, the dishes of the fixed-price menu seem to me a parody of *nouvelle cuisine*—as if the chef had seen a movie on the presentation of this style of cooking and then gone about reproducing it without any idea of what must first occur—namely, *cooking*. Let me temper these harsh comments by stating that I think the owner believes in what he's doing, believes he's doing the right thing; but as this is also one of the most expensive restaurants in Italy, the performance—for that's what eating at Vissani is finally all about—is something less than entertaining.

HOTELS

Maitani
via Maitani, 5
(0763) 42-011
AmX, Visa, Diners
Moderate

A simple but adequate hotel just across from the Duomo, with moderately comfortable rooms. As it's the only game in town, you might wish to drive the 5 kilometers out of Orvieto to stay at La Badia (see below).

In La Badia, 5 km
La Badia
(0763) 90-359
AmX, Visa
Closed Jan, Feb
Moderate

This hotel, a twelfth-century abbey, is charmingly situated just outside Orvieto. Most of the rooms are cell-like, and the help can be downright unfriendly, but there are some good-size suites available if you prefer not to stay in Orvieto, and the area is beautiful.

Padua/Padova

Bologna 115 km	*Ferrara* 73	*Mantua* 120
Milan 234	*Ravenna* 134	*Treviso* 50
Venice 37	*Verona* 81	*Vicenza* 32

This busy northern Italian city has an intellectual feeling about it. There's a resonance to its name for any schoolchild who studied the sciences. Padua, considerably older than Venice, has long been an important center of religion, scholarship, and art. It claims as its own the great Renaissance painter Andrea Mantegna, although he actually hailed from Isola Mantegna, a small town near Vicenza. Galileo taught at its university, which was founded in 1222; Copernicus and Tasso studied here, and Petrarch, Dante, and Andreas Vesalius were also connected to the university.

Have coffee at the famous Caffè Pedrocchi in piazza Cavour, near the Hostel of the Bo, an important meeting place since it opened in 1831. Then stroll through lovely piazza delle Frutta (the Square of Fruit) and piazza delle Erbe (the Square of Herbs) with its outdoor market. Petrarch lent his name to a dish still to be found on menus here: Petrarch salad, which is a potato-tomato mixture. Evidently Galileo and the other notables who lived here touched no gastronomic nerves. . . .

ANTICO BROLO

★ ★ ★ ½

REGION	Veneto
ADDRESS	vicolo Cigolo, 14
PHONE	(049) 664-555
CREDIT CARDS	AmX, Visa, Diners
CLOSED	Sun, Aug 1–21

CLASS	ATMOSPHERE	SERVICE	WINE	PRICE
3.5	3.5	3	3	E

A large, expansive room, with pillars, wood-beam ceilings and handsome wood appointments, ceiling-high arched windows, and lush palms. Soft brown and pink tablecloths, comfortable leather chairs, pale yellow walls, a stained-glass door all work together to produce a very upscale look. Antico Brolo, the very recent incarnation of the now defunct Al Falconiere, has been thoughtfully and tastefully designed by a husband-and-wife team: he markets and tends the dining room, she oversees the kitchen, taking special care with the preparation of pastas and pastries.

Directions. The restaurant is in a very small alley just off the large grassy circle called Prato della Valle.

SUGGESTED DISHES

crostini gratinati al radicchio trevigiano   Slices of toasted bread topped with ham, *radicchio,* and *fontina* cheese.

tagliatelle all'antica   Long flat noodles with sausage, artichokes, and cream.

garganelli allo scalogno e aceto balsamico   Freshly made quill-shaped pasta tubes with sausage, shallots, balsamic vinegar, cream.

lingua di vitellone in salsa di aceto balsamico   Veal tongue, sliced thin and served with a sauce of meat juices and balsamic vinegar.

dolci   The desserts change daily and should be sampled here.

WHAT TO SEE IN PADUA

Cappella degli Scrovegni
(open daily)

In this chapel are the extraordinary frescoes by Giotto depicting the lives of Christ and the Virgin.

Basilica del Santo
(Sant'Antonio)
(open daily)

This church, dedicated to St. Anthony, draws pilgrims from far and wide. Donatello's equestrian statue of the Venetian condottiere Erasmo da Narni, called Gattamelata, dominates the church square. Donatello also created the sculptures on the high altar of the church.

Museo Civico
(closed Mondays and afternoons)

The painting gallery here contains works by Giotto, Giovanni Bellini, Giorgione, Bassano, Tintoretto, and Veronese.

SUGGESTED WINES

White

Soave Classico di Monteforte, Capitel Foscarino, Anselmi A pretty pale yellow color, with tartness and good subtle fruit. Refreshing, cool nose. A fresh, active, bright white.

Red

Corbulino, Tobia Scarpa di Trevignano A blend of Merlot, Cabernet, and Pinot Nero. Delicate in taste and scent, but definite about its makeup; both the Cabernet and Pinot Nero are in evidence. Soft and pleasingly acidic at the same time. Medium-bodied but intense without any heaviness.

Plaza
corso Milano, 40
(049) 656-822
AmX, Visa, Diners
Moderate

Parma

Bologna 96 km   *Brescia* 114
Florence 184   *Genoa* 198   *Milan* 122
Modena 56   *Verona* 101   *Venice* 214

Parma, which translates "shield" in Latin, is magical in part because of the quality of its air and the light that passes through it and around the pastel, off-red of the buildings. It's no surprise that the best thing to do here is walk. The shops are lovely, and the buildings are colored in a way that when they marry the Parmigiana light an atmosphere is sparked that will cater to your most fanciful imaginings. It's a wealthy, well-dressed city.

Stendhal, author of *The Charterhouse of Parma,* lived here, as did the sixteenth-century artist Parmigianino; Arturo Toscanini was born in Parma, and the renowned Teatro Regio, Parma's opera house, carries his legacy. The Galleria Nazionale (closed Mondays and afternoons) has works by Leonardo da Vinci, Fra Angelico, El Greco, Parmigianino, Correggio, and Annibale Carracci.

The Centro Episcopale is a beautiful grouping of buildings in the center of town, which includes the Baptistry, the Duomo, and the Church of San Giovanni—all three worth investigating. Works by Correggio can be seen in the Duomo and in San Giovanni.

Surprisingly, Parma is not the true home of Parmesan cheese, which hails from nearby Reggio nell'Emilia; it's now made in Parma, certainly the most convenient place to make this purchase. Valentina Harris notes, "Every morning at dawn and each evening in the provinces of Parma, Reggio Emilia and Modena, about 100,000 people in 35,000 stables milk 350,000 cows to produce 1,300,000 liters of milk, out of which 879,000 cwts [hundredweights] of Parmesan are produced!" Parma ham (*prosciutto*) too may be purchased here; the best are cured in nearby Langhirano, where the air is said to be perfect.

PARIZZI

★ ★ ½

REGION	Emilia-Romagna
ADDRESS	strada della Repubblica, 71
PHONE	(0521) 285-952
CREDIT CARDS	AmX, Visa, Diners
CLOSED	Sun dinner, Mon, July 21–Aug 17

CLASS	ATMOSPHERE	SERVICE	WINE	PRICE
3	2	3	2.5	M

A modern space, clean, but one would not accuse it of being good-looking: the lights in the ceiling, for example, are covered with pastel-colored plastic squares, and the decor approaches the downright unattractive. But the food is prepared thoughtfully, with care and considerable pride.

SUGGESTED DISHES

*culatello   A sweet, prime cut of *prosciutto*—the rump, or "heart."

sacchetti di asparagi in fonduta di grana   Little pasta packages of cheese and asparagus, first boiled, then baked.

stinco di santo   Slices of beef with a rich gravy sauce; not dissimilar to brisket.

asparagi alla parmigiana   Asparagus with a Parmesan and butter sauce.

*parmigiano   Try a chunk of this city's claim to fame, Parmesan cheese.

SUGGESTED WINES

Sparkling

Malvasia dei Colli di Parma Torrechiara di Lamoretti   A sparkling local wine with a winning floral bouquet. Served successfully with the *culatello*.

White

Pinot Grigio del Collio di Mario Schiopetto A rich, round wine showing excellent fruit and structure.

Red

Sangiovese di Romagna, Vigneti delle Lepri, Fattoria Paradiso Deep red to purple, with a keen, appealing floral nose and plenty of fruit in the finish. A rich-tasting wine with depth and youthful spunk.

OTHER RECOMMENDED RESTAURANTS

La Greppia
strada Garibaldi, 39
(0521) 33-686
AmX, Visa, Diners
Closed Thurs, Fri, July, Dec 24–Jan 2

One of the better restaurants in town, especially handy if you're staying at the Park Hotel Stendhal, which is only a hundred yards away. A straightforward, Mediterranean restaurant, with quite an impressive wine list and some good dishes: *culatello di Zibello,* a *prosciutto; crespelle ai cipollotti novelli,* pancakes stuffed with small onions; *pappardelle alla Greppia,* thick flat green pasta with cream and dried *porcini* mushrooms; and *carré di vitello in salsa di noci,* rack of veal in a nut sauce.

HOTELS

Park Hotel Stendhal
piazzetta Bodoni, 3
(0521) 208-057
AmX, Visa, Diners
Moderate

For the moment, this is by far the best hotel in Parma—perfectly located for walks in this beautiful town. The rooms are simple but comfortable; ask for one of the higher ones that face the back.

Hotel Baglioni
viale Piacenza, 14
(0521) 292-929
AmX, Visa, Diners
Expensive

This new hotel, part of the COGETA/Palacehotels chain, is scheduled to open in 1990. It promises to be an excellent, first-class hotel.

F O O D   A N D   W I N E   S H O P S, M A R K E T S

Food

Salumeria Garibaldi
via Garibaldi, 42

A good selection of local products.

Otello dall'Asta
via E. Copelli, 2

The place to go for Parmesan—fresh (*tenero*) to well-aged *parmigiano-reggiano*.

Perugia

L'Aquila 171 km	*Arezzo* 74	*Assisi* 26	
Borgo Pace 99	*Florence* 154	*Gubbio* 39	*Lucca* 228
Milan 449	*Pescara* 281	*Ravenna* 196	*Rome* 172
Siena 107	*Torgiano* 16	*Urbino* 101	

One of the most charming and active hill towns in Italy, and an important Etruscan and medieval city, Perugia is the birthplace of two important artists, Perugino and his student Pinturicchio; Perugino also taught young Raphael. In the Galleria Nazionale dell'Umbria (closed afternoons, except Thursdays) you'll find works by Perugino, Pinturicchio, Fra Angelico, and Piero della Francesca.

Perugia has a large population of students who come from all over the world to learn Italian at the Università per Stranieri, the university for foreigners. This international student population transforms Perugia into a rather cosmopolitan community, adding something festive and youthful to the life

SIDE TRIPS
FROM PERUGIA

Deruta

It's worth taking the short trip to Deruta to have a look at the majolica produced here. This style of pottery reportedly first appeared in Majorca and became popular during the Renaissance. Deruta is an ideal place to pick up the necessary gifts and mementos—soup and pasta bowls, plates, platters, and so on. I shop at FIMA, which is pleasant and reliable and has one of the best selections. Ubaldo Grazia is also very good. Both will ship to the U.S., with a little urging.

Gubbio

A wonderful drive on Route 298 from Perugia takes you on the back road to Gubbio, through the mountains of Bosco and Mengara. It doesn't take long, just over an hour. The scenery is lovely, and it's worth your while to fit this town in—and awaiting you is a considerable restaurant to take care of your midday meal: Taverna del Lupo (see page 189).

of the town. Walking here is a major occupation, and there are few squares in Italy more pleasant than piazza 4 Novembre, with its liberating feeling of openness, the cathedral, Palazzo dei Priori, and Fontana Maggiore, the wonderful fountain that commands the center of the square, built by Nicola Pisano and his son Giovanni in the thirteenth century. Take in the shops that line the small winding streets such as via delle Volte and via dei Priori, which descend from the square and the connecting corso Vannucci, the main shopping street. Perhaps a coffee and a pastry at the Pasticceria Sandri, at corso Vannucci, 32.

Among the regional specialties to be sampled here is *porchetta,* a spit-roasted suckling pig with a generous application of herbs, especially fennel and rosemary, and garlic. It should not be missed. And this is the original home of Perugina chocolates, for those with a yen.

Monterchi, Sansepolcro, Anghiari, and Arezzo

One of the most moving experiences for me in Italy is a day trip from Perugia to the tiny cemetery chapel just outside Monterchi, which houses one of the great paintings of the Renaissance: Piero della Francesca's *Madonna del Parto ("The Pregnant Madonna")*. And after you've experienced this painting, it's just a short drive to Sansepolcro, Piero's birthplace, and its Museo Civico (open daily, mornings and afternoons), where you'll find Piero's *Resurrection,* which Aldous Huxley called *the* greatest painting. Lunch at Ristorante Paola e Marco (just outside town), or take the beautiful road to the hill town of Anghiari, a few kilometers away, where you can eat at Locanda al Castello di Sorci, a rustic, family-style farm restaurant that serves honest, filling homemade fare. Or you might want to lunch at the Buca di San Francesco in Arezzo and then have a look at Piero's spectacular fresco cycle depicting the legend of the Holy Cross, in the Church of San Francesco (closed during lunch hours).

Lake Trasimeno

Another fine trip is around this beautiful lake. You can take a boat or ferry to Isola Maggiore for lunch at the rustic and picturesque restaurant Sauro. If you wish to remain on the mainland, try Cacciatore–Da Luciano in Passignano sul Trasimeno.

LA ROSETTA				
★ ★ ★				
REGION	Umbria			
ADDRESS	piazza Italia, 19			
PHONE	(075) 20-841			
CREDIT CARDS	AmX, Visa, Diners			
CLOSED	Mon			
CLASS	ATMOSPHERE	SERVICE	WINE	PRICE
3	3	3	3	M

One of the better hotel restaurants, La Rosetta is especially festive in the summer months, when the patio in front of the hotel is used for dining. Inside you'll find a bright space with walls and vaulted ceilings, pleasant murals, and a palm tree. It's a modest restaurant, but my favorite in Perugia. Try a sampling of the dried sausages, *salsicce secche*.

SUGGESTED DISHES

crostini con fegatini di pollo   Slices of toasted bread with a topping of puréed chicken livers.

carciofi cimaroli alla romana   Whole artichokes cooked in oil and herbs, stuffed with a mixture of chopped artichokes, bread crumbs, oil, and white wine.

tagliatelle di casa con tartufi   Flat noodles tossed with black truffles in a cream sauce.

**tagliatelle di carote al gorgonzola*   Flat noodles made with carrots, in a *gorgonzola* sauce—a beautiful and delicious dish, which isn't always available.

vol au vent di tortellini Rosetta   Gratinéed *Tortellini* with cream and ham.

paillard di mongana grigliato   A steak cut from a milk cow, beaten thin and grilled.

salsicce alla griglia   Grilled sausages.

spiedini misti alla perugina   Mixed grill: beef, sausage, veal, pork, chicken, all grilled with fresh sage leaves.

choux à la pompadour   Balls of chocolate and whipped cream served with a cream-filled pastry, as in profiteroles.

SUGGESTED WINES

White

Torgiano, Torre di Giano, Lungarotti   A simple, clean, fruity wine, pale yellow in color with nice floral notes in the bouquet. It's more substantial than the Lungarotti Chardonnay, and I think a more pleasant drink.

Orvieto, Antinori   A mild, slightly fruity wine, without a great deal of personality, but worth sampling while in Umbria.

Red

Torgiano, Rubesco, Lungarotti   Grapey, simple, full of good fruit when drunk young. A good, clean Italian red.

OTHER RECOMMENDED RESTAURANTS

La Lanterna
via Rocchi, 6
(075) 66-064
Closed Sun, Aug 1–26
    Simple but well-cooked food. Everything tastefully prepared and served without fanfare.

See restaurant suggestions on p. 243 under "Side Trips from Perugia."

HOTELS

Brufani
piazza Italia, 12
(075) 62-541
AmX, Visa, Diners
Expensive
    The most comfortable and well-run hotel in Perugia, with lovely views of the Tiber Valley and elegant rooms. Notable former guests include Louis Armstrong and Charlie Chaplin. The hotel runs simply but smoothly under the direction of Maurizio Ferrante.

La Rosetta
piazza Italia, 19
(075) 20-841
AmX, Visa, Diners
Moderate
    Placed perfectly in the Old Town, near Perugia's most important square, piazza 4 Novembre. The rooms are simple but comfortable, and it's an easy hotel to negotiate, welcome after a day's driving. A hotel attendant will park your car, leaving you to rest before you walk through the square. Perhaps you can enjoy the *Tribune* over an *espresso* before the dinner in La Rosetta's fine dining room, or better—in good weather—on the terrace.

Chocolates

Perugina
via M. Angeloni, 59

One of Italy's most famous makers of chocolate candy. It is they who created *bacio* ("kiss"), the ingenious and delicious little foil-wrapped chocolate and nut candies.

Wine

Enoteca Provinciale di Perugia
via Ulisse Rocchi, 18.

A fine selection of Umbrian wines, in a notable setting.

Pesaro

Ancona 76 km	*Bologna* 150	*Florence* 196	*Forlì* 87
Perugia 134	*Ravenna* 92	*Rimini* 40	*Urbino* 36

The area around Pesaro is perhaps known best for its fine Adriatic beaches, which support a water-loving summer population. The city is the birthplace of Gioacchino Rossini, and home to an important ceramics industry and to Verdicchio, the white wine that's been produced in the Marches for 2,000 years.

Take in the Musei Civici, consisting of a painting gallery and ceramics museum (closed Sunday afternoons, Mondays, and all afternoons October through March). Here you'll be treated to an altarpiece and other works by Giovanni Bellini and a fine collection of ceramics, including work by Mastro Giorgio (Andreoli) da Gubbio and Niccolò Pellipario. And be sure to allow your itinerary to take you through the mountains outside Pesaro on a great morning excursion to the medieval hill town of Urbino. It's a pleasant 36-kilometer drive, and the paintings that await you in Urbino's Galleria Nazionale delle Marche in the Ducal Palace are among the most important in the country (see page 314).

One of the important dishes of this region is the ubiquitous fish soup called *brodetto,* a relative of the French *bouillabaisse;* it employs a large variety of fish, but necessarily *scorfano* (known locally as *scarpena*), or scorpion fish, along with olive oil, saffron—and then any number of other ingredients. *Brodetto* is a dish with a history: Homer has Achilles and Agamemnon partaking of this chowder, and it's reported that Dante nourished himself with it while in exile. Of the cuisine here, Waverley Root writes: "The cooking of The Marches is not as heterogeneous as one might expect. One noted gastronomic writer has tried bravely to sum it all up in a single phrase as 'rough and savory,' but it is difficult to arrive at a description of The Marches cuisine which will apply everywhere, for The Marches do not have one cuisine, they have at least two. 'Rough and savory' fits the inland cuisine (symbol, *porchetta*), which bows to Roman-Umbrian-Etruscan influence, but the coastal cooking (symbol, *brodetto*) casts a nostalgic glance toward Greece."

LO SCUDIERO
★ ★ ½

REGION	The Marches
ADDRESS	via Baldassini, 2
PHONE	(0721) 64-107
CREDIT CARDS	AmX, Visa, Diners
CLOSED	Thurs, July

CLASS	ATMOSPHERE	SERVICE	WINE	PRICE
2.5	2.5	2.5	2.5	M

The restaurant, in the heart of the old part of town, is in the cellar of a former palace and as might be suspected is somewhat cavelike—vaulted brick ceilings, wooden sconces on the walls, high-backed chairs. The feeling is that of a family restaurant: good spirit, lots of movement, and some decent, simply prepared seafood.

SUGGESTED DISHES

zuppa di pesce in ciotola   Fish soup.

scorfano in zuppa leggera   Scorpion fish in a light broth.

aragosta con salsa rosa   Lobster in a tomato sauce.

scampi dell'Adriatico a piacere   Adriatic scampi, any way you like them.

spigola   Sea bass, grilled.

gran fritto di carne e verdure allo Scudiero
Mixed fried meats and vegetables.

capretto   Roasted leg of goat.

SUGGESTED   WINES

White

Bianchello del Metauro   A must while in Pesaro, and
perfect with the Adriatic seafood dishes here. Victor Hazan
writes of this wine: "Bianchello may be translated as 'little
white,' and of the thousands of Italian wine names none is
so aptly descriptive. Little should not be confused with in-
significant. This is the very model of a fresh, charming
young white, small but comely."

Red

Sangiovese dei Colli Pesaresi   A decent, unremarkable drink, but tasty enough for a red from this region.

OTHER   RECOMMENDED RESTAURANTS

Da Teresa
viale Trieste, 180 (in the Hotel Principe)
(0721) 30-096
AmX, Visa, Diners
Closed Jan, Dec

HOTELS

Vittoria
piazzale della Libertà, 2
(0721) 34-343
AmX, Visa, Diners
Moderate

Piacenza

Bergamo 109 km *Bologna* 150 *Brescia* 84
Florence 240 *Genoa* 148 *Milan* 64
Parma 62 *Turin* 190 *Verona* 145

Piacenza was founded by the Romans and later destroyed by the barbarians. Take a walk through its old narrow streets before or after your meal. "Artists will find Piacenza delightful," wrote Augustus Hare in 1884, "and will be filled with admiration of the lovely effects of colour formed by its great houses, palaces, and churches standing out against the clear sky and ever-delicate distances; and the architect will be enchanted with the grandly-colossal forms of its buildings, enriched here and there by the most delicate tracery of terracotta, and shaded by vast projecting roofs supported on such huge stone corbels as a northern architect has never dreamt of. On the whole, this is one of the most picturesque and full of colour of all the Lombard towns."

ANTICA OSTERIA DEL TEATRO
★ ★ ★ ★

REGION	Emilia-Romagna
ADDRESS	via Verdi, 16
PHONE	(0523) 23-777
CREDIT CARDS	AmX, Diners
CLOSED	Sun dinner, Mon, Jan 1–6, Aug 1–25

CLASS	ATMOSPHERE	SERVICE	WINE	PRICE
3.5	3.5	3.5	3	E

This fine restaurant is housed in a charming old theater behind piazza Cavalli, in the old part of Piacenza. High ceilings, dark beams, and antique furniture contribute to the ambience in no small way. Only the high-backed light wood chairs seem oddly out of place here, although they are surprisingly comfortable and will carry you through the meal, regardless of how long you linger over the last of your bottle of wine.

SUGGESTED DISHES

piccione in insalata con vinaigrette all'olio di nocciola A tossed salad with pieces of pigeon in a vinaigrette of hazelnut oil.

tortelli dei Farnese A *ravioli*-like pasta stuffed with ricotta, spinach, nutmeg, and sage in a butter and cheese sauce.

spaghetti con astice in salsa all'anice selvatico Spaghetti with lobster in a sauce of wild anise.

treccia di branzino all'olio vergine–timo–pomodoro–sale grosso Sea bass served with olive oil, thyme, and tomatoes.

sella di coniglio con pere glassate e patate al timo Sliced rabbit stuffed with carrots, parsley, and onion, with a centerpiece of rabbit kidney, all garnished with layered red and white slices of stewed pears (some stewed in red wine, some in white), and then a circle of potatoes.

SUGGESTED WINES

White

Sauvignon, Colli Bolognesi A locally produced white, golden in color with appealing green highlights. With its big aromatic fruit, this is a simple but tightly made wine to begin your meal with.

Red

Gutturnio, Colli Piacentini, Vigna del Ronco A blend of Bonarda and Barbera grapes. Deep red in color, big and basic though not unrefined. It's clean and slightly hot, with 13.5 percent alcohol.

Pisa

Bologna 179 km   *Florence* 77   *Genoa* 175

Livorno 22   *Lucca* 22   *Milan* 275

Parma 190   *La Spezia* 75   *Viareggio* 20

Pisa is an earnest town, seemingly easygoing. Galileo was born here and taught in the university. It's difficult to think of Pisa without the image of the Leaning Tower popping into your mind. When you see it for the first time, no matter how many pictures you've seen, this wonder of the world is more *itself* than you imagined—bigger not in size, but in affect. The Leaning Tower, or Torre Pendente, was started in 1173 by Bonanno Pisano and completed in 1350. It now leans nearly fifteen feet from the perpendicular, and it continues to move, despite attempts by various architects and engineers to prevent it from further movement. Don't ignore the other "miracles" in the Campo dei Miracoli, the Field of Miracles: the Duomo—especially Giovanni Pisano's pulpit—and the Baptistry.

SERGIO
★ ★ ★

REGION	Tuscany
ADDRESS	lungarno Pacinotti, 1
PHONE	(050) 48-245
CREDIT CARDS	AmX, Visa, Diners
CLOSED	Sun, Mon lunch, Jan 15–31, July 15–31

CLASS	ATMOSPHERE	SERVICE	WINE	PRICE
3	3	3	3.5	E

Ask to sit in the upstairs room, by far the most pleasant eating area. Stone walls on one side, dark wood on the other, large glass chandeliers, and handsome dark wood floors. Numerous contemporary paintings, some more engaging than others, hang on the walls. This restaurant, like Sergio, its chef-owner, is simultaneously somber and amused. No doubt about it, the place has character, and is capable of some well-executed dishes.

SUGGESTED DISHES

filetti di triglia allo zafferano   Fillets of red mullet with a subtle saffron sauce.

tagliatelline con carciofi   Narrow *fettuccine*-like pasta served with sliced artichokes.

tortelli di tartufi, mascarpone e fonduta   Large *ravioli*-like pasta stuffed with mascarpone and black truffle and tossed in a *fontina* sauce.

portafoglio alla Sergio con salsa al vino bianco   Sliced pieces of lamb scented with thyme and rosemary, garnished with a potato-nest full of peas and served with a sauce of white wine and lamb juices.

petto di faraona ai lamponi e vino rosso   Breast of guinea hen in a sauce of raspberries and red wine.

pecorino   A soft, fragrant, fresh version of the cheese.

torta alla spuma di mirtilli   Cake with a whipped bilberry (or blueberry) sauce.

SUGGESTED WINES

White

Chardonnay, San Felice, Castelnuovo Berardenga   A very pale, steely Chardonnay. Mild, subtle fruit, low acidity and alcohol, no sign of wood or butter; shows more like Sauvignon than Chardonnay.

Red

Chianti, Castello di Querceta, La Corte   This fine Chianti, aged in small *barriques,* announces itself as well made; an elegant garnet red, a noble Chianti nose with a long, interesting finish. The wine tends to flatten out a bit after twenty or thirty minutes.

OTHER RECOMMENDED RESTAURANTS

Al Ristoro dei Vecchi Macelli
via Volturno, 49
(050) 20-424
AmX, Visa, Diners
Closed Sun lunch, Wed, Jan 1–8, Aug 10–24

Lo Schiaccianoci
via Vespucci, 104
(050) 21-024
Visa
Closed Sun dinner (summer, all day), Mon, Aug, Dec 27–
Jan 5

HOTELS

Cavalieri
piazza Stazione, 2
(050) 43-290
AmX, Visa, Diners
Expensive
There's not much choice in Pisa. This hotel is serviceable,
but slightly depressing, even though it belongs to the CIGA
chain. It might be worth the commute to spend the night in
Viareggio.

Ponte a Moriano

Bologna 166 km   *Florence* 83   *Livorno* 55   *Lucca* 9
Milan 283   *Parma* 198   *Perugia* 237   *Pisa* 31
Pistoia 52   *Siena* 151   *Viareggio* 36

Ponte a Moriano is in the heart of the Garfagnana region, in the valley of the Serchio River, an area noted for its trout, mushrooms, strawberries, and chestnuts.

LA MORA
★ ★ ★ ★ ★

REGION	Tuscany
ADDRESS	via Sesto di Moriano, 1748
PHONE	(0583) 57-109
CREDIT CARDS	AmX, Visa, Diners
CLOSED	Wed dinner, Thurs, June 27–July 8, Oct 10–20

CLASS	ATMOSPHERE	SERVICE	WINE	PRICE
4	4	5	4.5	E

Located just outside Lucca, La Mora has been here for over a hundred years; it was founded by the Brunicardi family in 1867. Sauro Brunicardi is a handsome, intelligent man, welcoming but not overly so, whose enthusiasm for his restaurant is immediately apparent. He'll show you his impressive *enoteca* (wine shop) across the road from the restaurant, and the dining rooms and kitchen, and then let you eat.

There are four dining rooms on two floors. Executed with considerable taste, each varies in atmosphere and appointments. It's certainly one of the most elegant of the country restaurants in Italy. Everything on the walls seems suitable, attractive, necessary—plates, a cuckoo clock, brass pots, and so on. The rooms here are, happily, filled with Italians—my table was the only exception. You'll be pleased by the generous and intelligently selected wine list, with modest prices, from Sauro's *enoteca*. Numerous regional wines are represented and offered with pride. Serious and at the same time festive, the restaurant attends to the small things: the mineral water is served ice cold, the crockery consists of plates from Ginori, the highly polished waiters never let you down.

To provide an indication of some of the ingredients in the plate you're being served, each dish is "signed" with a garnish, as is common in both Italy and France: the partridge leg in the risotto, a sprig of fresh mint, or a flame of emmer (a kind of wheat) to accompany the *gran farro*. The level of gastronomical wisdom among the diners is also considerable here. An elderly woman at the table next to mine, upon discovering the Vin Santo she was after was unavailable that day, asked for a Moscato or Malvasia. There is a plethora of game to pick from, all of it fresh and from the area. Ask to be served by Carla.

Directions. From Lucca, take Highway 12 toward Abetone to Ponte a Moriano, about 9 kilometers. La Mora is on the far side of town (don't cross the river), to the right of the road, immediately before a small overpass; there are signs for the restaurant, which is in a narrow street parallel to the main road.

SUGGESTED DISHES

filetti di trota ai fagiolini Trout fillets on a bed of green beans, sauced with a light mayonnaise—memorably delicate.

fritto di pesciolini del Serchio Deep-fried whitebait, served with a little lemon.

insalatina di pollo ai pinoli Slices of chicken paired with matching slices of *porcini* mushrooms, accompanied by toasted pine nuts, oil, and just enough balsamic vinegar to stain the meat and mushrooms.

ravioli di ricotta al tartufo bianco *Ravioli* stuffed with spinach and ricotta, tossed in a light sauce of butter and beef stock and topped with white truffle. The *ravioli*, made in a back room of the kitchen by Mamma, are *ravioli* as they were meant to be—so light as to seem, in memory, transparent.

risotto sulla pernice *Risotto* made with a partridge sauce, and garnished with a partridge leg placed in the middle of the dish.

gran farro A rich but surprisingly light emmer soup, a house specialty; olive oil is added at the table.

cinghiale in umido con olive Thinly sliced wild boar cooked in a red wine sauce and served with *polenta*.

agnello della Garfagnana al forno Roasted lamb in a wine sauce, served with spinach on the side.

semifreddo allo zabaione con salsa di fragole A whipped semifrozen *zabaione* ice cream, served with a strawberry sauce.

SUGGESTED WINES

White

Bianco di Cercatoia, Montecarlo, Fattoria Buonamico A wine with some complex perfume in the nose, which arrives with a trace of orange. Elegant and graceful, light and soft, golden-colored, with an excellent display of fruit. Alive in the mouth. A perfect match for the trout.

Red

Rosso di Cercatoia, Montecarlo, Fattoria Buonamico Balanced, deep, spicy, rich, and a beautiful dark garnet—this is a very clean, well-made wine, with the smoothness of a good red Burgundy." Made with Sangiovese, Cabernet, and Sirac grapes from the region, it's one of the most agreeable wines on the list, and a house recommendation.

Quistello

AMBASCIATA

★ ★ ★ ½

REGION	Lombardy
ADDRESS	via Martiri di Belfiore, 33
PHONE	(0376) 618-255
CREDIT CARDS	AmX, Diners
CLOSED	Wed, Jan 7–23, Aug 4–21

CLASS	ATMOSPHERE	SERVICE	WINE	PRICE
4	4.5	5	3.5	VE

Although in easy striking distance of Mantua, Verona, and Genoa, Ambasciata feels isolated; if Romano Tamani, the chef and co-owner with his brother Francesco, greets you at the door your first impression will be even more intense. He's an ecstatic character, very much taken with his part in all this; in fact, Romano, a man who's comfortable with the outer limits of humor, is the spirit here and his presence is felt everywhere. You are received like a long-lost relative who has finally arrived, such is the warmhearted urgency.

The floors here are covered with Oriental carpets, and there are beautiful flowers everywhere, including on the tables. The center table is a tableau of roses, damask, brocade, silver, and china. You'll be struck by the abundance of silver—plates, urns, candelabra, bowls, tureens. At one end of the dining room is a large window into the spotless kitchen. The *fantasia* of the designer is expressed in dramatic if not downright grand gestures (sometimes perhaps even mad) at every turn, from the details of the room to the waiters, who appear at your table with trays to transport new plates and carry off the old, each tray balanced with a small vase of flowers. Napkins are changed after the first course; dishes are warmed before receiving food; and everything is served from copper pots and pans, with copper utensils. Sixteen-inch tapers burn wildly around the room and on the tables; Rossini is played at high volume on the tape deck. Part of the etiquette here is that women sit on the red plush chairs, while the men inherit the less comfortable cane chairs, as Romano wishes. The atmosphere is festive and personal, as if you were eating in Romano's own home; it's even a little like Christmas all year round.

Directions. From Mantua, take the road to Cerese, where you'll arrive at a set of traffic lights. Go left toward Modena, straight on through Bagnolo and San Benedetto, following the signs for Quistello. You will cross a river, where the road ends. Go left, and the restaurant is immediately on your left.

SUGGESTED DISHES

frittata di cipollotti e aceto rosato quistellese Basically, a great omelette, with the essence of onion and a vague splash of local rosé vinegar.

culatello con mostarda di mele campanine "Heart" of *prosciutto,* from a two-year-old pig, marinated fifteen days in red wine. If you show even the slightest interest, the whole prosciutto will be brought to your table. Served with a *mostarda* of apples preserved in a honey, wine, and mustard syrup.

maccheroni al pettine al sugo di coniglio e rosmarino Macaroni, handmade on a special instrument with strings like a mandolin (*pettine* actually means "comb"), with a sauce of rabbit and rosemary.

tortelli di cima di ortiche A green pasta stuffed with nettles and ricotta, served with a butter and cheese sauce.

tortelli di zucca e mandorle *Ravioli*-like pasta stuffed with pumpkin, preserved fruit (*mostarda*), crumbled *amaretti,* and nutmeg, topped with chopped pine nuts and sauced with a little butter and Parmesan.

braciole di maiale Long thin pork chops, flavored with rosemary and lemon.

zabaglione al marsala De Bartoli e dolci Ambasciata A rich, deep orange *zabaglione* whipped with a special Marsala, accompanied by a sampling of house sweets.

torta di tagliatelle An unusual sweet cake made with long, thin flat noodles, and nuts and chocolate.

Sparkling

Ca'del Bosco, Dosage Zero The *aperitivo* here. One of the most beautifully made sparklers in Italy—subtle, complex, intense!

White

Bianco di Quistello, Cantina Sociale Cooperativa di Quistello The house white: slightly cloudy, as it's not filtered, it's a naturally sparkling, spritely, pleasant, light, and amusing. A wine with a little Romano in it.

Red

Pinero, Ca'del Bosco Reads like a Burgundy, with floral notes to its perfume. Soft, luscious, it's certainly one of the very best reds produced in this country. Warm and endearing.

Dessert

Moscato di Mezzocorona Secco, Conti Martini A pleasant, well-modulated dessert wine from Trentino-Alto Adige. Flowery and pretty to look at.

Ranco

Aosta 190 km	*Bergamo* 114	*Milan* 67
Novara 51	*Sesto Calende* 12	*Stresa* 37
Turin 146	*Varese* 27	*Verona* 220

Ranco is a quiet little town on the Lombardy side of Lake Maggiore. The drive along this side of the lake into Ranco is lovely, and the atmosphere considerably more relaxed and easygoing in an everyday sort of way than on the more fashionable Piedmont side of the water.

DEL SOLE

★ ★ ★ ★ ½

REGION	Lombardy
ADDRESS	piazza Venezia, 5
PHONE	(0331) 976-507
CREDIT CARDS	AmX, Visa, Diners
CLOSED	Mon dinner, Tues, Jan 1–Feb 11
7 ROOMS	Elegantly appointed and very comfortable modern accommodations. A great breakfast! Moderate.

CLASS	ATMOSPHERE	SERVICE	WINE	PRICE
4.5	4.5	4	3	VE

This restaurant presents a clean, gracious look—white stucco walls, dark wood trim, tile floors, bentwood chairs—and has been decorated with a light but elegant hand, sparely. Flowers are nicely arranged, the Venetian glasswork is well selected. All in all, very airy and light, white with blue and black accents, a contemporary feel cast with a distinctly Mediterranean air. The service is delicate, caring, and gentle. This is dining at its most comfortable, by way of Itala Brovelli, a genius at anticipating a diner's every need, and her husband, Carlo, the gifted presence behind the flames. The trademark of many a dish here is a garnish of candied finely sliced lemon and orange rind. Because of the disappointing representation of Lombard wines on the wine list, I have suggested wines from other regions—neighboring Piedmont and Friuli.

If you don't like the idea of driving into Milan upon arrival in Italy after a long flight, Ranco is only thirty minutes from Malpensa airport. Dinner with the Brovellis and a good night's sleep in their charming *albergo* is an excellent and civilized way to begin your Italian journey, and can certainly help cure your jet lag.

Directions. Take the *autostrada* that goes from Milan to Varese, and then go toward Sesto Calende. Just before you reach the bridge, make a left for Angera and proceed to Ranco.

carpaccio di salmone e persico Raw salmon and perch from Lake Maggiore, with caviar, red pepper, and oil. It's beautifully presented: pinwheels of salmon with inserts of the white fish.

bignè di gamberi e foie gras al vapore A deep-fried shrimp fritter with a light, tasty dough, presented with a square of steamed *foie gras* in a little olive oil.

lavarello affumicato con caviale di melanzana alle erbe di giardino Smoked lake fish and eggplant caviar with garden herbs.

fagottino di gamberi e crema di carciofi Ravioli-shaped bundles of an artichoke and crayfish mousse, tied neatly with carrot strings. Beautifully presented, with each taste asserting itself independently.

lasagne di fegato d'oca fresco in crema di tartufo e sedano fritto A light green lasagne with foie gras and a delicate cream sauce containing white truffles, served with fried celery.

lasagne al ragù di seppia con fagiolini verdi al profumo di basilico Alternating layers of black (from cuttlefish ink) and white lasagne choreographed over a stuffing of vegetables and cuttlefish, with a sauce of oil and basil. The entire structure looks a little like the Duomo in Orvieto. Served with green beans tossed with a little oil and basil.

involtino di salmone in fili di patata con salsa tartara A fillet of barely cooked salmon in a bundle made with long strings of deep-fried potato. Served with a tartare sauce and garnished with a carrot and orange purée.

dorso di salmone con fondant di alloro, arancia, limone e pepe rosa Sliced salmon, garnished with bay leaves, candied orange and lemon rind, and toasted red peppercorns.

piccione caramellato al miele con uva al vino rosso Pigeon caramelized with honey and served with red wine grapes.

pesca tiepida di vigna con salsa di pesche e lamponi A slightly warm peach with a sauce of puréed peaches and raspberries.

sfogliatina di pere caramellate allo zabaglione
A flaky pear tart presented with zabaglione, pepped up
with a shot of calvados.

SUGGESTED WINES

Spumante

*Gancia di Gancia, Chardonnay Brut, Fratelli
Gancia*   One of the richer, smoother *spumanti* in Italy.
The wines produced by this vineyard are up there with
those of Ca'del Bosco and the *spumanti* of Ferrari–Fratelli
Lunelli.

White

Collio Sauvignon, Borgo Conventi   There's a nice
initial fizz to this tart, intense, and very pale wine from
Friuli. Lovely floral highlights in a long, pleasing finish.

Ronco delle Acacie, Abbazia di Rosazzo   Another
white from Friuli—perfect for lunch at Del Sole. A graceful, balanced, elegant wine with an aromatic burst of fresh
fruit and flowers. And behind the perfume just the right
touch of oak emerges, with a moment of mesmerizing
wood.

Red

Nebbiolo d'Alba, Vignaveja, Gaja   Yet another
non-Lombard wine. Ronco is on the Piedmont border,
and this solid, robust Piedmont red was recommended by
the house.

Ravenna

Bologna 74 km	*Florence* 136		*Milan* 285
Pesaro 92	*Urbino* 128	*Venice* 145	*Verona* 216

Ravenna boasts of the finest Byzantine mosaics in Europe—
"a symphony of color," as they were described by Dante, who
lived in exile here until his death in 1321. He has been honored with a memorable tomb, austere and moving, near the
Church of San Francesco, and has in return honored Ravenna
with his spirit, which in some metaphysical way makes itself
felt in this solemn but elegant mausoleum. For a change of
pace, head for the amusing wine bar around the corner called
Cá de Ven (via Ricci, 24) and get something local to eat and
drink.

THE MOSAICS
OF RAVENNA

It's the Byzantine mosaics that bring most visitors to this charming city. The finest can be found in the locations listed below. All are open daily; the Battistero degli Ortodossi is closed on Sunday afternoons.

Mausoleo di Galla Placidia

San Vitale

Battistero degli Ortodossi (Neoniano)

Sant'Apollinare Nuovo

Sant'Apollinare in Classe (5 kilometers outside Ravenna)

TRE SPADE
★ ★ ½

REGION	Emilia-Romagna
ADDRESS	via Rasponi, 37
PHONE	(0544) 32-382
CREDIT CARDS	AmX, Visa, Diners
CLOSED	Mon, July 25–Aug 28

CLASS	ATMOSPHERE	SERVICE	WINE	PRICE
3	2.5	2.5	3	M

This is a dark restaurant with red floor tiles and a modern beamed ceiling. The dining room is split in half by a wall and a table covered with flowers and foods: whole *prosciutti,* fruits, and desserts. Green material covers the walls, and wainscotting and cabinets are of dark wood. It's a homey place, warm and friendly, happily straightforward.

SUGGESTED DISHES

sformato di fagiano con salsa ai porri A mold of chopped pheasant served with a leek sauce.

stringozze con pomodoro e crema di olive Home-made spaghetti-like pasta with fresh tomatoes and olive purée.

arista all'arancio con purè di mele Roast loin of pork with an orange sauce, garnished with applesauce.

pollo nostrano in casseruola con scalogno Local chicken prepared in a casserole with shallots.

formaggi Cheeses: select the fresh *pecorino* here—a soft, relatively mild cheese.

SUGGESTED WINES

White

Chardonnay, Terre Rosse, Vallania Apples and herbs mixed with some floral notes and a dash of vanilla in the first rush of the bouquet, then more fresh fruit filling the mouth. A terrific white, alive in its fruit-to-acid balance; delicate and elegant, it has a beautiful gold color with a slight green cast to it.

Red

Ronco delle Ginestre, Baldi, Castelluccio A big, rich, bright red with a good deal of complexity to work with. Burton Anderson writes: "From Sangiovese Grosso grown at Casale near Modigliana in Romagna's hills. Aged in small barrels of new French oak, [it develops] elegant tone in deep ruby color, flowery bouquet in dry but rich and complex flavor."

Sangiovese di Romagna, Zerbina The fruity, youthful house wine. No nose, but a fun, lively wine, grapey—Victor Hazan might say it "fills the mouth with forthright, abundant flavor."

HOTELS

Centrale-Byron
via 4 Novembre, 14
(0544) 22-225
Cash only
Inexpensive

A charming if minimal hotel, placed right off the main square, piazza del Popolo. The rooms, although basic, are just as comfortable as those in the expensive Jolly Hotel, which is less well situated and indisputably depressing.

Rome / Roma

L'Aquila 119 km   Assisi 177   Bologna 379
Florence 277   Milan 572   Orvieto 121   Perugia 172
Ravenna 366   San Vincenzo 260   Siena 230
Todi 130   Venice 528   Verona 503

Rome is the city I first fell in love with; it has all that's important to me about Italy—the endless list of things to see; the texture of the air in this Mediterranean city, found nowhere else; the Roman light, magical on the buildings; the color and smell of the buildings themselves. And I am excited by the prospect of dining on Roman *cucina,* the straightforward preparation of food in this region, Lazio. It's for these reasons I've included Rome in this book about "northern" Italy. But I've also included it because it's the southernmost city in northern Italy and in a number of significant ways relates as much to the North as to the South; it's where one ends and the other begins. And as a final justification, if one is needed, for including Rome, the intention of this book is to address the traveler's route from Milan to Rome—to me the happiest itinerary there is.

A list of dishes that should be sampled while in Rome might include a few old specialties, such as *rigatoni con pajata,* hollow pasta tubes with a sauce of milk-fed veal intestines cooked in bacon fat; *bucatini alla gricia,* long hollow pasta tubes sauced with bacon, cheese, oil, and black pepper; *trippa alla romana,* tripe, first boiled, then stewed with tomatoes, garlic, parsley, and mint; and *coda alla vaccinara,* oxtail served in a rich tomato sauce with pine nuts and raisins. They can all be sampled in a number of restaurants, but Checchino dal 1887 specializes in these and other Roman dishes. Also of note is the food prepared in the Jewish ghetto—for example, *carciofi alla giudea,* deep-fried artichokes. Keep in mind that Rome is known for its wonderful lamb, *abbacchio.* And it's also in Rome that you'll find a wonderful chicory-like salad green called *puntarelle,* typically dressed with oil, vinegar, garlic, and anchovies.

10 SPECIAL SIGHTS
OF ROME

The list of things to see in Rome is obviously endless. What follows are a few of the essential sights—what would be at the top of any list—in no particular order.

Roman Forum (closed Sunday afternoons, Tuesdays)

Palatine Hill Romulus, the founder of Rome, and his brother, Remus, were discovered on this hill, and from here the emperors ruled the world.

Colosseum (closed Sunday afternoons, Mondays) More accurately called the Flavian Amphitheater, it opened in A.D. 80 under the emperor Titus, but its construction was begun eight years earlier under Vespasian, the first Flavian emperor.

Pantheon (closed afternoons and Mondays) Built around 27 B.C. by Marcus Agrippa, it began as a temple celebrating all the gods. It became a Roman Catholic church in the seventh century.

Piazza di Spagna, Spanish Steps, Keats' House "Spagna" and "Spanish" are for the Spanish Embassy, which was once located here. The steps, also called Scala della Trinità dei Monti, date from the eighteenth century. The Fontana della Barcaccia, the Boat Fountain in the piazza, is by Pietro Bernini,

AL MORO
★ ★ ★ ★

REGION	Lazio
ADDRESS	vicolo delle Bollette, 13
PHONE	(06) 678-3495
CREDIT CARDS	Cash only
CLOSED	Sun, Aug

CLASS	ATMOSPHERE	SERVICE	WINE	PRICE
3.5	3.5	4	3	E

Opened in 1929, Al Moro is the epitome of a Roman restaurant, and year after year it continues to be one of the best in

Gian Lorenzo Bernini's less famous father. The Keats House (closed Saturdays and Sundays), where the poet died in 1821, is filled with correspondence, memorabilia, even a lock of Shelley's hair.

Via Appia Antica   The link between Rome and the South, the Old Appian Way was built some 300 years before Christ. Visit the catacombs along the way.

Vatican City   An endless city within the Eternal City: St. Peter's Square, St. Peter's Basilica; the Vatican Museums, including the Sistine Chapel (see page 268).

Piazza Navona   This comfortable square contains Gian Lorenzo Bernini's seventeenth-century Fontana dei Quattro Fiumi (Fountain of the Four Rivers) and a few very pleasant outdoor cafés.

Trevi Fountain   The massive construction celebrates the end of the Baroque. Tourists are encouraged to throw two coins over their shoulder into the fountain: one to ensure a return to the Eternal City, the other to fulfill a secret wish.

Protestant Cemetery at Testaccio   (closed at lunch) Keats and Shelley, among others, are buried here. A special place, unlike any other cemetery.

the city. It's where Romans and foreigners who know anything about anything go to eat. Just ask Burt Lancaster, who's a regular. You could say Al Moro has about it a little of the Stork Club, circa 1945.

There are three small rooms, filled primarily with wonderfully chic and hip Romans; the back room tends to be reserved for foreigners, and this is a good thing, because it is the domain of Rome's greatest waiter: Stefano Pace, an informed, witty, patient man, full of important suggestions which he delivers in nothing less than a Scottish brogue—picked up from his Scots wife. All the waiters here are the real thing—experienced professionals, serious and seemingly dour, but ready to rock and roll when you show the right enthusiasm. The owner, whom you encounter at the door, controls only the front room, which he peoples with his

4 MUSEUMS OF ROME

Vatican Museums (closed Sundays except for the morning of the last Sunday of the month; Saturday afternoons; and afternoons except in July, August, September)
In the Pinacoteca are works by Fra Angelico, Filippo Lippi, Giovanni Bellini, Leonardo, Pinturicchio, Perugino, Raphael, and Caravaggio. In the Sistine Chapel are frescoes by Botticelli, Perugino, and Michelangelo.

Borghese Museum (closed Mondays and afternoons)
The museum displays works by Raphael, Caravaggio, Titian, Gian Lorenzo Bernini, and Canova. The important, upstairs part of this museum was closed for renovation as of this writing, but it's worth checking to see if it's open when you're in Rome.

Doria Pamphili Gallery (closed all day Mondays, Wednesdays, Thursdays, and all other afternoons)
Here are works by Titian, Tintoretto, Caravaggio, Correggio, and Velázquez.

Palazzo Barberini (closed Sunday afternoons and Mondays)
The gallery in this palace exhibits works by Fra Angelico, Raphael, and Titian, among others.

Roman pals. Pass through the door and continue on without looking back. The pleasures lie in the back room, with Stefano as your guide.

The restaurant is put together in a straightforward fashion, which is to say, serviceable; oak wainscotting, sconces, white tablecloths, and for character, a number of Hirschfeld-style drawings of the owner and others, pictures that allude to subjects not immediately available to tourists—this, of course, pleases the anti-tourist in tourists, who for the moment, and after some glasses of well-selected wine, feel like citizens. The atmosphere is sophisticated Roman, comfortable and warm, and the staff seems pleased to be serving some of the best food in this ancient city. Because the wine list doesn't contain a very interesting selection of Lazio wines, I've suggested some from other regions that go well with the food.

6 CHURCHES OF ROME

Basilica di San Pietro You must see all of St. Peter's, and especially Michelangelo's *Pietà*, the throne by Bernini, and Canova's *Tomb of Clement XIII*.

San Luigi dei Francesi (closed Thursday afternoons)
This church has three breathtaking paintings of the life of St. Matthew by Caravaggio.

Sant'Agostino Here you'll find Caravaggio's *Madonna of the Pilgrims*.

Santa Maria del Popolo Two paintings by Caravaggio are here: *The Conversion of St. Paul* and *The Crucifixion of St. Peter*. When you're finished looking at them, you might stop for coffee at the conveniently located Caffè Rosati, on the other side of piazza del Popolo.

Santa Maria della Vittoria Bernini's magnificent *Ecstasy of St. Theresa* is required seeing.

San Pietro in Vincoli Here you'll view Michelangelo's *Moses*.

SUGGESTED   DISHES

*radicchio di Treviso ai ferri con gorgonzola Grilled *radicchio* with *gorgonzola* melted on top.

*spaghetti alla Moro Prepared like a *carbonara*, with bacon, Parmesan, onions, and a little red pepper.

rigatoni alla baronessa Hollow tube pasta with a sauce of chicken livers, mushrooms, and butter.

abbacchio romanesco al forno con patate Traditionally prepared roasted lamb with potatoes. Lamb isn't served rare in Italy; this is baby lamb, very tender.

ossobuco in bianco con purè Braised veal shin in a white sauce, with a touch of cream, tomato, and white wine. Accompanied by peas and mashed potatoes. (Served on Thursdays.)

spigola alla Moro One of the best bass fillets served anywhere, expertly baked, boned, and served with a little butter and lemon.

puntarelle con la salsa A chicory-like salad green found only in and around Rome, served with a vinegar, oil, and anchovy dressing. This should be tried at least once while in Rome.

semifreddo di zabaione con cioccolato A soft *zabaione* ice cream (made with eggs, sugar, and Marsala), served with a chocolate sauce.

SUGGESTED WINES

White

Müller Thurgau, Feldmarschall, Tiefenbrunner
A lively, winningly tart wine from Trentino–Alto Adige. Plenty of energy and life; wonderful fruit, perfume, and taste. A good choice for the food served at Al Moro. One of the best whites I've tasted; if you've never had it, you'll be pleasantly surprised.

Red

Chianti, Castello di Ama, Vigneto Bellavista
Fine, elegant nose. A light clear wine, representative of fine Chianti, and quite upper-class.

ALBERTO CIARLA
★ ★ ★ ★

REGION	Lazio
ADDRESS	piazza San Cosimato, 40 (in Trastevere)
PHONE	(06) 581-8668
CREDIT CARDS	AmX, Visa, Diners
CLOSED	lunch, Sun, Aug 12–29, Dec 23–Jan 6

CLASS	ATMOSPHERE	SERVICE	WINE	PRICE
4	3.5	3.5	3.5	VE

A radically *designed* restaurant. Black tablecloths and chairs with red seats and black wood. Black walls with mirrors and large fish tanks that project a soothing fish metabolism into the dining rooms. You may feel as if you were below water level—calming and charming. The wine is handsomely stored in glass display cases, the ceiling too is mirrored, and the red and black motif is repeated thoughtfully throughout the three rooms. Alberto takes as much care with the preparation of his food as he has with the atmosphere he's created in which to consume it. My only argument is that the tables are slightly crowded.

SUGGESTED DISHES

insalatina al crudo Slices of raw salmon, bass, and shrimp on lettuce, with a mustard vinaigrette.

**cevice di pesce crudo* Marinated fish with parsley and hot red pepper—quite spicy . . . an Italian *seviche*.

bombolotti allo sparaceddo Short tubular pasta with a tomato and a *sparaceddo* sauce (*sparaceddo* is a vegetable from Calabria).

zuppa di pasta e fagioli Bean soup with bits of pasta, mussels, squid, and miscellaneous fish, hot red pepper, and a fish stock base—the combination of beans and fish may be more unusual than delicious.

**filetto di spigola Roscoff* Fillet of sea bass steamed with herbs.

SUGGESTED WINES

White

Velletri, Vigna Ciarla Almost clear it's so pale. Very light to the palate, with minor fruit and a wallflower nose. This wine is bottled specially for the restaurant.

Fiorano, Boncompagni Ludovisi A fairly substantial white grown along the Appian Way near Rome. Some good depth and grace come from this luxuriously colored wine.

Fiorano Semillon, Boncompagni Ludovisi Floral, semidry, an unusual white worth trying while in Rome.

Red

Torre Ercolana, Anagni An important regional wine that employs Cesanese, Cabernet, and Merlot grapes; it shows a little initial fizz and then some serious earth and herbs. Rich, luscious, and elegant in a powerful way, with mint in evidence on the finish. An intelligent wine and one of the best "moderns," which in Italy means there's Cabernet in the blend. There's a very limited production of the wine, one of Lazio's showpieces, which must be experienced. Burton Anderson describes it as "opulently perfumed with an authoritative concentration of flavors that explode on the palate and linger there."

Dessert

Aleatico, Vergaro   Ask for a glass of this—a friend of the wine steward makes it. It's an unusual wine: almost jamlike in affect, it's a cautiously sweet, intensely colored red made from the antique Aleatico grape. A must.

PATRIZIA E ROBERTO DEL PIANETA TERRA
★ ★ ★ ★

REGION	Lazio
ADDRESS	via Arco del Monte, 94
PHONE	(06) 686-9893
CREDIT CARDS	AmX, Visa, Diners
CLOSED	Lunch, Mon, Aug

CLASS	ATMOSPHERE	SERVICE	WINE	PRICE
4	3	4	3.5	VE

A cavelike restaurant, with an impressive vaulted brick ceiling and parquet floors. The dining room is divided in half by a brick wall, which supports an arrangement of fresh flowers. It's serious here without being overly elegant: handsome perhaps, but not grand, despite the ambition of the young and talented owners. It can be quite cold in chilly weather if you sit at certain tables; sit away from the wall on the right as you enter the dining room. Great energy here goes into tending the cellar and procuring the best available foodstuffs. Excellent breads are served throughout the meal.

SUGGESTED DISHES

insalata di spinaci e caviale   A salad of spinach, sturgeon caviar, and pine nuts. This is a dish from the fifteenth century.

*carpaccio d'oca con tartufo bianco   *Carpaccio* of goose breast, with slices of white truffle and Parmesan.

minestra di piselli A pea soup with pasta squares, whole peas, and Parmesan in a hearty stock.

ravioli di fegatini *Ravioli* stuffed with chicken liver in a sauce of stock, livers, and hearts; the dish is based on a sixteenth-century recipe.

*_riso con ovuli_ A beautifully executed *risotto* with butter, mushrooms, and rosemary.

risotto di cicoria *Risotto* with chicory—very green, quite subtle, and *not* bitter in the least.

filetti di spigola alle erbette fine e tartufo bianco Fillets of bass with herbs, white truffle, and oil.

scorfano con cozze Scorpion fish topped with mussels, tomato, and a little olive oil.

sella di capretto al miele e aceto balsamico Saddle of goat with honey and balsamic vinegar.

marchesa al cioccolato Chocolate marquis.

sorbetti misti Assorted sorbets: lemon, grape, strawberry, wine, and peach.

SUGGESTED WINES

White

Tristo di Montesecco, Fattoria di Montesecco A wine that hails from The Marches. Almost no bouquet, amber-yellow, and pleasantly earthy. Not a major wine but interesting for The Marches, and one you're not likely to find elsewhere.

Vintage Tunina, Jermann A beautiful white from Friuli, composed of Chardonnay, Sauvignon, and Pinot Bianco. Some say it's the best white in Italy, some say it drinks like a good Burgundy. Whatever the case, it must be sampled at least once while in Italy.

Red

Colle Picchioni, Vigna del Vassallo, Paola di Mauro A fresh, if slightly weak, well-made wine from Lazio. Light in the eye and on the nose, a taste focused and fine for a wine with so little body. Overall, it's subtly eager, nearly elegant.

AL 59 · DA GIUSEPPE

★ ★ ★ ½

REGION	Lazio
ADDRESS	via Brunetti, 59
PHONE	(06) 361-9019
CREDIT CARDS	Cash only
CLOSED	Sun, Sat in June and July, and Aug

CLASS	ATMOSPHERE	SERVICE	WINE	PRICE
3	3	2	2	M

Located between the Mausoleum of Augustus and piazza del Popolo, this small Bolognese establishment is frequented by a serious Roman clientele. A stone's throw away from the Tiber, it's a simple but finely executed space: vaulted ceiling, white lace curtains, pale green walls decorated with bird paintings, wooden floors, and finally the columns, which make themselves a presence in the room, all play a part.

Don't allow yourself to be rushed—you'll be asked to order pasta within minutes of being seated; ask for a menu and order your *acqua minerale* and *vino*. The waiters can be downright unpleasant to outsiders, but eating here is satisfying revenge. Lunch is a better idea than dinner. The wine list is basic, with very little choice and almost nothing from this region. I've listed two safe and pleasant wines.

SUGGESTED DISHES

prosciutto di Langhirano   High-quality *prosciutto* from Langhirano (near Parma), said to have the perfect air for curing this ham.

carciofi alla romana   Boiled artichokes served with oil and herbs.

*gramigna alla romagnola   Short, thick, spaghetti-like pasta served with a sausage and cream sauce.

misto di pasta   A plate of mixed pastas: *tortellini,* little doughnut-shaped pasta, with a cream sauce; *tortelloni,* large *tortellini,* stuffed with pumpkin; and green-noodle lasagne, made in the traditional Bolognese way.

braciola di maiale   A pork chop, prepared simply.

lombata di vitello   Loin of veal.

bollito misto   Mixed boiled meats served with a green sauce and *mostarda,* a sauce made with preserved fruits suspended in a thick syrup of mustard, wine, and honey.

SUGGESTED WINES

White

Galestro, Capsula Viola, Antinori   A clean, decent white—modest color, fruit, body, and flavor . . . a modest wine.

Red

Cabernet, Santa Margherita, Lison-Pramaggiore   A light but decently refined Cabernet. No depth or surprise; a well-made, easy drink. Closed nose. Not much fruit, and slightly tart on the finish.

CHECCHINO DAL 1887
★ ★ ★

REGION	Lazio
ADDRESS	via di Monte Testaccio, 30
PHONE	(06) 574-6318
CREDIT CARDS	AmX, Diners
CLOSED	Sun dinner, all day Sun June–Aug, Mon, last week of July to last week of Aug, Christmas week

CLASS	ATMOSPHERE	SERVICE	WINE	PRICE
3	3.5	3.5	3.5	E

This very hip, slightly out-of-the-way restaurant, which recently celebrated its centenary, is in the Testaccio district, once the location of slaughterhouses, and caters primarily to Romans in groups enjoying their indigenous cuisine. It's loud and bright, and if you're in the right mood a fine place to spend a Roman evening. Tile floors, fake wood wainscotting, and amusing drawings by the artist Anfa on the white stucco walls provide a festive atmosphere. The restaurant is famous for its Roman specialties—primarily dishes that use as ingredients what the Italians call *il quinto quarto,* the fifth quarter: intestines, tail, feet, and so on; but more standard fare is available for the less adventurous. It's casual and fun, and because of its popularity a reservation is mandatory. It was here that the famous Roman dish *coda alla vaccinara* was invented in 1890 by Sora Ferminia, the daughter of the restaurant's founders. You'll need to take a taxi, as the restaurant is quite a way from the center of town—out near the Pyramid of Caius Cestius and the Protestant Cemetery, where Keats and Shelley are buried.

SUGGESTED DISHES

insalata di zampi A salad of veal trotter (calf's foot and shin) and celery, beans, carrots, and olives.

*rigatoni con pajata A tube-shaped pasta with a sauce of intestines of milk-fed veal cooked in bacon fat.

tonnarelli al sugo di coda Thin pasta squares with an oxtail and tomato sauce.

bucatini alla gricia Long hollow pasta sauced with an extraordinary bacon, and cheese, oil, and black pepper.

arrosto misto Roasted meats: sweetbreads, liver, lung, "mountain oysters," and marrow.

trippa alla romana Tripe Roman style, first boiled, then stewed with tomatoes, garlic, parsley, and mint.

coda alla vaccinara Oxtail served in a rich tomato sauce with pine nuts and raisins.

*gorgonzola, miele e marsala A slice of *gorgonzola* covered with honey and served with a glass of De Bartoli's Vecchio Samperi (see below).

SUGGESTED WINES

White

Colle Picchioni, Paola di Mauro Good body and appealing gold color. Fruit much in evidence, and just enough acidity to keep it all in harmony.

Red

Colle Picchioni, Vigna Vassallo (Selezione per il Centenario di Checchino), Paola di Mauro This bottling, produced especially for the restaurant's centenary, is considerably heavier than other bottlings of the same wine; there's a slight pitchlike front taste and an interesting thickness. A well-made wine that comes off determined, tannic, and knottish.

Fiorano, Boncompagni Ludovisi   Alive, Bordeaux-like nose, with a touch of tomato. Intense, rich fruit, and good depth.

Dessert

Vecchio Samperi, De Bartoli   Although not a true Marsala, it's wonderfully mellow, rich, and well-balanced.

PIPERNO
★ ★ ★

REGION	Lazio
ADDRESS	Monte de' Cenci, 9
PHONE	(06) 654-0629
CREDIT CARDS	AmX, Visa, Diners
CLOSED	Sun dinner, Mon, Easter, Aug, Dec 23–Jan 2

CLASS	ATMOSPHERE	SERVICE	WINE	PRICE
3	3	3	3	E

There are a number of restaurants in the Jewish quarter that serve traditional Jewish specialties (not to be confused with "delicatessen" food), and Piperno is probably the one to try first. Immediately upon entering this festive establishment, you'll step before one of Piperno's victories, a colorful display of fresh seafood; whole fish a few hours out of the water, wait on ice to be selected by one of the patrons and cooked to order: *triglia,* red mullet; *sogliola,* sole; *orata,* bream; and *spigola* or *branzino,* sea bass. This is a handsome restaurant, comfortable and popular, serving the best specialties of Jewish cuisine in the Ghetto, as the neighborhood is called in Rome. The waiters recall those good men at Ratner's; don't be put off. They can be stern but in the end they will respond to any enthusiasm you make manifest; they are very Italian in this—seasoned, impatient, caring. You'll want to sit in the front room—dark green walls with attractive dark paintings—by far the more attractive of the two dining rooms, and it will allow you to see much more of the restaurant's activities. The back room can be a family room, noisy and crowded, and there it's easy to be ignored by your waiter, who's also interested in what's going on in the front room.

The meals are heavy, with plenty of deep-fried foods. You might want to balance your selection with a salad and a piece of fruit at the end. Be sure to try the excellent *puntarelle;* this salad green is available only in and around Rome. Start out a little early for dinner so you can take a leisurely walk through the streets of the Ghetto, a very different atmosphere from the rest of Rome.

SUGGESTED DISHES

carciofi alla giudia Flattened, deep-fried artichokes, Jewish style.

fiori di zucca ripieni e fritti Deep-fried squash flowers stuffed with mozzarella and anchovies.

supplì Deep-fried rice balls stuffed with ham and mozzarella.

gnocchetti alla Piperno Very light potato dumplings with a meat and tomato sauce.

filetti di baccalà Deep-fried salt cod fillets.

fritto di mare Mixed fried fish.

crostata della casa: ciliegie, aranci e ricotta Three types of tarts: cherry, orange, ricotta.

SUGGESTED WINES

White

Müller Thurgau, Feldmarschall, Tiefenbrunner A lively, winningly tart wine from Alto Adige. Plenty of energy and life, wonderful fruit, perfume, and taste. One of the best whites I've tasted; try it, you'll be pleasantly surprised.

Red

Torgiano, Rubesco, Lungarotti A bright, deep, fruity, and finally simple wine—smooth, rich, and soft, with an inviting nose. Among the *tastiest* red wines Italy has to offer.

Dal Bolognese
piazza del Popolo, 1
(06) 361-1426
AmX
Closed Sun dinner, Mon Sept–May, Aug 5–20

This restaurant has enjoyed considerable fame over the years, boasting of a clientele that includes famous practitioners of the *dolce vita*. The quality of the Bolognese cuisine served here has declined somewhat since those happy, carefree days, but it's pleasant enough and well located in piazza del Popolo. A specialty of the house, and of Emilia-Romagna, is *bollito misto,* served here from a silver cart that contains, in two compartments of heated water, boiled tongue, beef, ham, *cotechino* sausage, chicken, and a few other miscellaneous cuts. To accompany this display of tasty meats—don't be put off by the notion of boiled meat—you will receive a piquant green sauce and a bowl of *mostarda,* preserved fruits suspended in a mustard-honey-wine syrup. The *risotto al salmone,* risotto with salmon, is also excellent.

Vecchia Roma
piazza Campitelli, 18
(06) 686-4604
Cash only
Closed Wed

In the heart of the Ghetto, the Jewish quarter, this cavelike restaurant, coolish and damp in the winter, is best experienced on a fine Roman night in the warmer months, when you can eat outside on the charming little patio. The *antipasti misti,* a mixed assortment of fish, is the thing to start with. Follow with a simple meat or grilled fish—anything more elaborate is less than advised. Try a bottle of Torre Ercolana, Anagni (see the description under "Alberto Ciarla," page 271).

Tavola d'Oro
via Marianna Dionigi, 37
(06) 312-317
Cash only
Closed Sun, Aug

If you happen to find yourself on the other side of the river after visiting the Vatican or walking in Trastevere, there's a neighborhood hole-in-the-wall specializing in Sicilian cooking that happens to be quite wonderful, just off piazza Cavour. It's a family-run affair, with Mamma very active in the kitchen. If you've never tasted traditional Sicilian *caponata*, or even if you have, nowhere will you get it better—eggplant, capers, olives in an extra virgin olive oil, and tomato purée. Sicilian *antipasti* are fresh and energetic. Follow with the *cavateddri con melanzane*, a potato-based pasta with tomato sauce and eggplant. The Sicilian sausage with *caciocavallo* cheese, spiced with coriander seeds, is worth trying. For dessert the *zabaglione*, served hot, and the *cannoli* are memorable. Delicious pizza bread soaked with olive oil, impregnated with garlic, and served hot will precede your meal. Order the sturdy Sicilian house wine.

RESTAURANTS TO AVOID

Papa Giovanni
via dei Sediari, 4

Expensive and very poorly run. The food is aggressively mediocre and the dining room severely depressing. It's mentioned here because it does have a reputation, based on another generation's experience.

Relais Le Jardin
via De Notaris, 5 (in the Lord Byron Hotel)

Despite the fact that this restaurant receives the highest ratings in Rome from the Michelin and *Espresso* guides, it's outrageously expensive and marked by seriously amateurish cooking. The food was nothing less than embarrassing on three different occasions—and at no small cost.

La Rosetta
via della Rosetta, 9

You might hear that there's a nice little fish restaurant next to the Pantheon. Save yourself a great deal of money and the possibility of an extremely unpleasant night. Aside from the fact that the owner is capable of achieving great heights in the realm of the offensive, the last time I visited La Rosetta he suggested a small tasting menu of fish and two bottles of a simple, inexpensive white wine for my party of four; the bill came to $120 per person—rather excessive for a basic and only moderately comfortable *trattoria*. One can do surprisingly well without this experience.

Hassler
piazza Trinità dei Monti, 6
(06) 679-2651
AmX
Very expensive/Luxury

Located at the top of the Spanish Steps above Piazza di Spagna, this is one of the most popular hotels in the country. The owner, Roberto Wirth, an extremely charming man, and watches over his hotel with the care of a new father; the hotel was opened by his family back in 1885 and they've run it ever since. Floor by floor, the rooms are all being renovated, with attention paid to every detail, from the color of the paint and the texture of the materials, to the "hardware" of the room. It's of particular interest to Wirth that whenever possible the rooms command interesting views. This is a magical place, whether you're dining in the garden restaurant, looking over the city from the rooftop restaurant (great for New Year's Eve, breakfast, and lunch), or merely waiting for your partner in the handsome lobby, where you are likely as not to be standing next to Jean-Paul Belmondo. A favorite resting spot for the elite—European and American alike. For any piece of information or reservations, ask Alberto Olmeda, the concierge who knows everything.

Excelsior
via Vittorio Veneto, 125
(06) 4708
AmX, Visa, Diners
Very expensive/Luxury

Being located on via Veneto means there's a lot of activity in and around the hotel; there are always dignitaries or celebrities staying here, which can make for a great deal of excitement. A world class, deluxe hotel, if slightly stuffy; and always comfortable and professional, although lacking that sometimes welcome warmth received in many of the less formal establishments.

Le Grand Hotel
via Vittorio Emanuele Orlando, 3
(06) 4709
AmX, Visa, Diners
Very expensive/Luxury

A sister to the Excelsior, it could be described in exactly the same way, although this is by far the more comely of the two—grand in the Belle Époque tradition. Beautiful rooms, impeccable service.

Grand Hotel de la Ville
via Sestina, 69
(06) 6733
AmX, Visa, Diners
Expensive
Just down the street from the Hassler and considerably less expensive. A favorite among Europeans.

D'Inghilterra
via Bocca di Leone, 14
(06) 672-161
AmX, Visa, Diners
Expensive
To my mind the prime location in Rome—right in the middle of the best Roman shopping streets, between via dei Condotti and via Borgognona. There's a sweet little bar for cocktails or coffee after dinner, and the rooms, mostly on the smallish side, are very nicely finished with antique furniture and cheerfully colored material on the chairs, beds, and curtains; rugs add a warm touch. All in all, it's the epitome of a charming, if not luxurious, hotel; it's run by Nushin Mozaffari in a low-key but carefully observant way. The list of those who have spent nights here includes Ernest Hemingway, Franz Liszt, Mark Twain, Hans Christian Andersen, and Henry James—not in that order, of course.

Plaza
via del Corso, 126
(06) 672-101
AmX, Visa, Diners
Moderate
After the Hotel d'Inghilterra this seems to me the best hotel location in Rome: a minute from the shopping streets between the Corso and piazza di Spagna—via Frattina, via Borgognona, via dei Condotti and via della Croce—which makes for easy, short outings to pick up a little something in one of the stores or just to wander a bit. And you're minutes from the Pantheon and piazza Navona, and from piazza del Popolo at one end of the Corso and piazza Venezia at the other. The rooms are straightforward with no extras, but the hotel is very smoothly run.

La Residenza
via Emilia, 22
(06) 474-4480
Cash only
Moderate

Good, comfortable rooms within walking distance of via Veneto.

Gregoriana
via Gregoriana, 18
(06) 679-4269
Cash only
Moderate

Located off a street at the top of the Spanish Steps. The rooms are sweetly decorated, moderately quiet, and comfortable year-round.

Hotel Raphael
Largo Febo, 2
(06) 650-881
AmX
Moderate

A handy location, especially if wandering in piazza Navona is one of the special activities for you in Rome. The rooms are simple, although some effort has obviously been made in decorating them. It's more a high-end *pensione* than a hotel, but the prices are reasonable and its location on a tree-lined street keeps you pleasantly out of the mainstream, despite its proximity to piazza Navona.

FOOD AND WINE SHOPS, MARKETS

Food

via della Croce

There are a number of fine food shops on this street—among them Panetteria Nanni at #25, which sells bread; the very good *salsamenterie,* Fabbi at #27–28 and Focacci at #43 which sell cheese, various cured meats such as *prosciutto* and *bresaola,* dried mushrooms, and other foodstuffs; and Fratelli Roffi Isabelli, a wonderful wine store (see below).

Volpetti
via della Scrofa, 31-32

A fine *salsamenteria* just up from the Church of San Luigi dei Francesi, with its three fantastic Caravaggios. A good place to have a snack from the *tavola calda,* or to pick up some cold cuts, cheese, and a bottle of wine to consume in nearby piazza Navona after a morning of Caravaggios.

Caffè Giolitti
via degli Uffici del Vicario, 40

Some say the best ice cream in Rome is to be found here. You can also have pastries, sandwiches, drinks, and coffee, standing or sitting at a table. Minutes from the Pantheon.

Wine

Fratelli Roffi Isabelli
via Bocca di Leone, 40 (at via della Croce)

Once a workingmen's bar, this charming *enoteca* was renovated a few years ago and is now a wine-tasting bar and shop, where you can sample the wines of Italy and then purchase a bottle to take home. If you go on a Friday or Saturday afternoon, look for Edward Steinberg, the resident wine expert by way of Harvard University; he's extremely knowledgeable about regional wines, and he will explain anything you want to know about the latest Italian wines, and will gladly offer suggestions as to what might interest you.

Enoteca al Parlamento
via dei Prefetti, 15

A large selection of old vintage wines from the very best producers.

Enoteca Trimani
via Goito, 20

A wide selection of wines and olive oils.

Enoteca Elsanino Mario
via del Pantheon, 56

In this tiny store just off piazza della Rotonda, where the
Pantheon is located, you can find a surprising range of wines
at very good prices. The owner is a sweet man who will do
his best to find you something useful, if you give him an idea
of what it is you're after.

Buccone
via di Ripetta, 19–20

A good selection of wines from all over Italy, just off piazza
del Popolo.

Markets

The market of piazza Campo dei Fiori, one of Rome's most
festive piazzas, may also be the most interesting in Rome.
When you've finished looking at the stands of fruits and vegetables, meats and fish, flowers and plants, purchase an orange and wander over to the nearby Palazzo Farnese, now
the French Embassy, and then down via Giulia, to see what's
going on in the art galleries. The market is open Monday
through Saturday, mornings only.

San Vincenzo

San Vincenzo is being turned into a quiet, low-key resort town, with new hotels and restaurants opening up. It's out of the way, to be sure, but you won't go wrong taking a day to drive down the beautiful coast from Livorno—or from Pisa, Lucca, Viareggio, or even Florence—and stopping in Bolgheri, just outside San Vincenzo, to visit the vineyard that produces Sassicaia, one of the great Italian red wines. In the center of small, focused San Vincenzo is a picturesque marina, which can be quite convincing at sunset. Then a stroll through town, coffee, and finally the evening meal.

GAMBERO ROSSO
★ ★ ★ ★

REGION	Tuscany
ADDRESS	piazza della Vittoria, 13
PHONE	(0565) 701-021
CREDIT CARDS	AmX, Visa, Diners
CLOSED	Tues, Nov, lunch June 15–Sept 15

CLASS	ATMOSPHERE	SERVICE	WINE	PRICE
4	4.5	2.5	3.5	E

Gambero Rosso, "The Red Shrimp," is the creation of Fulvio and Emanuela Pierangelini. With its mellow color theme—yellow and white marble floor, white walls with yellow trim, pale yellow tablecloths—the restaurant reminds you that it's located near the water. The casement windows facing the sea are especially pretty with their dark wood. A little balcony separates the main room with the water view from the passage into the back room. In this airy, romantic setting, filled with flowers, and cane and wicker chairs, you can sample some of the best seafood in Italy. Unfortunately, the service here is surprisingly underwhelming—and very much out of league with the very high quality of the kitchen. But as waiters are the link between the kitchen and diners, this is something the gifted chef-owner might want to rectify. Be sure to sit in the room with the view of the sea.

passatina di ceci con gamberi   Shrimp set on a sauce of puréed chickpeas, with olive oil poured around the shrimp.

*insalata di sogliola   A salad composed of greens on the bottom, a little layer of puréed foie gras and truffles, a slice of grilled sole, and finally avocado, oil, and a sprinkling of lemon. Garnished with diced tomato and asparagus spears. Masterful.

ravioli di pesce alla crema di frutti di mare   Black and white *ravioli* (the black are made with cuttlefish ink) stuffed with a fish mixture and sauced with cream and finely chopped seafood—octopus, mussels, and so on.

raviolone di zucchine con gamberi   One large *ravioli* stuffed with zucchini purée and shrimp, served with a sauce of seafood stock, butter, and finely shredded seafood.

ranio con carciofi   Sea bass—called *branzino* in the North, *spigola* in the South, and *ranio* (from *ragno*, "spider") in San Vincenzo—covered with a layer of sliced, parboiled artichokes. Other fish may be served this way as well.

*budino alle confetture della casa   A cube of white mousse made with secret ingredients and filled with puréed figs whipped with chocolate. The same fig stuffing is heated and placed in a light pastry shell.

SUGGESTED WINES

White

Pinot Bianco, Fulvio Pierangelini   The house white, made for the restaurant. A simple, straightforward wine with a slightly bitter finish.

Bianco di Cercatoia, Montecarlo, Fattoria Buonamico   A wine with some complex perfume in the nose, which arrives with a trace of orange. Elegant and graceful, light and soft, golden-colored, with an excellent display of fruit. Alive in the mouth.

Grattamacco, Piermario Meletti Cavallari   A wonderful Tuscan white: pears in the nose, delicate and seductive, and a beautiful lemon color. A good explosion of fruit in the mouth, with a noticeable kick of acidity to tighten the focus. A smart wine, ready to go and very with it. More *there* than most Italian whites.

OTHER RECOMMENDED RESTAURANTS

La Bitta
via Vittorio Emanuele II, 119
(0565) 704-080
AmX
Closed Mon, Oct 15–Nov 15

HOTELS

Grand Hotel I Lecci
via della Principessa, 114
(0565) 704-111
AmX, Visa, Diners
Moderate to expensive

   A relatively new hotel, five minutes from the center of town. It's an airy, pleasant if antiseptic place for your overnight stay; after dinner at Gambero Rosso there's nowhere else to go. The rooms have terraces for morning coffee among the trees and birds. And then you're off.

Siena

Arezzo 89 km	Assisi 131	Florence 68	Grosseto 73
	Livorno 116	Lucca 128	Orvieto 123
	Perugia 107	Pisa 106	Sinalunga 45

Siena is well known not only for its rivalry with big sister Florence and as one of Italy's most beautiful hill towns—it's actually built on three hills—but also as home of Duccio di Buoninsegna, the Sienese painter who straddled the Byzantine and Gothic traditions, and of Jacopo della Quercia, Siena's greatest sculptor, who lived during the fifteenth century. The Palio, the world-famous horse race that takes place in piazza del Campo, Siena's central square, on July 2 (the Feast of the Visitation) and August 16 (the day after the Feast of the Assumption) has drawn visitors to Siena since the seventeenth century.

Piazza del Campo itself is an important central square in Italy, one of the choicest places in which to sit and enjoy a cup of coffee, if you don't mind a goodly number of fellow travelers doing the same thing. Palazzo Pubblico, a memorable Gothic construction that dominates the piazza, is the seat of government in Siena.

The Duomo, an imposing Gothic cathedral with a façade of black, white, and pink marble, was completed in the fourteenth century. Especially noteworthy is the interior floor, an inlaid-marble "pavement," executed by forty or so Renaissance artists. Nicola Pisano's thirteenth-century pulpit is remarkable, and in the Museo dell'Opera del Duomo, the cathedral museum (closed afternoons from November to mid-March), you'll see Duccio's *Maestà*. In the library are frescoes by Pinturicchio. From the Duomo, walk over to the Pinacoteca (Picture Gallery, in Palazzo Buonsignori, closed Mondays, and afternoons), where you'll find works by Duccio, Pinturicchio, and Sodoma.

The rich earth of Siena's three hills is responsible for the name of a color: sienna, the memorable reddish brown in which this town is cast. What Siena is not known for is its native cuisine—or these days, its restaurants—which is surprising, given the number of tourists who visit this fine medieval city with its narrow and colorful streets, churches, palaces, and ramparts. There is one exception, noted below.

ANTICA TRATTORIA BOTTEGANOVA
★ ★ ★

REGION	Tuscany
ADDRESS	via Chiantigiana, 29
PHONE	(0577) 284-230
CREDIT CARDS	AmX, Visa, Diners
CLOSED	Sun

CLASS	ATMOSPHERE	SERVICE	WINE	PRICE
3	2.5	2.5	3	M

Although not immediately impressive, this *trattoria* has a charm of its own, and more than you might first have thought. It is simply and thoughtfully laid out, with vaulted brick ceilings, stone walls, arched lamps; the feeling is warm and cozy, familial. And it is a typically family-run restaurant, with Mamma in the kitchen, the children serving, and the

head male running the establishment. The winning wine cellar is stocked with well-selected local Chianti and other Tuscan wines at good prices. And the owner has carefully placed a few tables in this excellent little cellar, for the special parties.

Directions. From the center of town follow the green signs toward Rome. After you cross the bridge, continue straight; do not follow the main road, which swings to the right. Go up the hill; the restaurant is on the left. If you don't want to drive, take a taxi, it's a five-minute drive outside the center of town.

SUGGESTED DISHES

passato di ceci con taglierini Chickpea purée with a little pasta and oil added.

taglierini al limone Thin noodles served with a light cream and lemon sauce.

*coniglio arrosto Roast rabbit, perfectly executed—not in the way it was shot but in the way it's prepared here. Tender, moist, and delicate of flesh.

*lombo di suino alla Chateaubriand Roasted fillet of pork, sliced and served with a small showering of "out of season" white truffles, here called *martzoli*.

pecorino delle crete senesi A soft, slightly aged *pecorino* with truffle oil on top.

i dessert di Nonna Argia Surprise desserts.

SUGGESTED WINES

White

Cervaro della Sala, Antinori Composed of Grechetto and Chardonnay and aged in French oak. A big, tasty white, still youthful, even a little green, but rich and generous, and worth trying while you're here.

Red

Coltassala, Castello di Volpaia A blend of Sangioveto and Mammolo grapes, this wine has a slightly orange cast moving from its garnet center. It's powerful without being luscious, on the austere side, with good earthy fruit and enough acidity to keep the wine steady.

HOTELS

Park Hotel
via di Marciano, 18
(0577) 44-803
AmX, Visa, Diners
Expensive
   One of the CIGA chain, set on beautiful property a few minutes outside the center of Siena. The rooms are attractive, but they are *not* the most comfortable rooms of the CIGA chain. Nevertheless, walking around the lovely grounds after breakfast seems to correct anything that was less than perfect the night before.

FOOD AND WINE SHOPS, MARKETS

Wine

Enoteca Italica Permanente
Fortezza Medicea
   A large selection of wines from all over Italy, set dramatically in the Medici fortress. Wine by the glass available.

Sinalunga

Arezzo 44 km   *Assisi* 86   *Florence* 103   *Gubbio* 95

Orvieto 78   *Perugia* 65   *Rome* 188   *Siena* 45

In Sinalunga, you are close to a number of other hill towns of interest to lovers of Tuscan wine and food, such as Montepulciano, where a very pleasant lunch can be had at Fattoria Pulcino (see page 230), or Montefollonico and its first-class restaurant La Chiusa (page 228), and then there's Antica Trattoria Botteganova (page 289) in Siena.

LOCANDA DELL'AMOROSA

★ ★ ★

REGION	Tuscany
ADDRESS	2 km south of Sinalunga
PHONE	(0577) 679-497
CREDIT CARDS	AmX, Visa, Diners
CLOSED	Mon, Tues lunch, Jan 20–Feb 28
7 ROOMS	On the pricey side, without matching comfort. Expensive.

CLASS	ATMOSPHERE	SERVICE	WINE	PRICE
3	4	3	3	E

The approach to this working *fattoria* (farm), which dates back to the fourteenth century, is impressive indeed: it's on a hill at the end of a long line of cypresses, with vineyards and a forest sprawling around it. If brick floors please you, you'll love them here; the floors of Locanda dell'Amoroso are among the most beautiful I've seen in any restaurant. The dining room, once the site of the stables, illustrates just how an old country restaurant should look: ancient beams in the vaulted brick ceilings, dark wood all around, neat, handsome tables—and near the kitchen, in the front of the restaurant, bottles of olive oil from the farm's olive trees, wine from its vineyards, honey from its bees, and jars of marmalade. And then there are the enthusiastic and appealing women who wait on tables.

Directions. The restaurant is located outside Sinalunga. If you are coming via the Siena–Perugia road, exit at Sinalunga and go through the town; the restaurant is just beyond it, and is announced by the long tree-adorned driveway mentioned above. Sinalunga is very close to the Florence–Rome *autostrada.*

SUGGESTED DISHES

*ravioli al burro e salvia Large *ravioli* filled with spinach and sauced with sage-impregnated butter.

risotto al radicchio rosso A rose-colored *risotto* made with *radicchio* and red wine. Garnished with shredded *radicchio*.

pollo alle erbe Roasted chicken with herbs: a simple dish, well executed.

braciola di maiale alla salvia Pork chop prepared with sage.

fagioli all'olio Simple and excellent Tuscan beans and oil.

formaggi Have a selection of the cheeses.

*focaccia di mandorle An almond cake.

SUGGESTED WINES

White

Amoroso Bianco This wine is made at the Locanda. Good balance of acidity and fruit with some subtle floral notes. Crisp and spritely, this cheerful white finishes with a slight floral perfume.

Red

Amoroso Rosso, Riserva Also made here, it's a very full, robust Chianti, earthy, herbal, deep garnet in color, with some worthwhile complexity.

S o r i s o

Alessandria 118 km   *Aosta* 179   *Arona* 20
Genoa 199   *Milan* 78   *Novara* 40   *Ranco* 41
Stresa 36   *Turin* 130   *Varese* 46

Soriso is the town, Al Sorriso the restaurant. *Sorriso* means "smile," but even with a smile Soriso is not an easy town to find, especially at night, when you're likely to arrive without one. Happily, the difficulties are well rewarded if your goal is a meal at Angelo and Luisa Valazza's world-class restaurant.

The road into Soriso *ends* in Soriso. Once there, you're close to the charming town of Orta, which feels more like North Africa than Italy. It's on Lake Orta and there's nothing in Italy quite like it. Certainly it's worth visiting for a late-afternoon coffee; and if you have the time, take the short boat ride to the beautiful little island of San Giulio. It's a pleasant forty-five-minute drive to Stresa from Soriso; there you can walk along Lake Maggiore, gaze at the Borromean Islands, and perhaps take a light lunch at Emiliano.

AL SORRISO
★ ★ ★ ★ ★

REGION	Piedmont
ADDRESS	via Roma, 18
PHONE	(0322) 983-228
CREDIT CARDS	Visa
CLOSED	Mon, Tues lunch, Jan 10–31
8 ROOMS	Small but very comfortable rooms, all with nice views. Moderate.

CLASS	ATMOSPHERE	SERVICE	WINE	PRICE
5	4.5	5	4	VE

Not a single false note from beginning to end, this is dining at its most elevated. Al Sorriso is a handsome restaurant—refined and elegant. It is decorated with plants, paintings on the white walls, pink tablecloths, dark burl appointments, etched glass, Italian design Jill lamps, orchids in various-sized vases, soft music creating what might even be called a "romantic" atmosphere. There are only ten tables here—spacious but intimate.

Although the restaurant is a little out of your way wherever you're coming from (the Milanese who frequent this establishment make the trip in under an hour), it's a wonderful drive during the day through the hills near Lake Orta to reach it. Angelo Valazza, who runs the restaurant with his wife, Luisa, is very involved in Le Soste (see page 7); he is supremely informed about Italian cuisine and is happy to answer any questions you might have. Remember only that northern Italians tend to think Italy ends before you reach Tuscany.

Directions. From Milan take the *autostrada* Milano–Laghi and get off at the Sesto Calende exit. Go in the direction of Arona and follow the signs to arrive in Borgomanero. Follow the signs for Orta and continue for 7 or 8 kilometers, until you see a sign for Soriso on your left—you're about 2.5 kilometers from the restaurant. Go left at that sign and at the next stop sign go left again, and follow the signs for Ristorante Sorriso. It's on your left as you enter the village.

S U G G E S T E D   D I S H E S

piccolo carpaccio di fegato grasso An amazing *carpaccio* of foie gras marinated in oil and salt for twenty-four hours, served on a bed of sliced apple and *radicchio* with red *mirtilli* (similar to bilberries or blueberries), which give the plate a little color. The geese for this dish are raised by a woman in Ferrara.

giambonetto di galletto farcito, con insalatina novella Sliced cock's leg stuffed with "gray" truffle (called *crostone di Monferrato* in Soriso; see page 36) and pistachios. Served with a green salad.

foglie di verza ripiena con fonduta di fontina al tartufo Cabbage leaves stuffed with a *fontina* and truffle mixture.

fantasia di scampi con porri farciti in salsa di patate Scampi boiled for two minutes in *fumetto* (fish stock)—as tender as any I've tasted—and placed on a ring of leeks stuffed with chopped scampi, which in turn is set atop a mound of puréed potatoes.

cuore di carciofo e animelle gratinati al dragoncello Artichoke hearts stuffed with sweetbreads, all gratinéed with a little tarragon. Beautifully presented.

ravioli di formaggio dell'Ossola al tartufo nero
Ravioli filled with ricotta and served with "gray" truffles (see p. 36). A dish as light as air.

fassone piemontese al vino rosso con midollo
Strips of braised beef presented in a reduction of the braising liquid, red wine, and for added richness, bone marrow. Served with a purée of potatoes and parsley. This is recommended even for those who don't like braised beef.

petto di piccione al porto con fonduta di porri
Breast of pigeon—gamey in the best way, full of flavor, tender—perfectly cooked with a sauce of port and leeks. Served with a purée of pigeon kidney, liver, and other internal organs, white bread, parsley, and other herbs.

il formaggio delle nostre valli Cheese(s) "from our valleys." Ask for a selection of all the Piedmontese cheeses available; you'll be advised in what order to taste them.

bavarese di torroncino in salsa di caramello A mousse of hazelnut nougat in a caramel sauce.

parfait di agrumi in salsa di arancie sanguigne Parfait of citrus fruits—tangerines, blood oranges, lemons—in a sauce of blood oranges and passion fruit.

SUGGESTED WINES

White

Erbaluce di Caluso, Colombaio di Candia Pacchiè A most unusual nose: a little caramel, a little leather. A sunny color, very fresh, and much livelier than most Piedmontese whites.

Red

1982 Barbaresco, Gaja The first hit of scent will conjure up the bouquet of good Bordeaux. Deep garnet color, very rich, very soft, everything in perfect balance. Although still young, with something serious held back, it's an intense, complex, and gorgeous red.

Stresa

Take a nostalgic walk along Lake Maggiore at sunset, with the Borromean Islands softly afloat in a green haze on the water. Especially in the late fall, when the tourists have returned home and bats weave the lake-softened air that has an idea of winter in it, the light is nineteenth-century and hermetic. In Stresa, you're within striking distance of two important restaurants: Del Sole, across the lake in Ranco (page 260), and Al Sorriso, in Soriso (page 294). Both are worth considering seriously.

EMILIANO
★ ★ ★

REGION	Piedmont
ADDRESS	corso Italia, 52
PHONE	(0323) 31-396
CREDIT CARDS	AmX, Visa, Diners
CLOSED	Tues, Nov 15–Dec 20

CLASS	ATMOSPHERE	SERVICE	WINE	PRICE
4	3.5	2	3	VE

If you enjoy walking to dinner, Emiliano is an easy and very romantic ten-minute walk from the lakeside hotels. The dining room is large and bright, decorated with light brown floor tiles, Oriental carpets, and a great deal of wood paneling. Lovely fresh flowers are set in black vases placed casually but correctly around the room. Silver sconces and pink candles complete the subdued Oriental decorative theme here.

S U G G E S T E D   D I S H E S

stringozze in ricetta di Felisi A bed of flat pasta topped with peas, shrimp, lobster, salmon, and mussels in a sauce of fish stock, curry, and a touch of cream.

tortelli di ricotta e erbette al burro di noci Large *ravioli*-like pasta stuffed with ricotta and herbs, served with a nut-butter sauce.

---

scaloppa di salmone al vino rosso   Salmon fillet with a red wine sauce, garnished with peas and zucchini.

SUGGESTED WINES

White

Chardonnay Gaia & Rey, Gaja   Clean, hay-colored, everything in perfect balance: wood, fruit, acid. Soft, gauzy, rich, and deep, with a long finish. Very elegant.

Red

Bricco dell'Uccellone, G. Bologna   Here is Barbera at its very best and most graceful, a wine Burton Anderson says is "filled with fantasy and humor." Powerful color, nose, and flavor; big and rich, alcoholic, fruity and earthy, this is a wine of the earth with a moment of cherry in the finish. It comes on like Mike Tyson!

HOTELS

Des Îles Borromées
lungolago Umberto I, 67
(0323) 30-431
AmX, Visa, Diners
Very expensive/Luxury
   A beautiful hotel overlooking Lake Maggiore and the Borromean Islands. Elegant, spacious, deluxe rooms, which very much reflect the ninteenth-century atmosphere of Stresa.

Regina Palace
lungolago Umberto I, 27
(0323) 30-171
AmX, Visa, Diners
Moderate
   Also on the lake, overlooking the Borromean Islands. Less grand than Des Îles Borromées, but very atmospheric, with lovely comfortable rooms. It suggests a hotel that once really had its day; although that day has passed, the substance of that period remains in the air.

Torgiano

Assisi 27 km   *Deruta* 7   *Florence* 170   *Orvieto* 60
Perugia 16   *Rome* 158   *Siena* 123   *Terni* 69

There's nothing of note in this city, aside from the Museo del Vino, an interesting wine museum run by Giorgio Lungarotti, the most important winemaker in Umbria. Nevertheless, Torgiano, like Perugia, provides a good base from which to investigate the numerous hill towns in the area—Assisi, Todi, Perugia, Spello, Spoleto, Gubbio, Monterchi to see Piero della Francesca's *Madonna del Parto,* and Sansepolcro to see his *Resurrection.* If you're adventurous, you could drive as far as Arezzo to see Piero's amazing frescoes that bring to life the legend of the Holy Cross in the Church of San Francesco.

LE TRE VASELLE	
★ ★ ★	
REGION	Umbria
ADDRESS	via Garibaldi, 48
PHONE	(075) 982-447
CREDIT CARDS	AmX, Visa, Diners
CLOSED	Open daily
47 ROOMS	Pleasant, serviceable rooms, on the noisy side but otherwise comfortable. Moderate.

CLASS	ATMOSPHERE	SERVICE	WINE	PRICE
3	3.5	2.5	3	E

This restaurant is in the Relais & Châteaux hotel of the same name, owned by the famous Umbrian winemaker Giorgio Lungarotti. A large fireplace at the end of the dining room makes the space extremely intimate and friendly, especially in the colder months; pre-dinner drinks are served in another room, in front of another fireplace, of this hotel. The dark brick floors are unusually handsome, even in a country that boasts of an infinity of beautiful brick floors. Elegant glass, silver, and china adorn the red-clad tables.

The hotel is basic but comfortable, and it's a good stopping place on your way to or from Rome. Le Tre Vaselle is the showpiece of the Lungarotti vineyard.

SUGGESTED DISHES

imbrecciata A soup composed of beans, chickpeas, dried peas, and lentils in a vegetable stock.

pennette Tre Vaselle Small quill-shaped pasta, sauced with mushrooms, cream, and parsley.

frascarelli alla crudaiola Rice-shaped pasta with a tomato and basil sauce.

filetto di bue in salsa balsamica di uva Steak grilled with rosemary and balsamic vinegar.

SUGGESTED WINES

As only Lungarotti wines are served here, I have listed recommended vintages.

White

1984 Torre di Giano, Vigna Il Pino A clean, fruity wine, with some perfume to it. It is more substantial than the Chardonnay and considerably more pleasant.

Red

1971, 1975 Rubesco, Vigna Monticchio Smooth, rich, and soft with an inviting nose; garnet-colored. These are good years of one of the better wines Italy has to offer.

Tossignano

Bologna 47 km	*Florence* 84	*Forlì* 44	*Imola* 14
	Ravenna 59	*Rimini* 93	

Arriving at the Locanda della Colonna in Tossignano is a little like coming into a sultry, sleepy village in Mexico. At the lunch hour there's no one on the streets, and from the outside the little unmarked restaurant has the look of a *cantina*, with its columns, palm trees, and unassuming façade. It's a beautiful, in fact memorable, drive once you've exited the *autostrada* at Imola, going by way of Borgo Tossignano and then up the hill to Tossignano itself.

LOCANDA DELLA COLONNA

★ ★ ★ ★

REGION	Emilia-Romagna
ADDRESS	via Nuova, 10–11
PHONE	(0542) 91-006
CREDIT CARDS	AmX, Visa, Diners
CLOSED	Sun, Mon, Jan 10–Feb 10, Aug 15–31

CLASS	ATMOSPHERE	SERVICE	WINE	PRICE
4	4	3	4	E

The restaurant is simple and elegant, understated and warm. You'll begin in one of the black lacquered chairs or at a banquette with jade-turquoise upholstery, both of which are comfortable enough. Dark green candles in fine silver holders adorn the tables and easygoing indirect lighting and hanging gold lamps set the mood. Salmon-colored marble surfaces suit the earth tones of the tiled floors. The small front room is divided in half by two square white-brick columns and two bamboo plants. Pastel colors and bronze urns flush with colorful flowers dominate the room.

There are four tasting menus to choose from; nothing is offered à la carte. The service is slow and not completely professional, but what does it matter? Take your time, the restaurant is especially pleasant and the food good. Reservations required.

Directions. From Bologna take the *autostrada* toward Ravenna and exit at Imola. Follow the signs to Imola/Florence, then the signs for Florence to Borgo Tossignano. In the middle of Borgo Tossignano turn left at the sign for Tossignano and drive up the hill. At the statue, stay to the left. The restaurant, on the left, is the terra-cotta structure with columns and green windows. It has no sign.

SUGGESTED   DISHES

insalata di carciofi, parmigiano e bresaola all'olio extra vergine A salad of julienned raw artichokes, slices of Parmesan, and *bresaola* (air-cured beef) with a dressing of oil and lemon.

zuppa imperiale A rich chicken stock with small squares of bread and cheese.

lasagne ripiene in brodo di cappone   A soup made with capon broth and tiny, quarter-inch trapezoids of stuffed pasta—really irregularly shaped *quadrucci*. That they're called "lasagne" is a little gastronomical joke. You have to be Italian.

*filetti di coniglio all'aceto, peperoni al pane   Very moist pieces of loin of rabbit, sliced thin and served with a light sauce of balsamic vinegar and rabbit juices. Garnished with a rolled red pepper stuffed with bread crumbs and chopped nuts, and topped with a sprinkling of the nuts.

nocette e coratella di agnello al forno all'aglio dolce   Medallions and *coratella* (heart, liver, lung, and spleen) of lamb, baked with garlic and served with a subtle meat reduction. Garnished with vegetables.

crema al forno con frutti di bosco   A rich custard cream served with strawberry sauce and fresh wild strawberries.

SUGGESTED   WINES

White

Sauvignon, Colli Bolognesi, Monte San Peitro, Terre Rosse, Vallania   A simple Sauvignon, pale and fresh; light grass, good fruit and acidity balance. Most agreeable at lunch, or with a simple first course at dinner.

Red

Ronco dei Ciliegi, Modigliana, Baldi   A Bordeaux-like nose greets you first, immediately followed by something slightly metallic—but happily this seems to fade with time. A warm, generous, rich wine made from Sangiovese Grosso grapes. Upper-class color; focused, fine, luscious.

Treviso

Bologna 170 km	*Bolzano* 197	*Mantua* 169
Milan 264	*Padua* 50	*Trieste* 145	*Venice* 30
	Verona 130	*Vicenza* 82

Treviso, a city of water and bridges, was the birthplace of Lorenzo Lotto. You can view some of this Renaissance painter's work in the Church of San Nicolò and the Museo Civico.

Treviso is known also in the name of an important Italian vegetable: *radicchio di Treviso.* Every December, in fact, Treviso puts on a *radicchio* fair, during which local restaurants celebrate this red edible in a number of preparations. There are four distinct varieties of *radicchio,* but we're concerned here only with the long and leggy type; according to the citizens of Treviso, this is the *only* true *radicchio.* Related to endive, *radicchio* is a reddish-purple, slightly bitter, chicory-like vegetable, used in numerous ways, especially in salads and—my favorite preparation—grilled, often with a little *gorgonzola, fontina,* or other cheese melted over it. Waverley Root quotes a little Treviso jingle that says it all:

If you keep it, that is nice;
Eat it, and it's Paradise:
The *radicchio* of Treviso.

It's a 29-kilometer trip from Treviso to Maser, where one of Palladio's most famous villas, built in 1560, is situated. The villa is decorated with arresting frescoes by Veronese.

ALFREDO–RELAIS EL TOULÀ
★ ★

REGION	Veneto
ADDRESS	via Collalto, 26
PHONE	(0422) 540-275
CREDIT CARDS	AmX, Visa, Diners
CLOSED	Sun dinner, Mon, July 26–Aug 25

CLASS	ATMOSPHERE	SERVICE	WINE	PRICE
3	2.5	2	2.5	E

Hokey in that El Toulà way (this is the original El Toulà)—memories of *la dolce vita,* with salmon-colored tablecloths, fancy curtains, and colorful murals of virginal maidens *in natura* (butterflies and flowers aplenty)—the lower dining area here is dominated by a Japanese painting of a breaking wave. There's an old-world atmosphere, a Europe-in-decline charm, promoted here, with antique mirrors and lamps and candelabra—actually, it's even worn out, like an old European bar. Whimsical white plastic fans in the corners of the room and American rock-and-roll on the tape deck further an impression that it's a little too disorganized—too many hands, too little focus.

After your meal, take a walk up corso del Popolo to piazza dei Signori, in the historic center of Treviso, which contains three handsome buildings: Palazzo del Podestà, Palazzo dei Trecento, Palazzo Pretorio.

SUGGESTED DISHES

sarde in saor Fried and marinated sardines.

ravioli di branzino al ragù di capesante Ravioli stuffed with sea bass, served with a sauce of scallops, herbs, and butter.

risotto all'aragosta e cuori di carciofo Risotto with lobster and artichoke hearts.

petto di fagiano al tartufo nero e pepe rosa Breast of pheasant in a game sauce with black truffle, red peppercorns, parsley, and other herbs. Garnished with potatoes, spinach purée, and a little buckshot, to keep the dish honest.

casatella A creamy white cheese.

sorbetto al limone Lemon sorbet.

SUGGESTED WINES

White

Tocai della Casa Pleasant enough—honest fruit in a dry format.

Red

Venegazzù della Casa, Gasparini Loredan Put together like a Bordeaux, this is an enjoyable, lovely wine with good color, some depth, and a clever, well-bred nose; all in all, a focused production of serious intent, yet not overly austere, tasting fresh and lively. Cabernet in evidence with everything up front: what you taste the first time around is what you get.

OTHER RECOMMENDED RESTAURANTS

In Pieve d'Alpago, 67km
Dolada
(0437) 479-141
AmX
Mon (except in July and Aug), Jan 9–Feb 3
7 Rooms, moderate

HOTELS

Continental
via Roma, 16
(0422) 57-216
AmX, Visa, Diners
Moderate
 A very pleasant, very well-located hotel. Comfortable, thoughtfully run, and low-keyed. The perfect base for walks in this charming town.

Turin/Torino

Alba 59 km *Aosta* 113 *Asti* 55 *Cremona* 214
 Cuneo 94 *Genoa* 170 *Milan* 140 *Piacenza* 180
  Soriso 130 *Stresa* 134 *Vercelli* 73

Turin, the capital of Piedmont, is the home of *grissini*, breadsticks, and Peyrano chocolate, and the birthplace of Fiat and Lancia automobiles. In some scholarly quarters it's considered, along with Prague and Lyons, one of Europe's three "magical" cities. Turin is known for its grand squares and parks, arcades, bookstores, and cafés. Be sure to stop in for coffee at the popular Caffé Florio in via Po; it dates back to the 1800s and was frequented by Friedrich Nietzsche. In fact, it was near this café that the famous story has him embracing a horse. Turin is a beautiful city in which to walk with or without purpose; along via Roma, lined with elegant stores, from piazza Carlo Felice to piazza Castello by way of piazza San Carlo, with its impressive arcades that are said to have inspired the artistic imagination of the Surrealist painter de Chirico. You might want to stop at the Duomo, where, in the Chapel of the Holy Shroud, is kept what some say is the shroud that was wrapped around Christ after he was taken from the cross—and according to the Church retains the imprint of his body. Having said this, I should add that through recent scholarship this historic relic itself has been shrouded in controversy.

Turin has been called "the most Italian city of France [*sic*]." It is heavily influenced by its European neighbor, and it's understood that more interesting and characteristic regional cuisine is to be found in other towns of the Piedmont, such as Cuneo (Boves), Asti, and Alba. If one had to select the most famous and beloved food product of the Piedmont, it would have to be the white truffle, *Tuber magnatum,* harvested in the area of Alba—thus its regional appellation *trifola d'Alba* (it's also known as *tartufo bianco*). White truffles are in season from late fall to the beginning of January; gray truffles (called by different names in different places; see page 36) are available most of the year and are similar to white truffles but without their intensity and power. The Piedmontese can find an excuse to shave a few truffle slices—or more—on just about anything, from rice to turkey to the famous *fonduta,* made with *fontina,* eggs, milk, and butter.

Then there are the great Piedmontese wines, the most notable made from the Nebbiolo grape—Barolo and Barbaresco, as well as Gattinara, Ghemme, Carema, and Nebbiolo d'Alba.

LA SMARRITA
★ ★ ★ ★ ½

REGION	Piedmont
ADDRESS	corso Unione Sovietica, 244
PHONE	(011) 390-657
CREDIT CARDS	AmX, Visa, Diners
CLOSED	Mon, Aug 3–27

CLASS	ATMOSPHERE	SERVICE	WINE	PRICE
3.5	3	4.5	5	VE

It's a little out of your way, but don't come to Turin and miss La Smarrita. When you arrive, finally, you'll have to ring the bell. You'll enter the restaurant through a bar and circular sitting area. The dining room is also circular; brown carpeting, a stucco ceiling with wood appointments, circular tables with orange chairs, white tablecloths, German china, hardy flatware—and beautiful Reidel wineglasses, on which money was obviously spent. The room is simple and nearly cozy, with its plants, bottles, and glasses. The restaurant is nothing special as far as looks, but you've come to the right place to eat. My only quarrel is with the slightly comic and inappropriate attire of the chef/owner and his assistants: a bell-ringer's garb, which looks like a Roman toga (La Smarrita was the bell rung in the fourteenth century by certain knights, to call in lost travelers).

SUGGESTED DISHES

moscardini con pomodoro e basilico   Small octopuses served with arugula, basil, and fresh tomatoes.

noci sgusciate con fonduta e tartufo d'Alba   An unusual dish: three walnut shells, each still containing the nut meat and filled with *fontina* cheese and white truffle, presented on grape leaves.

spaghetti con vongole e broccoletti   Spaghetti with clams and broccoli rabe.

pesce spada Chateaubriand   Grilled swordfish steak, cooked rare and served with grilled *radicchio* and zucchini blossoms.

filetto di cervo al vino rosso   A filet of rare venison, served with a Barolo sauce and garnished with bacon. Applesauce is served on the side.

selezione di formaggi piemontesi   A selection of regional cheeses: *murazzano, robiola d'Alba,* and *trunchet.*

SUGGESTED WINES

White

Chardonnay, Marchese di Gresy   A straight-shooting Chardonnay, woodless, with a clean, clear, ethereal perfume. Elegant, showing a great deal of finesse.

Monteriolo (Chardonnay), Luigi Coppo   Big Chardonnay and big (French) wood. A very full white, complicated, thick, full of narrative. A wine that strives to make a statement. Good color, vanilla nose.

Opera Prima (Nebbiolo), Alfredo Roagna The first impression is the note of austerity in the nose, followed by some inviting floral signals emerging from the deep ruby liquid. Excellent fruit, dry and expansive. A wine that's well made, if not multidimensional.

Barolo, Cannubi Boschis, Luciano Sandrone A big wine, announced by nearly restrictive tannin, rough-and-tumble. Warm, striving for generosity, with plenty to share right now—and plenty to put aside for another day.

VECCHIA LANTERNA
★ ★ ★ ½

REGION	Piedmont
ADDRESS	corso Re Umberto, 21
PHONE	(011) 537-047
CREDIT CARDS	AmX, Visa, Diners
CLOSED	Sun, Sat lunch, Aug 10–20

CLASS	ATMOSPHERE	SERVICE	WINE	PRICE
4	3.5	2.5	3	VE

Vecchia Lanterna is a rather formal, old-world restaurant with gold flocked walls, Persian rugs, overwhelming Venetian chandeliers, lovely crocheted white tablecloths, and 130-year-old plates for the place settings. You might say this is an example of bad taste gone right, an observation reinforced by a rather schmaltzy piano player who will accompany your meal. Let the chef-owner—not the rather uninformed waiters—select a tasting menu for you.

SUGGESTED DISHES

*filetto di salmerino al vapore con insalatina all'aceto balsamico A rolled slice of steamed salmon trout—a pink-and-white-fleshed fish—with a mustard cream sauce, placed on a bed of chicory and parsley dressed with balsamic vinegar.

punte d'asparagi con morbidelle di piccione Asparagus tips, with quenelles of pigeon and pigeon brains in an asparagus sauce.

maltagliati tartufati con ragoût di Barbaresco
Light, flat, irregular pasta with pieces of duck in a Barbaresco wine sauce.

petto di anatra all'essenza d'arancia Sliced duck
breast in an orange sauce. Garnished with vegetables.

sella di cervo alla Monviso Saddle of venison.

mousse di cioccolato con panna montata Chocolate mousse with sweet whipped cream.

SUGGESTED WINES

White

Gavi, San Pietro Golden, fruity, light, simple, and
cheerful—not as dry or steely as Gavi from La Scolca.

Red

Darmagi, Gaja A giant red from this fine producer, its
first Cabernet grown in Barbaresco soil. Beautifully made,
elegant, showing some signs of softness and intense fruit,
but still a very young wine.

DEL CAMBIO
★ ★ ½

REGION	Piedmont
ADDRESS	piazza Carignano, 2
PHONE	(011) 546-690
CREDIT CARDS	AmX, Visa, Diners
CLOSED	Sun, July 27–Aug 27

CLASS	ATMOSPHERE	SERVICE	WINE	PRICE
3.5	3.5	3	3	E

Beautifully appointed, if a bit worn about the edges, old-world establishment (est. 1757). Tall mirrors, dark wood floors, plush red velvet chairs, large ornate glass chandeliers, and gold trim around everything but the waiters. The walls are decorated with paintings by the nineteenth-century painter Bonelli. A marriage of seedy and elegant. If you're staying at the Jolly Principe di Piemonte, it's an easy five-minute walk.

SUGGESTED DISHES

insalata di faraona al tartufo nero   A salad of guinea fowl with black truffle.

finanziera del Cambio   A "dry" stew (almost no liquid at all) of chicken and chicken liver, mushrooms, cocks' combs, sweetbreads, and truffles. Supposedly a favorite dish of nineteenth-century businessmen.

*involtino di salmone in fili di patate con salsa tartara   Long strings of deep-fried potato shaped into a bundle containing a fillet of barely cooked salmon. Served with a tartare sauce and garnished with carrot and orange purée.

fritto misto alla piemontese   Mixed fried food: beef, veal, liver, chicken, lamb, sausage, brains, sweetbreads, eggplant, zucchini, mushrooms—that is, almost anything the chef can lay his hands on. A typical dish of the Piedmont, and slightly on the heavy side.

spumone di cioccolato alla crema gianduja   Chocolate ice cream with a chocolate-hazelnut cream.

SUGGESTED WINES

White

Arneis, Blangè, Ceretto A refined and subtle white, it has been described gracefully by Victor Hazan: "Its rich straw yellow color with flashes of brilliant gold signal from the first Arneis's notable character. The aroma is subtly fruited, possibly recalling that of pears, and the bouquet is fine and forthright. The succulent taste flows with velvety smoothness toward a buoyant aftertaste.... Alcohol is substantial, between 12% and 13%, but in elegant balance with acidity and fruit."

Red

Nebbiolo d'Alba, Occhetti di Monteu, Ratti A light, simple wine with a charm that's of the moment, appropriate for lunch. Colored brown to orange at the rim; nevertheless, a pleasantly grapey wine, and without the complexity to tax your daytime palate.

OTHER RECOMMENDED RESTAURANTS

Al Gatto Nero
corso Filippo Turati, 14
(011) 590-414
AmX, Visa, Diners
Closed Sun, Aug

In Caselle Torinese
Antica Zecca
via della Zecca, 9 (in the Jet Hotel)
(011) 996-3733
AmX, Visa, Diners
Closed Mon, Aug 3–19

If you find yourself at the Turin airport, this is the place to eat—and the hotel is also excellent, if you need to spend the night. Try the mixed grill, or the fine *coniglio farcito con salsa tartufata,* stuffed rabbit with a truffle mayonnaise sauce made with a dash of raspberry vinegar.

Due Lampioni-da Carlo
via Carlo Alberto, 45

The place appears to be run by kids who don't have a clue about running a restaurant. The food is indifferent to bad—*risotto* in five minutes?—the service nonexistent, and the wine steward, a young man doing a poor imitation of Sal Mineo, pours himself a hefty half-glass of *your* wine, holds it up to the light (what's he looking for?), sets it down, pours your wine, and takes his glass to the other room, sipping as he goes, where he finishes it—at his leisure.

HOTELS

Jolly Principi di Piemonte
via Gobetti, 15
(011) 519-693
AmX, Visa, Diners
Expensive

Not an inspired hotel, but the most comfortable of those in town. Very well located. The rooms are nicer than the lobby might suggest.

Villa Sassi
strada al Traforo del Pino, 47
(011) 890-556
AmX, Visa, Diners
Expensive

Located on the edge of town, on the other side of the river, Villa Sassi is a small, excellent hotel that's slept travelers for over 200 years, evidently with considerable success. The hotel is a beautiful old villa with stunning grounds, peaceful and well-kept. It has been completely renovated, so the rooms are quite comfortable. The public rooms are grand, and the terrace is the place for afternoon tea or a drink.

Directions. Leave the Milan *autostrada* through the main Torino exit (Centro) onto corso Giulio Cesare. At the second light (there's an *automercato* there), go left onto corso Lungo Stura Lazio and cross the river (there's a little loop before you cross). Where the road splits, veer left to corso Casale. Go left for a short distance and turn right, onto strada al Traforo del Pino, which is a large two-way street with a grass divider. The hotel is just up the road, on your left.

Turin Palace Hotel
via Sacchi, 8
(011) 515-511
AmX, Visa, Diners
Expensive

Located just beyond piazza Carlo Felice and thus not as central as the Jolly, this was once a fine old world hotel. It has recently celebrated its hundredth year, and the rooms have been renovated and contain the basic modern conveniences, but most of the charm seems to have worn away with age. Maybe even a note of dreariness.

FOOD AND WINE SHOPS, MARKETS

Food

There are a number of excellent food stores along via Lagrange; three in particular, run by the Castagno family, are worth checking out: La Bottega del Maiale at 38, for meat; La Baita del Formaggio at 36, for cheese; and Salumeria Rosticceria Castagno at 34, for food that's already prepared and ready to go—salads, roast meats, various cooked vegetables, among others.

Peyrano
corso Moncalieri, 47

This shop/factory is famous for some of the best chocolate in the world.

Wine

Enoteca Casa del Barolo
via Andrea Doria, 7

A good selection of regional wines, as well as wines from all over Italy. Gigi Molinaro, the owner, will be more than willing to help you with any questions you might have.

Markets

The Porta Palazzo market, with its vast array of foodstuffs, is the one to visit in Turin. You can lose yourself for an hour or two, wandering from one seductive stack of fruits and vegetables to another. The general energy level of the market is intoxicating and infectious.

THE DUCAL PALACE
OF URBINO

This imposing palace, once home to the court of Urbino, contains an extremely important collection of Renaissance art in Italy. The Galleria Nazionale delle Marche, or National Gallery of the Marches, includes works by Paolo Uccello, Piero della Francesca, Raphael and Titian. The *studiolo,* or little study, of Federico, Duke of Montefeltro, features an outstanding example of trompe l'oeil wooden inlay, possibly designed by Botticelli. The gallery is closed afternoons except Fridays and Saturdays.

Urbino

Ancona 103 km	*Arezzo* 107	*Bologna* 186
Fano 47 *Florence* 164	*Gubbio* 72	*Perugia* 101
Pesaro 36 *Ravenna* 128	*Rimini* 76	*Siena* 172

One doesn't visit the walled town of Urbino, birthplace of Raphael, for the food: this is one of the necessary stops because of the art in the gallery of Palazzo Ducale, the palace of the benevolent Duke of Urbino, Federico da Montefeltro, who turned this town into something extraordinary during his years in the Renaissance. An aficionado of art as well as a soldier, the Duke surrounded himself with some of the most important artists of the time, including the master of the fifteenth century, Piero della Francesca. An interesting story is told about the Duke: evidently, there was a hunting accident in which a falcon clawed out his right eye. After the court surgeon took care of the injury, the Duke had his doctor cut a groove in the bridge of his nose, which would allow his ever-cautious left eye to detect and thereby avoid an attack originating from his right side. This story perhaps explains the strange profile of the Duke as painted by Piero in the portrait in the Uffizi.

Approaching Urbino is almost as good as the actual arrival, especially if you're coming through the mountains from the Umbrian side; one of the most spectacular drives in Italy. The nearly perfect hill town rises suddenly out of the softly rounded hills of the Umbrian Apennines, surrounded by grape vines and cypresses. The powerful sight of the turreted façade of Palazzo Ducale announces the town, with a breathtaking soberness and elegance.

NUOVO COPPIERE
★ ★

REGION	The Marches
ADDRESS	via Porta Maja, 20
PHONE	(0722) 320-092
CREDIT CARDS	AmX, Visa, Diners
CLOSED	Wed, Feb

CLASS	ATMOSPHERE	SERVICE	WINE	PRICE
2	2	3	1	I

It's a two-minute walk from Palazzo Ducale. It's modest, to be sure, with black cane chairs and a pleasant clutter of things placed happily around the room, including a rather bizarre collection of psychedelic and primitive, childlike paintings. But the proprietors, Benny and Lucia, are very nice and take a considerable amount of pride in their restaurant. A decent meal can be had here.

SUGGESTED   DISHES

tagliatelle di pasta fresca all'amatriciana   Fresh flat noodles, with a sauce of tomatoes, onions, bacon, and hot red pepper.

agnello nostrano al forno   Roast lamb from this area.

brasato al Barolo con crostone di polenta   Beef braised in Barolo wine and served with a slice of grilled *polenta.*

medaglione del Duca Federico   A thick slice of veal with a fresh tomato sauce.

filetto di bue alla brace   A charcoal-grilled beef fillet.

*tiramisù   Literally "pick-me-up": a rich dessert made with cream, *mascarpone, espresso,* liquor, ladyfingers, and chocolate.

The wine list won't make your day. I suggest the house wines, white Verdicchio and red Sangiovese di Romagna.

OTHER RECOMMENDED RESTAURANTS

Vecchia Urbino
via dei Vasari 3–5
(0722) 4447
AmX, Visa, Diners
Closed Tues, Oct 1–Feb 28

Venice/Venezia

Bologna 152 km	*Florence* 254	*Milan* 267	
Modena 189	*Padua* 37	*Parma* 214	*Ravenna* 145
Rome 528	*Treviso* 30	*Verona* 114	*Vicenza* 69

How does one recognize Venetian painting? By a brilliance of color, some say (Antonello's secret); by a greater luminosity, say others (the light of the lagoons). By the subject matter, many would confess, meaning the milky-breasted goddesses, with pearls braided in their gold coiffures, of Titian, Tintoretto, and Veronese, or the views of Guardi and Canaletto. I would say that it identifies itself—and it is always unmistakable—by an enhanced reality, a reverence for the concrete world

—MARY MCCARTHY

Chi no ghe piase el vin, Dio ghe toga l'acqua.
(God will take water away from him who does not like wine.)

—*Venetian saying*

Venice is located on over 100 islands, and it's reported there are 150 canals and nearly 400 bridges. The street terminology, perhaps demanded by the waterways, is a little different here: a "canal" is called a *rio,* with the exception of Canal Grande and Canale della Giudecca; "street" is *calle, calletta, callesella, ramo,* or *salizzada*; "quay" or "embankment" *riva, rio, fondamenta, larga, rughetta,* or *ruga*; and the passage under a house is a *sottoportego.* There's only one big "piazza" in Venice—piazza San Marco—and numerous "squares" of more moderate size, called *campi.* A "small square" is a *campiello* or *campazzo.*

There are those who argue that Venetians invented the fork and used it while the rest of the civilized world was still eating with their hands. Some say it was the Venetians who first thought to serve calf's liver with onions. And there are those who believe Marco Polo, a son of Venice, brought the first pasta to Italy. It's best not to argue these matters with Venetians. With regard to the last claim—and in the interest of native cuisine and historical accuracy—I quote Fred Plotkin: "If Marco Polo brought Chinese noodles back to Venice in 1279, it was probably to compare them with the pasta already made on the Italian peninsula. Spaghetti, it seems, first appeared in Sicily, though the date is uncertain." It *is* certain that Venice has been an important and creative gastronomical center, both in terms of its region, the Veneto, and nationally—and early on, Venice was Italy's supplier of spices. There are those who say the Venetian trademark dish has to be *risi e bisi,* a rice and pea combination that's considered a soup by some, a *risotto* by others. But another group will tell you it's the Venetian liver and onion dish mentioned above, *fegato alla veneziana,* that's most notable; and still others suggest it's the Venetian *scampi* that most epitomize Venetian cuisine. Again, to avoid unnecessary and unresolvable controversy, suffice it to say that Venice boasts of many, many dishes—especially those employing rice and seafood. Ironically, for all her involvement with the world of gastronomy, Venice remains without a truly notable restaurant.

The city has contributed in other ways to the evolution of Italian culture. The list of artists of the Venetian school is more than illustrious: the Bellinis—father Jacopo and sons Gentile and Giovanni, who's the most important of the three; Carpaccio, Giorgione, Lotto, Titian, Veronese, and Tintoretto. The composer Antonio Vivaldi was Venetian. Venice has always attracted important visitors, who have been profoundly affected by this hermetic city: Thomas Mann used Venice as the setting for his masterpiece *Death in Venice,* and Goethe wrote of the Grand Canal: "the most beautiful street in the world."

SPECIAL SIGHTS
OF VENICE

A few essential Venetian highlights:

St. Mark's Square This could be the most famous square in the world—if you're here during the high tourist months, it will certainly seem so!

Doges' Palace (closed Sunday afternoons)
The center of Venetian political power, the Palazzo dei Dogi or Palazzo Ducale was home of the doges from the ninth century until the collapse of the republic, at the very end of the eighteenth century. It now houses works by Giovanni Bellini, Carpaccio, Bosch, Titian, Tiepolo, Tintoretto (*Paradise*—one of the largest oil paintings in the world), and Veronese. And don't miss the Scala dei Giganti, the Giants' Stairs, and the Scala d'Oro, the Golden Stairs.

Bridge of Sighs (closed Sunday afternoons)
The famous bridge runs from the Doges' Palace to Pozzi Prison; the condemned would sigh for their fate when crossing it. Casanova made a daring escape from the prison in the eighteenth century.

Gallerie dell'Accademia (closed Mondays and afternoons)
The picture galleries of the art academy display works by Giovanni Bellini (*San Giobbe Altarpiece, Madonna with St. Catherine and the Magdalene, Madonna with Doge Mocenigo, Madonna and Saints*), Carpaccio (*Presentation in the Temple,* the St. Ursula cycle), Piero della Francesca (*St. Jerome*), Giorgione (*La Tempesta*), Mantegna (*St. George*), Tintoretto (*Miracle of St. Mark Freeing a Slave*), Titian (*Presentation of the Virgin, St. John the Baptist,* and his last work, a *Pietà*), Paolo Veneziano (*Coronation of the Virgin*), and Veronese (*Feast in the House of Levi*).

Collezione Peggy Guggenheim (closed November–March mornings, Tuesdays)
The collection, in Peggy Guggenheim's former residence, includes works by Picasso, Pollock, Chagall, Kandinsky, Ernst, Klee, Magritte, Bacon, Duchamp, Braque, Brancusi, Motherwell, and Rothko.

Scuola di San Rocco (closed afternoons November–February, except Saturdays and Sundays)
Fifty-six paintings by Tintoretto can be found in this "school," (these *scuole* were variously schools, meeting places for nobles, community centers). Note especially the *Crucifixion*, which Tintoretto considered his finest work.

Scuola di San Giorgio degli Schiavoni (closed Sunday afternoons and Mondays)
The sixteenth-century building is known for its works by Carpaccio, especially scenes from the life of St. Jerome.

Basilica di San Marco The glamour of St. Mark's has earned it the name Chiesa d'Oro, Church of Gold. A mix of styles—Byzantine, Romanesque, Gothic, and Renaissance—it contains important Byzantine and Renaissance mosaics. See especially the fourth-century bronze horses in the museum of the basilica; the tenth-century golden altarpiece called the Pala d'Oro in the chancel; and the Tesoro (Treasury).

Santa Maria della Salute This church, begun in 1631 by the architect Longhena and completed fifty-six years later, was the fulfillment of a pledge to the Virgin for delivering Venice from the plague. Here are works by Titian and Tintoretto (take special note of his great *Marriage at Cana*).

San Giorgio Maggiore A Palladian church built in the middle of the sixteenth century, it contains important works by Tintoretto, including a Last Supper and *The Shower of Manna*.

OSTERIA DA FIORE
★ ★ ★

REGION	Veneto
ADDRESS	calle del Scaleter, San Polo, 2202
PHONE	(041) 721-308
CREDIT CARDS	AmX, Diners
CLOSED	Sun, Mon, Aug 1–22, Dec 25–Jan 6

CLASS	ATMOSPHERE	SERVICE	WINE	PRICE
3	3.5	2.5	2	E

A long rectangular dining room, inviting and warm. A place for hip Venetians. The room is decorated sparingly, with dark wood paneling, comfortable, padded black chairs, white-striped yellow material on the walls, and yellow tablecloths. A nice array of flowers adds color and scent to the room. Maurizio Martin, the owner, will help you order, since there's no menu or wine list. Given the popularity of this place among Venetians, it's best to reserve ahead of time, a few days or more.

SUGGESTED DISHES

gamberetti alla griglia   Salted and grilled shrimp.

cappe lunghe e ostriche   Razor (or tube) clams and oysters with a sauce of cheese, cream, and white wine, placed under the broiler for a moment—similar to clams casino.

insalata di branzino e gamberetti   Sea bass and shrimp in a mayonnaise sauce.

taglierini gratinati con verdure e gamberetti Gratinéed thin noodles, with vegetables and shrimp in a green sauce.

SUGGESTED WINES

White

Chardonnay, Deroa   A highly perfumed white, pale yellow with green highlights and a hint of fizz. Delightful.

Pinot Grigio, Collio, Marco Felluga   The owner's suggestion: a crisp, well-balanced white from the Collio region of Friuli. Good acidity and a light finish; very pale, elegant. Friuli is known for its fine white wines.

CORTE SCONTA
★ ★ ★

REGION	Veneto
ADDRESS	calle del Pestrin, Castello, 3886
PHONE	(041) 522-7024
CREDIT CARDS	AmX, Diners
CLOSED	Sun, Mon

CLASS	ATMOSPHERE	SERVICE	WINE	PRICE
2	2	3	2	M

Corte Sconta, in the picturesque section of campo San Lorenzo, is a bare-bones restaurant with hard, uncomfortable chairs, white walls, crudely covered light bulbs, paper placemats and napkins: basic, that is. Now, as have many working-class *trattorie*—Il Latini and Antico Fattore in Florence, for example—it has been taken up by the *cognoscenti* of the eating world, Italian and foreigner alike. There's no menu here, but the waiters, almost entirely women, are supremely informed and helpful, if at times slightly impatient. The restaurant's reputation has gone up and down: first, the discovery—good cheap seafood; then, with popularity, the old story of prices up and quality down. But it's once again on the ascent and is certainly worth a visit for lunch in a town with too few exciting restaurants.

SUGGESTED DISHES

I've listed a few dishes sampled recently at Corte Sconta—in English, as the dishes defy naming. In any case, they change daily, as the chef employs the day's catch in inventive combinations. You're best advised to let one of the waiters make a selection from what's freshest.

*A plate of razor clams; mussels minced with garlic, bread, and parsley; and scallops grilled with oil and served in their shells with parsley, garlic, and a splash of cognac.

A salad of shrimp, octopus, scampi, sea snails, anchovies, and squid eggs.

A plate of sardines covered with sweet and sour onions, pine nuts, and raisins, served with grilled *polenta*.

Short, thick pasta with a sweet-and-sour sauce of sardines, mushrooms, tomatoes, and parsley; the mushroom flavor dominates the sardines.

White

Prosecco di Valdobbiadene   A still *prosecco,* pale, frail, and quite pleasant. The wine is brought in *barriques* from a local vineyard and is bottled by the restaurant.

Ronco delle Acacie, Abbazia di Rosazzo   A graceful, elegant wine with a welcome burst of fresh fruit and flowers. Behind the perfume just the right touch of oak emerges, with a moment of mesmerizing wood. From Friuli, a regional neighbor.

AL GRASPO DE UA
★ ★ ★

REGION	Veneto
ADDRESS	calle dei Bombaseri, 5094
PHONE	(041) 522-3647
CREDIT CARDS	AmX, Visa, Diners
CLOSED	Mon, Tues, Dec 20–Jan 3

CLASS	ATMOSPHERE	SERVICE	WINE	PRICE
3	3	3	2	M

In a city of endless charm, it is surprisingly difficult to find a memorable meal in a restaurant here. Al Graspo de Ua is quite traditional, but considerably warmer and cozier than most places in Venice. The chairs are comfortable and the yellow tablecloths cheerful. Much of the food is agreeably displayed in glass cases or on open plates: various fish and shellfish, spinach, onions, celery, carrots, red and yellow peppers, *porcini* mushrooms, kiwi, pears, apples, grapes, pineapples, melons, and so on. The owner, Andrea Moro, has seen to it that his establishment is run with care. It's clear that he's given considerable thought to the workings of his restaurant, the food, and the men who work for him. Al Graspo de Ua is in a back street, between San Marco and the Rialto Bridge, closer to the latter. Ask for Andrea himself, or the waiter Gianni.

SUGGESTED DISHES

schie con la polenta   Baby shrimp lightly spiced and served with the ubiquitous block of grilled *polenta*. A specialty of Venice, available from October to January.

vermicelli con gamberi alla busara Long, thin noodles served with vegetables and seafood—mussels, clams, baby shrimp—in a light tomato sauce.

cernia alla bragoseto Grouper served in a tomato-seafood sauce made with shrimp, mussels, and clams. Potatoes on the side.

*insalata verde A perfect green salad, dressed with vinegar or lemon—as you like it.

tiramisù An excellent rendition of this rich dessert made with *mascarpone*, cream, *espresso*, liquor, ladyfingers, and chocolate. Worth every calorie it tags you with.

SUGGESTED WINES

White

Pinot Bianco, Collio, Formentini Light, bright, and white. Good mellow fruit immediately evident, crisp and up-front. It's excellent with the seafood.

HARRY'S BAR				
★ ★ ½				
REGION	Veneto			
ADDRESS	calle Vallaresso, 1323			
PHONE	(041) 523-6797			
CREDIT CARDS	AmX, Visa, Diners			
CLOSED	Mon, Jan 3–Feb 3			
CLASS	ATMOSPHERE	SERVICE	WINE	PRICE
3.5	3	3	2	VE

Harry's, for all its grand tradition, is a spare, brightly lit restaurant, plain and rectangular, slightly reminiscent of a New York City men's club: dark wood wainscotting, leather chairs, and yellow tablecloths, with closely gathered tables. Its very legend seems the restaurant's primary claim to fame—that and the peach-juice-and-*spumante* Bellini; certainly it is not any longer the food or atmosphere. On one occasion the cheese I ordered was served straight from the refrigerator, with no taste at all. Nevertheless, it is one of the possible choices you can make while in Venice.

zuppa di pesce A soup of various fish, flavored with saffron.

cannelloni alle melanzane *Cannelloni* stuffed with veal and topped with eggplant and cheese.

fegato alla veneziana con polenta The traditional Venetian fare: liver cut into pieces and sautéed with onions and parsley, served with *polenta*.

castraure delle isole Baby eggplant cooked in oil, garlic, and parsley—a specialty of early spring.

S U G G E S T E D   W I N E S

Aperitivo

Bellini Harry's specialty, peach juice and Asti Spumante.

White

Bianco di Custoza, Tenuta di San Pietro A crisp, clean white with good fruit in the taste and a whiff of the floral in the nose. Not a big wine, but capable of producing pleasure.

Red

Valpolicella, Valpantena, Bertani A ruby-bright, grapey wine of medium weight. Playfully bitter on the finish.

ANTICO MARTINI
★ ★ ½

REGION	Veneto
ADDRESS	campo San Fantin, 1983
PHONE	(041) 522-4121
CREDIT CARDS	AmX, Visa, Diners
CLOSED	Tues, Wed lunch, Jan 10–March 15, Dec 12–21

CLASS	ATMOSPHERE	SERVICE	WINE	PRICE
3.5	3	3	3	E

The immediate and somewhat deceiving impression you get upon entering this well-known Venetian restaurant is one of elegance—tile floors, fine and unusual paintings, handsome curtains, an elaborate chandelier, beautifully set tables accompanied by very comfortable chairs. In the end, however, you're left with the impression that it's all a little too theatrical, if not downright stagey. The overproduced red and black menu, in Italian, English, French, and German, is unhappily reminiscent of the tourist menus seen around town. And then the set of questionable dishes: smoked salmon with caviar, Scottish salmon, Indian-style lamb kebab, and crêpes Suzette. Nevertheless, eating on the terrace here—which faces the lovely Teatro La Fenice—during the summer months is one of the "experiences" a diner can have in Venice. Although very few Italians have been in attendance when I've dined here (which is not a good sign), in a town that doesn't offer an abundance of choices, it's worth keeping this restaurant in mind. The wine list includes a good and inexpensive regional selection.

SUGGESTED DISHES

lasagnette con funghi porcini Irregularly shaped pieces of flat pasta with a *porcini* mushroom sauce.

filetto di sogliola Martini Fillet of sole served in a seafood sauce.

branzino alla griglia Grilled sea bass.

galletto novello alle erbe Roasted chicken flavored with a variety of herbs.

tiramisù Literally "pick-me-up": a rich dessert made with *mascarpone*, cream, *espresso*, liquor, ladyfingers, and chocolate.

SUGGESTED WINES

White

Breganze di Breganze, Maculan An excellent Venetian white. Dreamy pale yellow in color, it's spunky but elegant, with generous fruit. It's been described as buoyant and vivacious.

Red

Venegazzù della Casa, Gasparini Loredan Put together like a Bordeaux, this is an enjoyable, lovely wine with good color, some depth, and a clever, well-bred nose;

all in all, a focused production of serious intent, yet not overly austere, tasting fresh and lively. Cabernet in evidence with everything up front: what you taste the first time around is pretty much what you get — no second thoughts.

LOCANDA CIPRIANI
★ ★ ½

REGION	Veneto
ADDRESS	on Torcello Island
PHONE	(041) 730-150
CREDIT CARDS	AmX, Visa
CLOSED	Tues, Nov 11–March 18

CLASS	ATMOSPHERE	SERVICE	WINE	PRICE
2.5	3.5	2	1	E

A fine old rustic restaurant, appointed with dark wood, tiled floors, and blue tablecloths. Outside, beautiful gardens provide much of the atmosphere here. This means lunch on the terrace in good weather. It's absolutely worth the boat ride to picturesque Torcello, followed by a lovely five-minute walk to the restaurant, along a canal left over from some romantic Italian movie from the thirties. When you arrive at the Cipriani, ask for Dario De Zoazi, who will make certain nothing's lacking. The restaurant is not related to the hotel of the same name on Giudecca island. A fine outing if the weather's right.

Directions. Catch the boat marked "Torcello" in front of the Hotel Danieli. The fifty-minute ride costs about 17,000 lire. The boat leaves Venice at 12:30, and leaves Torcello for Venice at 3:30. You may also hire a private boat.

SUGGESTED   DISHES

brodetto di pesce   A very decent fish soup.

risotto di pesce   *Risotto* made with fresh fish.

*granceole all'olio e limone   Spider crabs served in the shell with a lively oil and lemon sauce. With its subtle taste, this is an elegant starter and a house favorite.

tagliatelle verdi gratinate   Thin green noodles, gratinéed with cheese and ham. The pasta is done exactly right, with the correct amount of cheese for the sauce.

---

coda di rospo alla griglia   Monkfish lightly grilled with a little parsley and oil; solid rich white meat, no bones. Monkfish is quite underrated in Italy, and consequently it's almost always reasonably priced.

SUGGESTED   WINES

Because there's no wine list to speak of, I recommend sticking to the house wines, both local products, serviceable if not unforgettable.

White

Soave   The house white: mid range, without obvious character defects, a quiet dining companion.

Red

Cabernet, Sant'Osvaldo   A local wine without any particular luster, but with its modest lightness pleasant enough for lunch.

OTHER   RECOMMENDED RESTAURANTS

Da Ivo
calle dei Fuseri, 1809
(041) 528-5004
AmX, Visa, Diners
Closed Sun, Jan

Best for lunch, Da Ivo is a cozy little eating establishment—apparently well-known to the British crowd. It's a place where for a decent price you can have very good grilled monkfish, *coda di rospo alla brace,* or grilled sea bass, *branzino alla brace.* The coals over which the food is grilled come from olive trees. You might want to start with the hearty *penne paesane cacciatore,* quill-shaped pasta with mushrooms, tomatoes, and wine. Simple, decent Venetian fare.

La Colomba
piscina di Frezzeria, 1665
(041) 522-1175
AmX, Diners
Closed Wed in winter

This used to be a quiet place where you went for solid, straightforward food in a clean-cut, white-walled restaurant.

The food hasn't improved, but La Colomba *has* become slightly overpopulated with tourists, so booking is now required. Still, it's a pleasant restaurant with contemporary paintings on the white walls. Many different dishes are offered on the ever-changing list of "Piatti del Giorno," or plates of the day. I recently sampled *schie con polenta*, baby shrimp served with *polenta*, a specialty of Venice available only from October to January; *moleche*, excellent deep-fried soft-shell crabs; and *tartufi e ostriche*, truffles and oysters. And there are old standards, such as *cannelloni Colomba*, prepared decently with cheese; *risotto ai frutti di mare*, a quite good seafood *risotto*; and *cartoccio Colomba*, fish baked in parchment paper.

R E S T A U R A N T S   T O   A V O I D

La Caravella
calle larga 22 Marzo, 2397
  A Venetian tourist trap. My opinion.

H O T E L S

Cipriani
Isola della Giudecca, 10
(041) 520-7744
AmX, Visa, Diners
Very expensive/Luxury
  This is without doubt one of the finest hotels in the world—certainly it can compete with any I've stayed in. Of course, there'a a price to pay for perfection, and you pay it here. If you decide to bite the bullet and book a room or suite here, you'll enter the kingdom of the gifted manager Natale Rusconi, who knows his business like nobody's business, and you'll be treated to what life at the top is supposed to be. The hotel itself is situated on the island of Giudecca, a five-minute boat ride via the hotel's gratis private launch, which runs as needed. It picks you up and drops you off in Venice at piazzetta San Marco, just off the larger piazza; if the boat isn't waiting for you, there's a free phone that connects you to the hotel, and the boat appears five minutes later if it's not already on its way. Nothing has been overlooked by Dottor Rusconi, from the soap and towels in the bathrooms to the beautiful antique furniture to the elegant public spaces around the ho-

tel. There are various places to eat, inside and out, near an incredible pool. An unforgettable breakfast is served as part of the ticket: fresh orange juice; hot and cold cereal; your choice of breads, croissants, and rolls; eggs as you like them; and a sumptuous buffet that beckons you with cheeses, cold cuts, fresh fruit, and so on and so on. Tennis courts and a fitness center with steam bath, sauna, and massage are also to be enjoyed. It's difficult to describe the pleasure of approaching the Cipriani in the little hotel launch after a busy day doing battle with the crowds of Venice. The peace, quiet, and luxury this haven offers its patrons should be tried at least once in this lifetime.

Gritti Palace
campo Santa Maria del Giglio, 2467
(041) 794-611
AmX, Visa, Diners
Very expensive/Luxury

When one thinks of Venetian hotels, it's often the Gritti that first leaps to mind: considerably romantic rooms on the Grand Canal, handsome sixteenth-century mullioned windows, elegant furnishings in the lobby, a portrait by Titian of the doge Andrea Gritti (for whom the hotel was named) hanging in one of the lounges—and the feeling of merely *being* in the hotel where such notables as John Ruskin, Charles Dickens, George Sand, Somerset Maugham, and Ernest Hemingway stayed during their sojourns in Venice. One of Italy's premier luxury hotels.

Londra Palace
riva degli Schiavoni, 4171
(041) 520-0533
AmX, Visa, Diners
Expensive

This hotel faces the Church of San Giorgio Maggiore and was Tchaikovsky's favorite in Venice—in fact, he wrote his Fourth Symphony here. The Londra Palace opts for warmth and comfort over surface glitz and fancy.

Danieli
riva degli Schiavoni, 4196
(041) 522-6480
AmX, Visa, Diners/Very expensive/Luxury

Monaco e Grand Canal
calle Vallaresso, 1325
(041) 520-0211
AmX, Visa
Expensive

Very well located, a few yards from the San Marco *vaporetto* landing, the Monaco is elegant, understated, and comfortable—and priced somewhat lower than the larger luxury hotels. Be sure to get a room on the Grand Canal; it will require a little haggling, but it's worth the effort in order to watch the hypnotizing comings and goings on the water.

FOOD AND WINE SHOPS, MARKETS

Food

Sbrissa
In the Rialto market

A reasonably good selection of local cheeses.

Wine

Al Volto
San Luca, calle Cavalli, 4081

The best place in Venice to sample wines from all over the country is from Giancarlo Carbon's cellar—by the glass or bottle, with a small but tasty bite to eat. Just a hole-in-the-wall, it's very atmospheric, both in the rustic decor and in the serious Venetian clientele.

Markets

The Rialto market, next to the bridge of the same name, is the largest in Venice, and by far the most colorful—especially that part which houses the incredible fish stalls. Plan to spend at least an hour here, the earlier the better. Elizabeth David calls this the most remarkable food market in Italy.

Verona

Verona is to my mind one of the most elegant and charming cities in Italy, which is to say anywhere in the world. Life begins in piazza delle Erbe, the Square of Herbs. Once the town's Roman forum, it now operates as a market, selling Verona's famous peaches and a variety of vegetables, as well as an assortment of Italian kitsch.

Verona is, of course, where Shakespeare set the story of the star-crossed lovers Romeo and Juliet, whose tragedy was acted out just as the 14th century was getting underway. If you're a believer, you'll want to make time to gaze on Juliet's balcony, located just off piazza delle Erbe at via Cappello, 23. If you're an opera buff, and perfect acoustics appeal to you, you'll want to investigate the Arena, a Roman amphitheater dating back to the end of the first century A.D.; said to be the third largest after the Colosseum in Rome and the amphitheater in Capua, it is now used for musical performances. And for those with a high regard for Dante, a coffee at Caffè Dante in piazza dei Signori is the required gesture; here you can take in the finely austere statue of the master, which holds center ground. (Dante came to Verona after he was exiled from Florence.) The Museo Civico d'Arte (closed Mondays) in the Castelvecchio, contains work by Pisanello, Jacopo and Giovanni Bellini, Mantegna, Veronese, Tintoretto, Lotto, and Tiepolo.

But for me the wonderful "sight" is the doors of San Zeno Maggiore. There are two things to pay attention to in this Romanesque church. First, the eleventh-to-twelfth-century bronze doors, with plaques depicting scenes from the Old and New Testaments and from the life of St. Zeno. Helen Langdon writes, "San Zeno is one of the masterpieces of northern Italian Romanesque architecture. The façade bears a charming and typical hodgepodge of relief sculpture, surrounding the celebrated bronze doors of the portal." The second item worthy of your attention is Mantegna's *San Zeno Triptych*. It was once "on loan" to Napoleon, and when it was returned it was missing the panels of the *predella,* which, not mysteriously, can be seen in the Louvre.

Verona, a Roman city situated on the Adige River, is a walking town. Begin at the Due Torri, a hotel in piazza Sant'Anastasia, and walk away from the river down corso Saint'Anastasia to piazza delle Erbe. Walk the length of this market square and on to the Arena by way of via Mazzini with its wonderful shops.

NUOVO MARCONI
★ ★ ★ ★

REGION	Veneto
ADDRESS	via Fogge, 4
PHONE	(045) 595-295
CREDIT CARDS	AmX, Visa, Diners
CLOSED	Sun

CLASS	ATMOSPHERE	SERVICE	WINE	PRICE
3.5	3.5	3.5	3	E

A warm restaurant patronized by plenty of the local well-to-do business people. A "serious" atmosphere, and yet completely affable. The tables, covered with yellow tablecloths, are quite close together, but the chairs are comfortable and the clientele is pleasant. The decorator must have favored variety, as evidenced by the mix of wood and other materials, and columns, arches, and other architectural elements. Eat upstairs or downstairs—your call. If your waiter forgets, ask for the *olive fritte* (fried olives).

SUGGESTED   DISHES

luccio marinato   A salad of chopped, marinated pike served with *polenta*.

*insalata di mare   A salad of lobster, shrimp, a variety of mussels, whitefish, squid, and octopus.

polenta e funghi   Sautéed mushrooms served on a blanket of soft *polenta* with the texture of mashed potatoes.

risotto all'anitra   A rich duck *risotto*, well made.

spaghetti alle seppie nere   Spaghetti with slices of cuttlefish, and the ink—very black.

trancio di branzino ai ferri   A thick slice of grilled sea bass.

trancio di salmerino alla rucola A thick slice of salmon trout served with a sauce of arugula and cream.

filetto alla Pavarotti A fine, very light, fillet of beef, with an unobtrusive but tasty Amarone wine sauce.

sorbetto al limone An intense lemon sorbet.

SUGGESTED WINES

White

Soave, Gini, La Frosca Solid if subtle fruit with mid-range body. Tasty and engaging but not demanding. The finish seems just this side of flat, but not enough to really detract from the wine. Soave is *the* Verona white and you are obligated to try it—if not this one, someone else's.

Red

Recioto della Valpolicella Amarone, Bertani This wine from one of the top producers is solidly traditional Amarone, an Italian wine in the old style, tough, opinionated, and in need of full attention. It shows a deep garnet color and is thick, rich, velvety, and full in the mouth. If you haven't had an Amarone, remember that *amaro* means "bitter," which is the way this big guy comes to a close.

Dessert

Prato delle Rose, Russolo A wine in good balance, whose sweetness is subtle and enjoyable. A little rose in the bouquet.

IL DESCO
★ ★ ★ ½

REGION	Veneto
ADDRESS	via Dietro San Sebastiano, 7
PHONE	(045) 595-358
CREDIT CARDS	AmX, Visa, Diners
CLOSED	Sun, Jan 1–10, June 12–28

CLASS	ATMOSPHERE	SERVICE	WINE	PRICE
3.5	3.5	3	3.5	E

This relative newcomer—bear in mind that in Italy anything established after the war is considered a newcomer—was a convent in the sixteenth century, and the original beams remain very much in evidence. Il Desco (literally, "the table laid for a meal") is a darkish, attractive restaurant with a contemporary feeling: light-chocolate-colored walls decorated with patchwork hangings that echo the ceiling, which is composed of painted wood squares; handsome murals illuminated by modern Italian lamps; a fine Oriental carpet over gold-colored tiles. For those who have walked away the afternoon, there is the welcome soft support of the cordovan leather chairs. The well-laid, well-spaced tables are laden with Ginori. The main dining room has nine tables, all with correct indirect lighting, not always available in Italian restaurants. Where Nuovo Marconi is close, spritely, and old-world, Il Desco features quiet and subdued open space, with a *nouvelle* orientation. Taste the excellent starting breads—onion, olive, herb . . .

I should add that because the chef seems ever-present in the dining room, and the not unrelated indifference of some of the offerings on three separate occasions, the rating for this restaurant is lower than it might be.

Directions. The statue of Dante in piazza dei Signori, looks directly at the restaurant, which is about three minutes away, straight ahead.

SUGGESTED DISHES

insalata tiepida di coniglio con olio al tartufo   A slightly warm salad of rabbit with truffle oil.

calamari allo scalogno   Squid in a cream sauce with shallots, served with a slice of beet. The season to order squid is late fall.

bigoli con le sarde   Short, brown spaghetti-like pasta tossed in a sauce made with sardines. A local specialty.

taglierini rosa con calamaretti e fagioli   Pink noodles with squid and beans.

*animelle, cipolla fondente e capperi   Sweetbreads sautéed lightly, served with marinated onions and capers.

rognone di vitello all'aceto di lamponi, e verze   Veal kidney with a raspberry vinaigrette and savoy cabbage.

*petti di piccione al tartufo con flan di verdure   Pigeon breasts in a truffle sauce, served with a vegetable flan.

carré di agnello al forno, flan di verdure   Roasted rack of lamb served with a delicate dark sauce with a hint of ginger in it, and a vegetable flan.

selezione di formaggi con pane ai fichi   A selection of cheeses, served with fig bread.

crostata di mele con caramello di vino e gelato di datteri   Apple tart with a wine-caramel sauce and date ice cream.

*torta di mele calda con gelato al caramello   Warm, moist apple cake with a caramel sauce and caramel ice cream on the side.

SUGGESTED WINES

White

Soave Classico di Monteforte, Capitel Foscarino, Anselmi   Pretty, pale yellow, with tartness and good subtle fruit. Refreshing cool nose—a fresh, active, bright white.

Red

Campo Fiorin, Masi   Handsome garnet color with an interesting, slightly "old" nose (probably because this wine, basically a Valpolicella, is refermented on the skins of the grapes used to make Amarone). A trace of very appealing rose petals and other floral notes. Rich, deep, muted fruit—a luscious wine.

1981 Recioto della Valpolicella Amarone, Quintarelli   Rugged, deep red with nothing even approaching brown at the rim. A hot wine, alive, almost electric, with the trademark bitterness keeping the whole balance honest. Fruit in appealing evidence.

Dessert

Recioto di Soave, dei Capitelli, Anselmi   Gold, Sauterne-like, more rich than sweet, but a wine that remains on the surface, showing little depth; a good closing wine nevertheless.

ARCHE
★ ★ ★ ½

REGION	Veneto
ADDRESS	via Arche Scaligere, 6
PHONE	(045) 800-7415
CREDIT CARDS	Cash only
CLOSED	Sun, Mon lunch, June 25–July 17

CLASS	ATMOSPHERE	SERVICE	WINE	PRICE
3.5	3	3	3.5	E

This straightforward fish restaurant is reliable, unassuming, old-world, comfortable, and quiet—one might even go so far as to say sedate. And best of all, it's truly concerned with getting good food to your table without an abundance of fuss—a worthy enterprise. While it might not be the place to celebrate a great event, neither is it a place you'd want to miss if you had a free night in this beautiful city. The owner is interested in your well-being and is only waiting for the chance to guide you, so gently, in the right direction; this means the day's catch, which his chef has transformed into something wonderful. I'd trust the suggestions of the waiter—or even better, the owner—to get in on the right fish, which will be perfectly prepared. Don't neglect the buttered rosemary bread that arrives at your table after you're seated. Note the thoughtful wine list with a number of whites you don't ordinarily see, reasonably priced and totally suited to the menu.

SUGGESTED DISHES

insalatina di cozze e tartufo nero alla Vivaldi
Mussels with black truffle, served with salad greens.

insalatina tiepida di astice al basilico e rucola
A slightly warm salad of lobster, with basil and arugula.

*tartare di branzino, salmone e capasanta Tartare of sea bass, salmon, and scallops, served with marjoram bread.

ravioli di branzino con vongole veraci e pinoli
Ravioli stuffed with sea bass in a sauce of fresh clams and pine nuts.

branzino con frutti di mare al cartoccio   Sea bass
stuffed with shellfish and cooked in parchment.

SUGGESTED WINES

White

Breganze di Breganze, Maculan   An excellent white
from this region. Dreamy pale yellow in color, it's spunky
but elegant, with nice fruit. It has been described as buoyant and vivacious.

Bianco di Custoza, Cavalchina   A simple white,
clean with clear fruit and a slightly floral nose. Just enough
acidity keeps it honest and fun to drink.

12 APOSTOLI
★ ★ ★

REGION	Veneto
ADDRESS	corticella San Marco, 3
PHONE	(045) 596-999
CREDIT CARDS	AmX, Visa, Diners
CLOSED	Sun dinner, Mon, June 16–July 6

CLASS	ATMOSPHERE	SERVICE	WINE	PRICE
3	3.5	3.5	2.5	E

A good-sized, colorful restaurant, where you feel as if you've
wandered into the Middle Ages: brick archways, heavy iron
sconces, simple bronze chandeliers, and medieval-style murals
celebrating the seasons, the doors of San Zeno, the city of
Verona, painted in the sixties by Maestro Casarini. The atmosphere is festive, as if a celebration were about to begin,
with you in the middle of it. It's not what you'd call a warm
restaurant, but it is friendly. There's a handsome wine cellar
downstairs, which is used for special dinners. The restaurant
has fallen a little in the past five years, and although it's still
possible to get a first-rate meal, you're in no way assured of
it. It's important to order thoughtfully and to make yourself
known to one of the proprietors, or to the one waiter who
speaks English—his name is Gianni. Let him know you're
serious about your meals in Verona.

SUGGESTED DISHES

zuppa di funghi   A thick, rich, tasty mushroom soup—very fine.

torta di tartufi   A baked dish of truffles and cheese.

funghi al forno   Grilled mushrooms topped with sweet and sharp Gorgonzola and a local cheese called *grasso monte,* and baked, to melt the cheese. Garnished with black truffle.

tagliatelle "erbe fini"   Thin noodles with a sauce of fine herbs, Parmesan, and sautéed eggplant; the home-made pasta is cooked perfectly.

pastissada de caval   A stew made with horse meat, vinegar, wine, and various spices. A traditional dish of the Veneto.

petto di faraona al radicchio   Breast of guinea hen, served with *radicchio.*

SUGGESTED WINES

White

Soave, Pieropan Riserva dei 12 Apostoli   A solid house white, bottled especially for the restaurant's owners, Giorgio and Franco Gioco.

Red

Valpolicella, Allegrini Riserva dei 12 Apostoli   Another wine bottled for the restaurant. Spicy and rich with a little confusion in the nose, this rustic wine has an honest fruit and body. A drinkable if not memorable house wine.

HOTELS

Due Torri
piazza Sant'Anastasia, 4
(045) 595-044
AmX, Visa, Diners
Expensive

This fourteenth-century guest house of the Scaligeri, and later the Grand Hotel Impérial aux Deux Tours, is easily the best hotel in Verona. It's placed prettily next to the fine little Gothic church of Sant'Anastasia (which houses Pisanello's *St. George and the Princess*), and a few blocks from piazza delle Erbe. Each room is decorated authentically with antiques dated between 1770 to 1870; if the hotel isn't too crowded, you can select your room, and its period atmosphere, from a slide display in the reception area. Everything here is elegant and well run. My only quarrel, and it's a small one, is that for all the beautiful antiques that occupy the rooms, a few rooms are without a place to sit comfortably. The welcoming bar area is the place for your late-afternoon drink and look through the day's *Herald Tribune*. The manager, Raimondo Giavarini, is a gifted man and should be consulted about anything that can't be taken care of by Orfeo Fort, the able concierge.

Accademia
via Scala, 12
(045) 596-222
AmX, Visa, Diners
Moderate

A very good small hotel, right where you want to be: in the middle of Verona's best shopping streets, a few minutes from piazza delle Erbe and piazza Bra, where the Arena is located. All in all, a reliable hotel in any season; the rooms are comfortable and reasonably priced.

FOOD AND WINE SHOPS, MARKETS

Wine

Istituto Enologico Italiano
via Sottorivia, 7

A good selection of Veneto and other Italian wines, housed in a fourteenth century *palazzo*. A little disorganized, but it's possible to make some real finds here.

Viareggio

Bologna 180 km   Florence 97   Genoa 138
Livorno 39   Lucca 27   Massa 26   Milan 255
Parma 170   Pisa 20   Siena 126   La Spezia 55

It was off these shores in the summer of 1882 that Shelley drowned, after his boat, *Ariel,* capsized. Viareggio, on the Tyrrhenian coast, is a popular and fashionable beach town for Florentines and other Italians, as well as for the many tourists looking for a spot on the water. This area of Tuscany is called Versilia, and it runs from Viareggio north through Forte dei Marmi for some 30 kilometers. Summer, the height of the tourist season, is the least amusing time to visit this romantic spot that boasts of beautiful parks and gardens, Lake Massaciuccoli, pine forests, and the backdrop of the Apuan Alps. In February you can attend Viareggio's Carnival—there's dancing in the streets, a parade with colored floats, and general merriment. It goes without saying that fish is the order of gastronomical business here.

ROMANO
★ ★ ★ ★

REGION	Tuscany
ADDRESS	via Mazzini, 120
PHONE	(0584) 31-382
CREDIT CARDS	AmX, Visa, Diners
CLOSED	Mon, Jan 9–27, July 3–10

CLASS	ATMOSPHERE	SERVICE	WINE	PRICE
3	3	3	2.5	E

The atmosphere will turn out not to be memorable, and the space is a little crowded. But it's okay here—the red tile floor, dark wood wainscotting, and white walls give this seaside restaurant a proper Mediterranean air. And if practical napkins turn you on, the napkins at Romano are soft, heavy, and very absorbent. This restaurant is most useful for a lunch of local wine and fish that's done to perfection. Put yourself in the able and interested hands of the owner, Romano Franceschini, and you'll have provided yourself with more than adequate gastronomical insurance.

SUGGESTED DISHES

insalatina di mare calda Warm seafood salad with squid, scampi, and very good olive oil.

*sparnocchi con fagioli, pomodori e basilico Jumbo shrimp with three kinds of beans, tomatoes, and basil.

*fiori di zucca con sogliola Squash flowers with a slice of sole over them, served with a black squid-ink sauce.

filetto di triglia Fillet of red mullet with basil, *fava* beans, and tomatoes.

orata al forno Baked sea bream with tomatoes, basil, and oil.

SUGGESTED WINES

White

Bianco di Cercatoia, Montecarlo, Fattoria Buonamico A wine with some complex perfume in the nose, which arrives with a trace of orange. Elegant and graceful, light and soft, golden-colored, with an excellent display of fruit. Alive in the mouth. It's better than the Franceschini, the house white bottled for the owner.

L'OCA BIANCA
★ ★ ★ ½

REGION	Tuscany
ADDRESS	strada statale, 1 (Via Aurelia N)
PHONE	(0584) 64-191
CREDIT CARDS	AmX, Visa
CLOSED	Wed, Thurs lunch, lunch July and Aug, Nov 15–Dec 15

CLASS	ATMOSPHERE	SERVICE	WINE	PRICE
3.5	3.5	4	4	E

L'Oca Bianca, "The White Goose," has blue flocked linen walls with dark wood appointments. Very much a "romantic" spot, but you'll recognize immediately the restaurant's serious intent, in the attention to detail combined with good taste. The owner is calm, friendly, and warm and will be helpful when it comes to ordering your meal. Plenty of flowers and plants adorn the room, and a pleasing collection of art hangs on the walls. Little red lamps on the tables create the proper lighting. There's something slightly French about the atmosphere here.

Directions. From the Astor Hotel on viale Carducci, go north; turn right at the third traffic light. Proceed about a kilometer. The restaurant will be in front of you, just off to the left.

SUGGESTED DISHES

porro gratinato di tartufo bianco di San Miniato   Leeks gratinéed with truffle and *fontina* cheese, in a sort of *fonduta*. Intense leek flavor.

sfogliatina calda con pâté di fegato d'oca in salsa Madeira   A puff pastry with foie gras, on a bed of julienned carrots with a Madeira sauce. As a slight supplement, a glass of Château d'Yquem is served on the side.

*pasta doppia di coniglio e olive   Four round large *ravioli*: two white, stuffed with rabbit, and two green, stuffed with olives. A tomato sauce covers the white *ravioli*, a purée of chopped olives covers the green.

pecorino toscano con cotognata di pere   A young, semisoft *pecorino* cheese, smooth and flavorful, served with a pear and quince jam.

SUGGESTED WINES

White

Roussanne Bianco, Fattori Michi   A light, subtle nose with muted floral notes. Muted in the mouth as well. Unobtrusive but attractive.

Red

Chianti Classico, Riserva, Riecine   A straightforward Chianti nose, and upfront taste of modest fruit, if a touch raw. The fruit tends to fade a bit, while the wine remains slightly dry and tannic; but it opens after an hour or two and becomes more accommodating.

Il Patriarca
viale Carducci, 79
(0584) 53-126
AmX, Visa, Diners
Closed Wed except June 14–Sept 15

A kind of Hollywood establishment—lots of fuss, flowers, and photos of American movie stars. On the expensive side, but the cooking can be quite good.

In Forte dei Marmi, 14 km
Lorenzo
via Carducci, 61
(0584) 84-030
AmX, Visa, Diners
Closed Mon, Dec 15–Jan 31

A pleasant white stucco *trattoria* that specializes in fish. Try the *antipasto della casa,* a mix of various types of seafood; the *scampi e fagioli,* scampi and beans; *bavette sul pesce,* or a pasta with a fish sauce. The restaurant does grilled fish very well, *pesce alla brace.*

In Montignoso, 23 km
Il Bottaccio
via Bottaccio, 1 (near Massa)
(0585) 340-031
AmX, Visa, Diners
Always open

This is not a recommendation, merely a commentary:

This sixteenth-century olive mill is now an absolutely spectacular-looking restaurant with an extraordinarily talented young chef; were it not for the fact that it's so poorly run, it would have received a full review with a very high rating. It's most unfortunate for the chef, Pina Mosca, who should not have her efforts wasted by the foolery that takes place in the dining room. Be warned that although one *can* order à la carte, we were told by the young man in charge (who claimed he was the director and, because the owner "wasn't involved," ran the restaurant himself; he turned out to be the director's younger brother) that menus were not available and that we would have to accept a menu of his construction. His tasting menu, listed at 60,000 to 80,000 lire in Michelin, as well as in the guide of Relais & Châteaux, of which this restaurant is a member, came to 120,000 per person—without wine or extras!

If you decide to try Il Bottaccio anyway, sit in the back room, next to the indoor pool that contains six fat colorful carp. There are potted palms around the pool, not to mention a winning ceramic tiger. Every one of the dishes up to the entrée was superb, from the opening scampi to the mussel soup to the *ravioli* with fish sauce. I say up to the entrée because the young man mentioned above forgot we had a main course on his tasting menu when he dismissed the chef—and the rest of the staff as well. We received a few pieces of dry, cold pheasant, and then a dish of pastries. It was, all in all, an exasperating experience—what you'd call expensive chaos! When we left he followed us to our car, where he implored me to write to Michelin, to suggest they give *his* restaurant two or three stars.

HOTELS

Astor
viale Carducci 54
(0584) 50-301
AmX, Visa, Diners
Expensive

Although this modern hotel is nothing to look at from the outside—you'll wonder if you're at the right Astor—the rooms are very comfortable, nothing fancy. It's well-run, and the best place to stay in Viareggio. Ask for room 523, which affords a view of the water but is off the main road. The manager, Caradio Esposito, has much to say about his part of Italy. Engage him in a conversation after you've checked in— he's very informative—and then take a swim in their indoor pool. There's also a health spa here for those of a mind.

Principe di Piemonte
piazza Puccini, 1
(0584) 50-122
AmX, Diners
Moderate

Unlike the Astor, this hotel has a considerably grand exterior. The rooms, however, are on the plain side, without a great deal of charm. But a good second choice.

Vicenza

Vicenza, "Venice without canals," as it's sometimes playfully called, is where Palladio, the great Renaissance architect, finally came to rest (he was born in nearby Padua in 1508), and it is in and around Vicenza that you can see many of his palaces and country houses, including one of his finest

Palladio's Villas

When you get near Vicenza (or Verona or Venice), tour the Palladian villas: *Villa Cordellina-Lombardi* at Montecchio Maggiore; *Villa Poiano* at Poiano; *Villa Malinverni* at Lonedo di Lugo; *Villa Zen* at Lisiera di Bolzano; *Villa Emo* at Fanzolo; and the famous *Villa Barbaro* at Maser, with its extraordinary frescoes by Veronese. All are within 40 kilometers of Vicenza. Contact the local tourist offices or a travel agent for further information.

La Rotonda (closed Mondays) Also called Villa Capra, this is Palladio's model villa, just on the outskirts of Vicenza. He began it in 1550, and it was completed by his student Vincenzo Scamozzi. Call the Vicenza tourist office if you want to see the inside of the villa; the grounds of the villa are open daily except Mondays.

    Nearby is the Villa Valmarana, not a work of Palladio's but beautiful nonetheless and notable for the handsome frescoes by Gian Domenico Tiepolo. It is open from mid-March to mid-November, afternoons only; also Thursday and Saturday mornings; and mornings only on Sunday.

Teatro Olimpico (closed Sunday afternoons) This classical theater in Vicenza, modeled after those of antiquity, is another Palladian construction completed by Scamozzi.

though less ornate constructions, La Rotonda. There's not a great deal to see in Vicenza beyond what Palladio left behind, so you're really here to honor the elegant, neoclassical work of this important architect. It's said that the first person in America to own a copy of Palladio's famous *Four Books of Architecture* was Thomas Jefferson, whose Monticello was influenced by the Palladian model. Spend some time walking the length of corso Andrea Palladio, the main street. Here and in some of the surrounding streets you will find many of the master architect's constructions. You must also take in piazza dei Signori, which features one of Palladio's masterpieces, the Basilica.

Be sure to sample the city's signature dish, *baccalà alla vicentina,* codfish braised in milk and served with *polenta.*

CINZIA E VALERIO
★ ★ ★

REGION	Veneto
ADDRESS	piazzetta Porta Padova, 65–67
PHONE	(0444) 505-213
CREDIT CARDS	AmX, Visa, Diners
CLOSED	Mon, Aug

CLASS	ATMOSPHERE	SERVICE	WINE	PRICE
3.5	3	3	3	M

A large rectangular dining room with white stuccolike walls, and beams and vaulted ceilings. The restaurant feels very Mediterranean. There is impressive flower work, fine antiques are placed at either end of the room; and the walls are covered with paintings you might expect to see for sale on the street—local art, which ranges from okay to not. Have fish or seafood; it's really all they wish to serve. This is a congenial place to lunch after visiting the various Palladian sights.

SUGGESTED   DISHES

fantasia di gamberetti con insalata   Shrimp on a bed of chicory with a dash of soy.

spaghetti all'anello di seppie   Spaghetti with perfectly cooked "rings" of cuttlefish served in their own black ink.

seppioline ripiene con orzo   Sliced "cuttlefish shells" filled with *orzo* (barley), and placed on a patterned sauce of black cuttlefish ink and white cream. Garnished with pieces of cuttlefish.

cappe lunghe ai ferri   Razor clams baked with tomatoes and cheese and finished under the grill.

*cappe sante alla brace   Scallops grilled in their shells—plain and excellent.

SUGGESTED   WINES

White

Breganze Bianco, Maculan   A fruity and easygoing wine made with the Tocai grape. On the slight side, but the acidity and a little shot of fruit hold things together and make this an even, subtle drink. Perfect for lunch with the seafood here.

Dessert

Moscato Rosa di San Michele, Zeni   A rose-colored dessert wine from Trentino–Alto Adige. Reads more bitter than sweet, but with very subtle and enjoyable sweet highlights. Reminiscent of bitters.

OTHER   RECOMMENDED RESTAURANTS

Tre Visi
contrà Porti, 6
(0444) 238-677
AmX, Visa, Diners
Closed Sun dinner, Mon, July 15–Aug 8, Dec 25–Jan 1

HOTELS

Europa
viale San Lazzaro
(0444) 564-111
AmX, Visa, Diners
Moderate
   The Italian version of a Holiday Inn. Certainly serviceable, and even comfortable, but don't go looking for charm. A place to spend the night while in Vicenza, that's all.

ITALIAN–ENGLISH GASTRONOMICAL GLOSSARY

Also see "Regional Food and Wine Specialties," pages 41–94, as well as the lists of terms related to restaurants, page 29; salads, page 33; seafood, page 30; birds, page 30; wine, page 89; and food shops, page 92.

abbacchio   Milk-fed baby lamb (Lazio).
abboccato   Slightly sweet, of wine.
abbrandato   Stockfish.
abbrustolito   Toasted.
all'abruzzese   Abruzzese style; for instance, prepared with hot red peppers, oil, and garlic.
acciughe   Anchovies.
acerbo   Tart; unripe.
aceto   Vinegar.
acqua   Water.
acquacotta   "Cooked water": a thick soup of seasonal vegetables poured over slices of toasted bread (Tuscany).
acqua minerale   Mineral water.
   gassata   Carbonated.
   non gassata, naturale   Not carbonated.
affettato   Sliced; sliced ham, sausage, or other cured meat.
affogato   Poached; steamed.
affumicato   Smoked.
aggiadda   Garlic sauce (Liguria).
aglio   Garlic.
aglio e oilo   Garlic and oil (sauce).
agnello   Lamb.
agnoli, agnolini   Stuffed pasta squares (Lombardy).
agnolotti   Crescent-shaped dumplings stuffed with a combination of meat, spinach, Parmesan, egg yolk, and nutmeg, and served with a meat or butter sauce (Piedmont).
all'agro   With oil and lemon dressing.
agrodolce   Sweet and sour.
agrumi   Citrus fruits.
ala, aletta   Wing, of chicken or turkey.

albicocca Apricot.

alici Anchovies.

alimentari Grocery store; foodstuffs.

alla, all' In the style of; with.

alloro Bay leaf.

alosa Shad.

amabile Semisweet, of wine; slightly sweeter than *abboccato*.

amaretto Almond liqueur.

amaretti Almond cookies somewhat like macaroons.

amaro Bitter.

all'amatriciana Amatrice style; prepared with a sauce of bacon, tomatoes, onions, and hot pepper (Lazio).

ammantato Covered, with cheese for instance.

ananas Pineapple.

anatra, anitra Duck.

anatra, anitra in salmì Duck marinated in red wine, garlic, onion, anchovies, and herbs, then fried.

aneto Dill.

anguilla Eel.

anguria Watermelon. Also called *cocomero*.

animella Sweetbread.

annegato "Drowned": cooked in wine.

anolini Small *ravioli*-like pasta stuffed with meat (Emilia-Romagna).

antipasto Appetizer.

aperitivo Aperitif.

aragosta Lobster; spiny or rock lobster; langouste; sea crayfish.

arancia, arancio Orange.

aringhe Herring.

arista Loin or saddle of pork, typically roasted with herbs.

armleti Dumplings (Tuscany).

aromi Spices; combination of herbs used in cooking, including rosemary, sage, thyme, parsley.

all'arrabbiata "Rabid": referring to a spicy hot tomato sauce for pasta.

arrostine Chop or veal fillet.

arrosto Roasted; roast beef or other meat.

arrotolato Rolled up.

arselle, telline Wedge-shell clams.

arzilla Skate; ray. Also called *razza*.

asciutto Dry.

asiago Hard, sharp cow's-milk cheese (Veneto).

asparagi Asparagus.

assortito, assortiti Assorted.

astice Lobster. Also called *astaco* or *gambero di mare*.

attorta S-shaped almond cake (Umbria).

avocado Avocado.

baccalà Dried cod; stockfish.

bacche Berries.

bagna cauda (caôda) Hot dipping sauce for vegetables, made of anchovies, garlic, butter, oil, and white truffles if in season (Piedmont).

balsamella Béchamel.

banana Banana.

barbabietola Beet.

barbio, barbo Barbel, a freshwater fish.

basilico Basil.

bavette Long thin noodles.

beccaccia Woodcock.

Bel Paese Soft, mild Lombard cheese.

besciamella Béchamel.

bevanda Beverage.

bianchetti Newly hatched, nearly fetal red mullets, sardines, or anchovies so small and young that they look more like shredded fish without skin than individual fish. Typically boiled for an instant and served with lemon and oil, and found in restaurants in February and March (in Liguria especially). Also called *gianchetti* or *schiuma di mare*.

bibita Beverage.

birra Beer.

biscotto Biscuit, cookie.

bistecca Steak.

bistecca alla fiorentina A large T-bone steak from Chianina beef, grilled over coals and served *very* rare (Tuscany).

bitto Lombard cheese.

bocconcini Small, bite-size pieces, as for instance cubes of veal.

bogoni Snails (Veneto).

boldro, coda di raspo Monkfish.

bollito Boiled.

bollito misto Mixed boiled meats, often served with a green sauce and/or *mostarda*.

alla bolognese Bolognese style; served with a *ragù* sauce, for example.

bonet Chocolate custard flavored with rum and crumbled *amaretti* (Piedmont).

bonito Small tuna.

borraggine Borage, an herb.

bosega Gray mullet. Also called *botolo*.

bottagio A stew of pork, sausage, cabbage and other vegetables, herbs, and white wine. Also called *cassoeula* (Lombardy).

bottarga Dried, pressed, and salted tuna roe.

bottiglieria Wine store.

boudin Blood sausage (Valle d'Aosta).

bovoli, bovoletti, bovoloni Snails, in various sizes (Veneto).

alla brace Charcoal-grilled.

braciola Steak, chop, or slice of meat.

bracioletta Lamb cutlet, steak, or chop.

braciolina Lamb steak or cutlet.

braciolone Stuffed slice of beef or veal.

branzino, spigola   Sea bass.

brasato   Braised.

bresaola   Air-cured dried beef, sliced very thin (Lombardy).

broccoli   Broccoli.

brodettato   With lemon and egg yolks added (referring especially to braised meats and stews).

brodetto   Soup or stew. Various dishes prepared differently by region go by this term.

brodo   Bouillon, broth, consommé.

brunoise   Mixture of carrots, parsley, and onions.

bruschetta   Toasted rubbed with garlic and topped with olive oil.

brut   Dry; dry sparkling wine.

alla bucaniera   Pirate's style; referring to pasta served with a sauce made of seafood, tomatoes, garlic, parsley, and olive oil.

bucatini   Hollow spaghetti-shaped pasta.

budelline   Innards.

budello   Intestine.

budino   Pudding; quenelle; mousse.

bue   Beef; ox.

bufala, bufalo   Buffalo. *Mozzarella di bufala* is the cheese made with buffalo milk.

burid(d)a   Fish stew (Liguria).

burro   Butter.

busecca   Tripe soup (Lombardy).

busola   Chocolate nut cake (Lombardy, Veneto).

cacciagione   Game.

alla cacciatora   Hunter's style; prepared with a sauce of tomatoes, onions, peppers, mushrooms, garlic, herbs, and wine.

cacciucco   Thick fish soup.

cacio   Cheese.

caciocavallo   Mild, smoky Campanian or Sicilian cheese.

caffè   Coffee; *espresso*.

caicco   Large pasta squares stuffed with meat and cheese (Lombardy).

calamaretto   Baby squid.

calamaro   Squid.

calcioni   Large stuffed *ravioli*, made with sugar and sweet pecorino (The Marches).

caldo   Hot; warm.

camoscio   Chamois.

campagna   Country, countryside.

alla campagnola   Country style.

candito   Candied. *Frutta candita* is candied fruit.

cannella   Cinnamon.

cannelloni   Dish consisting of pasta rolled into oblong shapes which are stuffed with meat or cheese, covered with béchamel, and baked in the oven.

cantucci   Tuscan almond biscuits.

cape, cappe   Assorted shellfish (Veneto).

cape lunghe, cape longhe, cappe lunghe   Razor clams (Veneto).

cape sante, cappe sante, capesante   Scallops (Veneto).

cappelletti   Stuffed hat-shaped pasta

capperi   Capers.

capponata   Sicilian dish of eggplant, celery, onion, olives, capers, pine nuts, and a sweet-and-sour sauce.

cappone   Capon.

cappon magro   Mixture of cooked vegetables, fish, and shellfish (Liguria).

capra   Goat.

capra di mare   Spider crab.

capretto   Kid, baby goat.

capriolo   Venison.

carbonade, carbonata   Beef stew made with red wine (Piedmont, Valle d'Aosta).

carbonara   Pasta sauce made with bacon, egg yolks, and Parmesan.

al carbone   Charcoal-grilled.

carciofi alla giudia   Deep-fried artichokes.

carciofi alla romana   Artichokes braised in oil and mint.

carciofo   Artichoke.

cardo   Cardoon.

carne   Meat.

carota   Carrot.

carpa   Carp.

carpaccio   Raw, lean beef, sliced paper-thin.

carrello   Trolley, as for hors d-oeuvres or desserts.

carta   Menu; paper.

al cartoccio   Referring to fish or meat baked in a paper bag.

casalingo   Homemade, house style.

cassoeula   Stew of pork, sausage, cabbage and other vegetables, herbs, and white wine (Lombardy, Piedmont).

castagna   Chestnut.

castrato   Mutton.

cavallo   Horse.

cavatappi   Corkscrew.

caviale   Caviar.

cavolfiore   Cauliflower.

cavolo   Cabbage.

cazzoeula   Lamb or mutton stew (Lombardy).

ceci   Chickpeas.

cefalo   Gray mullet.

cena   Supper.

cenci   "Rags": sweet bow- or knot-shaped fritters, often dusted with powdered sugar (Tuscany).

centerbe   Liqueur made from 100 herbs (*cento erbe*).

cernia   Grouper.

cervella   Brains.

cervo   Venison.

cetriolo   Cucumber.

Chianina   Breed of cows that produce the best steaks in Italy— or, some might say, anywhere.

chiocciole   Snails.

chiodi di garofano   Cloves.

chitarra   Guitar; special instrument with strings like a guitar's, used for cutting pasta in the Abruzzi.

cicchetti   Little snacks, literally "pick-me-ups," or hors d'oeuvres that accompany what the Venetians call *l'ombra* (the shadow), which is a glass of wine.

cicoria   Chicory.

cieca, cear, cia   Elvers, tiny eels (Tuscany).

ciliege   Cherries.

cima di rape   Turnip top.

cinghiale   Wild boar.

cioccolata, cioccolato   Chocolate.

cipolla   Onion.

cipollina   Small onion; spring onion.

ciriola   Tiny eel.

cisra   Chickpea soup (Piedmont).

cocomero   Watermelon. Also called *anguria*.

coda di bue alla vaccinara   Oxtail braised with wine, vegetables, raisins, pine nuts, and chocolate (Lazio).

coda di raspo (boldro)   Monkfish.

colazione   Breakfast. Also called *prima* or *piccola colazione*.

colomba pasquale   Dove-shaped Easter cake.

colombo   Wood pigeon.

composta di frutta   Stewed fruit; fruit compote.

conchiglie   Shells; shell-shaped pasta.

confettura   Jam.

coniglio   Rabbit.

alla contadina   Country style; referring to a sauce employing various ingredients, usually including some of the following: tomatoes, onions, garlic, capers, olives, parsley, vinegar, and wine.

conto   Bill, check.

contorno   Side dish (vegetable).

controfiletto   Sirloin steak.

coperto   Covered; cover charge.

coppa   Dried pork sausage (Emilia-Romagna, Lombardy).

coratella   Offal—heart, liver, lungs, spleen.

corte bandita   Open house.

coscetta, coscetto   Leg, of lamb for instance.

coscia, coscio   Leg, of lamb or goat; haunch, of venison.

costata   Steak, chop.

costoletta   Veal, pork, or lamb chop or cutlet.

cotechino   Large fresh pork sausage (Emilia-Romagna, Lombardy).

cotto   Cooked; baked.

cotto adagio   Braised.

cottura completa   Complete cooking.

cozze   Mussels.

crema   Custard; custard cream.

crema caramella   *Crème caramel,* flan.

crescione   Watercress.

crespella   Crêpe, normally stuffed.

alla creta   Cooked in clay.

crocchetta   Croquette.

crostata   Tart; pie.

crostata di ricotta   Ricotta pie or tart.

crostino   Piece of toast or fried bread, topped with chicken-liver paste, cheese, truffle, anchovies, and so on. Also crouton.

su(l) crostone   On toast.

crudo   Raw, uncooked.

cucina   Kitchen; cuisine.

culatello   Rump of pork cured like *prosciutto.*

cuoco   Cook, chef.

cuore   Heart.

dattero   Date.

datteri di mare   Date mussels, date shells.

delfino   Dolphin.

al dente   "To the tooth": cooked until *just* done, still firm.

dentice   Dentex, a Mediterranean fish similar in taste to sea bass.

alla diavola   Usually describing chicken that is cut in half, flattened, and grilled over coals. Also referring to a tomato sauce made with hot spices such as cayenne pepper.

digestivi   After dinner drinks made with herbs, roots and barks, meant to aid digestion.

dolce   Sweet; dessert.

dolcelatte   Milder version of *gorgonzola.*

doppio   Double.

dorato   Golden; glazed; fried until golden.

dragoncello   Tarragon.

echino   Sea urchin.

erbe   Herbs.

escabecio, scapece   Fried fish marinated in oil, vinegar, garlic, and herbs (Abruzzi; called *scabecio* in Liguria).

fagiano   Pheasant.

fagioli   Beans; white beans.

fagioli all'uccelleto   Beans (white) cooked in oil with tomatoes.

fagiolini   Green beans.

fagottini   Little bundles—of pasta, veal, or cabbage, for example—stuffed and cooked.

faraona   Guinea fowl.

farcito   Stuffed.

farfalle   "Butterflies": butterfly-shaped pasta.

farina Flour.

farinata Fried flat cake made of chickpea flour (Liguria).

farro Emmer or emmer wheat, a grain in the barley family with a slightly wheatlike taste.

fasoi Beans (Veneto).

fave Broad beans.

fedelini Thin-noodle pasta used in soups.

fegatelli Small pieces of pork liver.

fegato Liver.

ai ferri Grilled.

fettuccine Flat ribbon pasta.

fettunta Toasted sliced bread, rubbed with garlic and soaked with olive oil (Tuscany).

fiadone Tart filled with layers of eggs, ricotta, sugar, cinnamon, and lemon (Abruzzi).

al fiasco Cooked in a flask; by the flask.

fico Fig.

filetto Fillet.

finanziera Rich, hearty, even elaborate stew of chicken, chicken liver and giblets, cocks' combs, sweetbreads, mushrooms, and truffles; traditionally, leftover meats are used. Supposedly a favorite dish of nineteenth-century Piedmont businessmen–hence the name.

finocchio Fennel.

alla fiorentina Florentine style (usually similar to *alla toscana,* Tuscan style). Referring to a tomato sauce with a variety of other ingredients, including peas, spinach, and cheese; also describing chicken fried with lemon, and the famous Florentine steak, *bistecca alla fiorentina.*

fiori di zucca Squash flowers, typically served fried and stuffed.

fiori di zucchine, zucchini Zucchini flowers, typically stuffed with cheese and anchovies and fried.

focaccia Traditionally, a flat Ligurian bread often made with sage. Now made with various toppings or fillings—onions, cheese, tomatoes. The term is used also for other flat breads and cakes.

foglia Leaf, as of pastry.

fondante Small croquette.

fonduta Piedmontese specialty; *fontina* cheese melted with eggs, butter, milk, with white truffle sliced over the top.

fontina Cow's-milk cheese from Piedmont and Valle d'Aosta.

formaggio Cheese.

al forno Baked in the oven, roasted.

fragole Strawberries.

fragoline di bosco Wild strawberries.

frascarelli Small dumplings used in soups (The Marches). Sometimes a rice-shaped pasta (Umbria).

freddo Cold.

fresco Cool; fresh.

fricassea Light stew finished with egg yolks beaten with lemon juice.

frittata Omelette, served flat.

frittatina Pancake.

fritto misto Mixed fried platter that might include liver, brains, sweetbreads, kidneys, vegetables.

frumento Wheat.

frutta Fruit.

frutta fresca di stagione Fresh fruit in season.

fumetto Fish stock.

funghi Mushrooms.

funghi porcini Italy's most popular mushrooms—*cèpes, boletus*. Usually served grilled or sautéed with a little oil, parsley, and garlic.

funghi trifolati Chopped mushrooms sautéed with parsley, garlic, and lemon.

fusilli Corkscrew-shaped pasta.

galantina Galantine.

galletto Chicken.

gallina, gallinella Hen, boiling fowl.

gamberetti Shrimp.

gamberi di fiume Freshwater crayfish.

gamberi Prawns.

gamberi imperiali Large prawns.

gambero di mare Lobster.

gamberoni Giant shrimp.

garmugia, garmucia, gramugia Vegetable and bean soup from Tuscany.

garofolato With cloves.

gelatina Aspic, gelatin.

gelato Ice cream; frozen.

alla genovese Genoese style; often referring to dishes prepared with *pesto* sauce, or to meat and fish dishes made with potatoes, white wine, parsley, and various herbs.

ghiaccio Ice.

gianchetti See *bianchetti*.

gianduiotti, giandujotti Chocolates made with hazelnut creams, from Turin.

ginepro Juniper.

alla giudia Jewish style. See *carciofi alla Giudia*.

glassato Glazed.

gnocchi Dumplings made with flour and potatoes or semolina.

gorgonzola Italian blue cheese.

gramigna Short, hollow spaghetti-like pasta.

grana Cheese similar to Parmesan.

granceola, grancevola, granseola Spider crab.

granchio Crab; shore crab.

granciporro Crab.

granita Light ice, usually flavored with fruit juice.

grappa Spirit made from pomace (skins, seeds) and sometimes vines after the grapes have been pressed for wine.

grasso   Fat; rich.

gratinato   Gratinée, gratinéed.

gremolada, gremolata   Mixture of garlic, chopped parsley, and lemon peel, typically sprinkled over *ossobuco* before it's served.

alla gricia   With bacon.

alla griglia   Grilled.

grissini   Breadsticks.

guarnizione   Garnish.

imbottito   Stuffed. A *panino imbottito* is a sandwich.

imbrecciata   Soup made with beans, lentils, and chickpeas.

impanato   Breaded; with bread crumbs.

indivia   Endive. Also called *insalata belga* (Belgian salad).

insalata   Salad.

insalata caprese   A salad of tomatoes, mozzarella, and basil, dressed with oil and lemon juice or vinegar.

insalata di mare   Seafood salad.

insalata mista   Mixed salad.

insalatone   "Big salad": salad of various vegetables.

intingolo   Stew; sauce.

involtino   Slice of veal or other meat, stuffed, rolled, and then braised, roasted, or grilled on skewers.

kaiserfleisch   Smoked pork (Trentino–Alto Adige).

kanostrelle   Round cake from Valle d'Aosta.

alla lampada   Referring to a dish prepared at the table, over a burner.

lamponi   Raspberries.

lampreda   Lamprey.

langosta   Crayfish.

lardo   Salt pork; lard.

lasagne   Large, flat pasta layered with various ingredients, including meat, vegetables, and cheese, and baked in the oven.

latte   Milk.

lattuga   Lettuce.

lauro   Bay leaf.

lavarello   Salmon like fish from Lake Como. Also called *coregone*.

legume   Legume; vegetable.

lenticchie   Lentils.

lepre   Hare.

lesso, lessato   Boiled.

limone   Lemon.

lingua   Tongue.

linguine   Flat spaghetti-like pasta.

liquoroso   Referring to a wine, often fortified, with a high alcohol content.

lista   List; menu.

alla livornese   Livornese style; usually meaning prepared with tomatoes, garlic, parsley, and oil.

lombata, lombatina Sirloin; pork loin; saddle of hare or rabbit.

lonza Cured pork fillet.

luccio Pike.

luganega, lucanega Long, thin spicy pork sausage (Veneto).

lumache Snails.

maccheroni Macaroni.

macedonia di frutta Fruit salad.

alla macellara Butcher's style; referring to liver prepared with lemon and parsley.

macelleria Butcher's shop.

macinato Ground; minced; pounded.

magasso Wild duck (Veneto).

maggiorana Marjoram.

magnonese Mayonnaise sauce of the Veneto, served typically with fish and shellfish.

magro Thin, lean; referring to a dish prepared without meat.

maiale Pork.

maionese Mayonnaise.

malfatti Dumplings composed of cheese and spinach.

maltagliati Pasta in a variety of irregular shapes.

mandarino Tangerine, mandarin.

mandorla Almond.

maniche "Sleeves": short tube-shaped pasta.

mantecato Softened, pounded into a paste, often with butter.

manzo Beef.

alla marinara Sailor's style; referring to pasta served with a sauce of tomatoes, peppers, garlic, and capers; and to rice served with seafood.

marinato Marinated.

marrone Large chestnut; brown (color).

mascarpone Unsalted creamy cheese from Lombardy. Often served sweetened.

maturo Ripe.

mazzafegato Pork liver sausage made with a variety of spices, pine nuts and raisins (the Marches, Umbria).

mazzancolle, mazzancuogni Large prawns.

medaglioni Medallions, thick slices of meat.

melagrana Pomegranate.

melanzana Eggplant.

mela Apple.

melone Melon, cantaloupe.

menta Mint.

meringha Meringue.

merlo Blackbird.

merluzzo Cod.

mezzo cotto Half cooked.

miele Honey.

millefoglie A flaky pastry.

milza Spleen.

minerale   Mineral; mineral water.

minestra   Soup; the course following *antipasto,* usually soup, risotto, or pasta.

minestrone   Hearty vegetable soup made with pasta, rice, and/or beans.

mirtilli   There's some confusion surrounding these intense red berries. The word is usually translated as "bilberries" or "blueberries," both of which are blue. Waverley Root suggests that the *mirtillo* might be closer to our cranberry, which is related to the bilberry.

misto, misti   Mixed, assorted.

mitili   Mussels.

mocetta   Dried salted chamois or goat (Valle d'Aosta).

moleche   Soft-shelled crabs.

mongana   Milk cow.

montebianco   Chestnut purée with whipped cream.

montone   Mutton.

more (di rovo)   Blackberries.

morbidelle   Small soup dumplings.

morena   Lamprey.

mortadella   Large pork sausage seasoned with coriander and peppercorns—Bologna's flagship sausage.

moscardino   Small octopus.

mostarda   Chutney-like sauce composed of various fruits preserved in a syrup made of mustard, honey, white wine, and other seasonings. Often served with boiled meats.

mozzarella   Mild white cheese made of cow's or buffalo's milk.

mozzarella in carrozza   Bread-and-mozzarella sandwich dipped in an egg-and-milk batter and fried. An Italian version of the French *croquemonsieur.*

muggine   Gray mullet.

muscoli, moscioli   Mussels. Also called *mitili, moscioli,* and *peoci.*

nasello   Hake.

Natale   Christmas.

'ndocca 'ndocca   Powerful stew made of pig parts such as feet, ears, snout, skin, and chops, cooked with bay leaves, garlic, vinegar, pimientos, rosemary, and tomatoes (Abruzzi).

nero   Black.

nervetti   Salad made with calf's trotters (feet and shins). The meat is boiled, then removed from the bone, cut into strips, and dressed with oil, vinegar, and onions.

nocciola   Hazelnut.

noce   Nut; walnut.

noce di cocco   Coconut.

noce moscata   Nutmeg.

nodino   Veal, pork, or other chop.

oca   Goose.

occhiata   Sea bream.

odori "Odors"; mixture of finely chopped onions, celery, carrots, parsley, and garlic, used to flavor a dish.

olio Oil.

olive (nere, verdi) Olives (black, green).

orata Daurade; gilthead, sea bream.

orecchiette "Little ears": ear-shaped pasta.

origano Oregano.

ortica Nettle.

orzo Barley.

ossobuco Braised veal shin (see p. 57).

ostriche Oysters.

ovolo, ovulo Orange mushroom found in late summer and early fall.

alla paesana Peasant style; referring to a pasta sauce of diced bacon, mushrooms, tomatoes, herbs, and cheese.

paglia e fieno "Straw and hay": green and yellow *tagliatelle*.

pagliata, pajata Veal innards cooked with herbs and wine (Lazio).

paillard Veal steak pounded thin and grilled.

paiolo Pot used for cooking *polenta*.

palombaccio Wood pigeon.

palombo Dogfish; ring dove, wood pigeon.

panada Bread, cheese, and egg soup (Veneto).

panarda Legendary Abruzzi feast at which more than twenty dishes might be offered and consumed.

pancetta Unsmoked bacon, cured in salt and spices and usually rolled.

pancotto Bread soup, often with a variety of vegetables. Also called *pappa*.

panettone Dome-shaped cake made with raisins and candied fruit, usually associated with Christmas (Lombardy).

pane, pan Bread.

panforte "Strong bread": very tasty cake made with almonds, walnuts, honey, preserved fruit, and spices, and usually associated with Christmas (Tuscany, specifically Siena).

pan grattato Bread crumbs.

panino (imbottito) Sandwich.

paniccia, panissa Chickpea *polenta* of sorts: boiled chickpea flour baked or fried with onions, until crisp, then served with cheese (Liguria).

panna Cream; heavy cream.

pansôti *Ravioli*-like triangular pasta stuffed with a mixture of ricotta, spinach, chard, and sometimes brains and/or sweetbreads, usually served with *salsa di noci*, a creamy walnut sauce (Liguria).

panzanella Salad composed of chunks of bread, tomatoes, cucumbers, red onions, anchovies, oil, and spices (Lazio, Tuscany).

pappa A thick tomato and bread soup, made with oil and garlic.

pappardelle Long, wide strips of pasta.

alla parmigiana In the style of Parma; with Parmesan cheese.

parmigiano-reggiano Parmesan cheese (see p. 48).

Pasqua Easter.

pasquale, pasqualino Pertaining to Easter.

passatelli Strands of cheese, egg, and bread crumbs (formed by being pushed through a sieve) served in a boiling broth.

passato Strained, mashed, puréed.

passito Semidried; sweet wine produced from semidried grapes.

pasta Pasta; a pastry; dough.

pasta asciutta Pasta served with a sauce. Dry, commercially made pasta.

pasta in brodo Pasta served in a soup.

pasta e fagioli Pasta and bean soup.

pasticceria Pastries, cakes; pastry shop.

pasticciata Timbale of egg pasta with a meat sauce and cheese, baked.

pasticcio Baked pie of pasta, vegetables, or meat, usually employing cheese as a binder.

pastinaca Parsnip.

patata Potato.

pecora Sheep.

pecorino Hard, sharp, sheep's-milk cheese.

penne Quill-shaped pasta.

peoci Mussels.

pepe Pepper.

peperata, peverada Peppery sauce for roasts and boiled meat.

peperonata Stew of bell peppers, onions, and tomatoes.

peperoncino Hot red chili pepper.

peperone Bell pepper; sweet pepper.

pera Pear.

perciatelli Long hollow noodles.

pernice Partridge.

persico Freshwater perch.

pesca Peach. The plural is *pesche*.

pesca noce Nectarine.

pesce Fish.

pesce spada Swordfish.

pesciolini Small fry fish, like whitebait.

pesto Pasta sauce made with basil, garlic, pine nuts, Parmesan and/or pecorino, and olive oil (Liguria).

petto Breast, as of chicken or veal.

piccante Spicy hot.

piccata Thin-sliced veal scallop, often sautéed.

piccione Pigeon.

piccola colazione Breakfast.

piedini di maiale Pig's feet.

alla piemontese Piedmontese style; referring, for instance, to sauces made with truffles, meat, *fontina* and Parmesan cheese, cream, butter, and/or other ingredients.

pieno Full.

pignoli, pinoli Pine nuts.

pincinelle Long thin noodles.

pincisgrassi Sheets of pasta layered with various ingredients—including ham, sausage, chicken livers, sweetbreads, onions, truffles, butter, and cream—then baked with grated cheese over the top (Abruzzi; called *vincisgrassi* in the Marches).

pinoccata Umbrian cake made with pine nuts and sometimes almonds.

piselli Peas.

pistacchio Pistachio.

alla pizzaiola Pizza-maker's style; prepared with a sauce of tomatoes, garlic, oregano, and sometimes anchovies and capers.

polenta Boiled corn meal, prepared in various ways.

polipo, polipetto Octopus; small squid.

pollame Poultry.

pollo Chicken.

polpetta Meatball.

polpettone Meat or vegetable loaf (or baked mixture not necessarily in loaf form).

polpo Octopus.

pomodoro Tomato.

pompelmo Grapefruit.

porchetta Spit-roasted suckling pig, often cooked with garlic, fennel, and rosemary. Other meats and fish are cooked *alla porchetta*, using the same method and ingredients.

porcini A variety of edible wild mushrooms (see page 357).

porro Leek.

pranzo Lunch.

prataiolo Chanterelle.

prezzemolo Parsley.

prima colazione Breakfast.

primavera Spring, as in "spring vegetables."

primizie First or early fruits or vegetables.

profumato Scented; flavored.

prosciutto Salted, air-cured ham; *cotto* is cooked, *crudo* is raw. The best is from San Daniele, in Friuli, and Langhirano and Parma, in Emilia-Romagna.

provolone Sharp, spicy cheese.

prugna Plum; prunes.

punta di vitello Shoulder or breast of veal.

puntarelle Chicorylike green, typically served in a salad dressed with oil and vinegar, garlic, and anchovies (Lazio).

punto Cooked medium.

purè Purée; puréed.

alla puttanesca "Whore's style"; referring to pasta sauced with tomatoes, capers, hot red peppers, anchovies, and garlic.

quadrucci Small cubes of pasta used in soups.

quaglia Quail.

rabarbaro Rhubarb. Also a beverage made from rhubarb.

radicchio Slightly bitter red chicory that comes in four varieties:

Radicchio di Treviso has long thin leaves and is the tastiest; *radicchio di Verona* is round like a head of lettuce; and *raddichio di Chioggia* and *radicchio di Castelfranco* are leafier heads with green as well as red leaves. People from Treviso recognize only their *radicchio* as being the real thing; according to Waverley Root, the locals call their variety *un fiore che si mangia*, "a flower that is eaten."

radice Radish; root.

ragno di mare Spider crab.

ragù Thick pasta sauce made with pork or beef, onions, carrots, and tomatoes.

rana Frog.

rana pescatrice Monkfish.

rapa Turnip.

ravanello Radish.

ravioli Stuffed pasta envelopes.

razza Skate; ray. Also called *arzilla*.

reni Kidneys.

ribes (nero, rosso) Currant (black, red).

ribollita Bean, bread, and cabbage soup, reheated ("reboiled") for serving (Tuscany).

ricciarelli Almond biscuits (Tuscany, specifically Siena).

ricotta Moist sheep's-milk cheese. Eaten by itself, like other cheeses, and used in various pasta, vegetable, and dessert stuffings.

rigato Ribbed, as various pastas.

rigatoni Ribbed, tube-shaped pasta.

ripieno Stuffed.

risi e bisi Thick soup of fresh peas and rice, and sometimes a little onion, served with Parmesan cheese (Veneto).

riso, ris, risi Rice.

risotto Creamy preparation of rice, cooked slowly in broth with a variety of ingredients.

rognoncini Kidneys.

rognone Kidney.

alla romana Roman style; with rich sauce of meat, tomatoes, herbs (sometimes mint), wine, cheese, and different vegetables; or with a butter and cheese sauce.

rombo Turbot.

rosmarino Rosemary.

rospa, rospo Monkfish.

rosso Red.

rosticceria Delicatessen specializing in roasted meats.

rotelle Spiral-shaped pasta.

rotolo Roll.

rustico Rustic.

salame Salami; salt-cured sausage.

sale Salt.

in salmì Marinated and cooked in a rich wine sauce.

salmone Salmon.

salsa   Sauce.

salsiccia   Sausage.

saltato   Sautéed.

saltimbocca   Veal scallops layered with *prosciutto* and fresh sage, and sautéed in butter and wine. (Lazio).

in salto   Reheated or fried, and thus flipped over, as with *risotto in salto.*

salumeria   Delicatessen specializing in *salumi.*

salumi   Salted or cured meats, including *salame, prosciutto,* and *coppa.*

salvia   Sage.

sambuca   Licorice-tasting liqueur.

sangue   Blood.

al sangue   Rare.

sanguinaccio   Blood sausage.

sapore   Taste, flavor.

ai sapori   With herbs.

saraceno   Buckwheat.

sarago, sargo   Sea bream. Also called *sarpa, sparaglione.*

sarde, sardelle, sardelline   Sardines.

sbira   Tripe served with a meat sauce (Liguria).

scabecio, scapece, escabecio   Fried fish marinated in oil, vinegar, garlic, and herbs (called *scabecio* in Liguria; the other two terms are used in the Abruzzi).

scalogno   Shallot.

scaloppina   Thin-sliced scallop, usually of veal, typically flattened and sautéed in butter.

scampi   Scampi; despite popular belief, crustaceans of the lobster family, not large shrimp; also called Dublin Bay prawns, langoustines, Norway lobsters, or saltwater crayfish.

sciarrano   Sea perch.

sciatt   Buckwheat fritters made with *grappa* and served with cheese (Lombardy).

sciroppo   Syrup.

scorfano   Scorpion fish (called *scarpena* in the Marches).

scorza   Rind, as of lemon or orange.

secco   Dry.

secondo   Entrée or main course of a meal; second; according to.

sedano   Celery.

sella   Saddle of lamb, veal, rabbit, and so on.

selvaggina   Game.

selvatico   Wild.

semifreddo   Soft, rich ice cream with whipped cream folded in; semifrozen pudding or mousse. Literally, "half cold."

senape   Mustard.

seppia   Cuttlefish.

seppiolina   Small cuttlefish.

sesamo   Sesame seed.

sfilatino   Loaf of bread (Tuscany).

sfilato   Boned, cut into small pieces, as with rabbit.

sfoglia   Sheet of dough; puff-pastry "leaf" or layer.

sfogliata   Flaky pastry; puff pastry.

sformato   Timbale of vegetables or rice; molded dessert.

sgombro   Mackerel.

sidro   Cider.

soffritto   Mixture of vegetables and herbs, including celery, carrots, onions, garlic, and parsley, sautéed in olive oil; the basis for many soups and stews.

sogliola   Sole.

sopa   Soup (Veneto).

soppressa   Sausage.

soppressata   Rough-cut pork sausage, often with herbs.

sorbetto   Sorbet, sherbert.

(pesce) spada   Swordfish.

spalla   Shoulder, of veal, beef, or lamb.

spanocchi   Large prawns.

speck   Smoked ham (Trentino–Alto Adige).

spezia   Spice.

spezzatino   Stew of veal, rabbit, or chicken sautéed in a sauce of wine and vegetables.

spiedo, spiedino   Spit, brochette.

allo spiedo   Cooked on a spit.

spigola, spinola, branzino   Sea bass.

spinaci   Spinach.

spremuta   Squeezed juice, as of citrus.

spremuto   Squeezed, as for citrus juice.

spugnole   Morel mushrooms.

spuma   Mousse.

spumone   Type of soft ice cream with fruit and nuts.

stagione   Season.

di stagione   Of the season.

in stagione   In season.

stinco   Shank, typically of veal.

stoccafisso   Dried cod; stockfish.

storione   Sturgeon.

stracchino   Soft, full cow's-milk cheese.

stracciatella   Light soup made with chicken stock and "rags" (*stracci*) of beaten eggs and semolina, served with Parmesan. Also chocolate chip ice cream.

stracciato   Scrambled.

stracotto   Braised, stewed; beef stew.

strascinati   Type of macaroni (Umbria).

stravecchio   Very old, as cheese or liquor.

stringozzi   Short pasta noodles, served usually with an oil and garlic sauce, sometimes with a tomato sauce.

stufato   Stew; stewed. For beef, a stew with red wine, vegetables, and herbs.

succo   Juice, as of fruit.

sugo   Sauce.

suino   Pork.

supplí   Fried rice croquettes.

tacchino Turkey.

tagliarini, taglierini, taglioni Long, thin noodles.

tagliatelle Long, flat noodles.

tagliato Cut; sliced.

tajarin Thin *tagliatelle* (Piedmont).

tapulòn Thin-sliced donkey meat stewed with cabbage, cauliflower, garlic, rosemary, and red wine (Piedmont).

tartaruga di mare Turtle. Also called *testuggine marina*.

tarteletta Tartlet.

tartufato Truffled; with truffles.

tartufo Truffle.

tavola Table.

tavola calda "Hot table"; snack bar that serves lunch items and snacks, both hot and cold.

tè Tea.

in tegame In a casserole.

telline, arselle Wedge-shell clams.

tenero Fresh, tender.

terrina Terrine, pâté.

testa, testarella, testina Head, of pig or calf; cap, of mushroom.

testa di maiale Pig's head.

tiepido Tepid, slightly warm.

timballo Mold; pie.

timo Thyme.

tiramisù Dessert made with *mascarpone,* cream, *espresso,* liquor, ladyfingers, and chocolate.

tofeja A hearty pork and bean soup/stew.

tonnarelli Square-shaped spaghetti. Called *maccheroni alla chitarra* in the Abruzzi.

tonno Tuna.

torcetti Biscuits from Piedmont and Valle d'Aosta.

tordo Thrush.

torrone White nougat candy with almonds and hazelnuts (Piedmont).

torta Tart; cake; pie.

torta pasqualina Traditional Easter pie with a filling of artichokes, possibly chard, eggs, ricotta, Parmesan and/or *pecorino,* and classically made with thirty-three ultrathin layers of dough (Liguria).

tortelli Large stuffed pasta.

tortellini Little doughnut-shaped pasta generally filled with cheese or meat (Emilia-Romagna, specifically Bologna).

tortellini alla panna *Tortellini* served with thick cream and Parmesan.

tortelloni Large *tortellini,* usually stuffed with cheese.

tortiglioni Spiral-shaped pasta.

tortino Omelette, served flat.

tostato Toasted.

totano Flying squid.

tramezzino Sandwich. Also called *panino.*

trancia, trancio   Slice.

trenette   Long, thin noodles, typically served with *pesto* and potatoes (Liguria).

trifola   Truffle, in Umbria dialect, and the Piedmont.

trifolati   Used to describe a variety of dishes, prepared in such a way as to suggest the richness of truffles. Often used to describe mushrooms that have been sautéed with garlic, parsley, and lemon.

triglia   Red mullet. Also called *trigghia, tregghia*.

trippa   Tripe.

trippa alla milanese   Tripe Milanese style, served with a meat sauce and Parmesan.

trippa alla romana   Tripe Roman style, braised in a tomato and meat sauce with mint and cheese.

troffie   Small pasta spirals, served with *pesto*.

trota   Trout.

trota salmonata   Salmon trout.

all'uccelletto   Cooked like (little) birds, on skewers, with sage.

uccelletti   Small birds, traditionally grilled on skewers.

in umido   Cooked in a sauce; stewed.

uovo   Egg.

uva (bianca, rossa, nera)   Grapes (green, red, black).

uvetta   Raisins.

vainiglia, vaniglia   Vanilla.

al vapore   Steamed.

verde   Green.

verdura   Vegetable.

vermicelli   Thin noodles.

verza   Savoy cabbage.

vincisgrassi   Sheets of pasta layered with various ingredients—including ham, sausage, chicken livers, sweetbreads, onions, truffles, butter, and cream—then baked with grated cheese on top. (The Marches; called *pincisgrassi* in the Abruzzi).

vino, vin (bianco, rosso)   Wine (white, red).

virtù   Thick vegetable soup from the Abruzzi, traditionally made with seven ingredients and cooked for seven hours.

vitello   Veal.

vitello tonnato   Thinly sliced braised veal, served cold with a tuna, caper, and mayonnaise sauce.

vongole   Clams.

zabaglione, zabaione   Pudding made with egg yolks, sugar, and Marsala.

zafferano   Saffron.

zampone   Fresh pork sausage stuffed into a pork trotter.

zenzero   Ginger.

zeppole   Sweet fritters.

zesti   Candied orange and lemon rinds.

zimino Fish stew from Liguria.

zite, ziti Short, wide tube-shaped pasta.

zucca Pumpkin; squash.

zucchero Sugar.

zucchine, zucchina, zucchette Zucchini, green squash.

zuppa Soup.

zuppa inglese Dessert composed of layers of light sponge cake with creamy custard, Alchermes, and candied fruit between the layers, coated with a final layer of meringue.

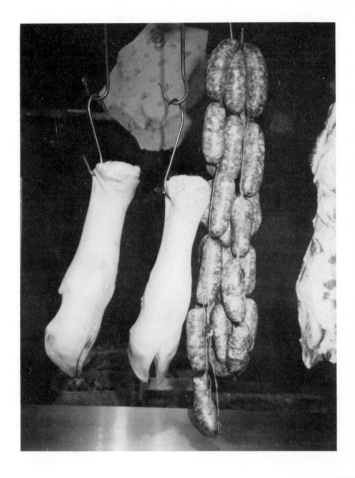

READING
LIST

Anderson, Burton. *The Simon and Schuster Pocket Guide to Italian Wines.* (revised ed.) Simon & Schuster, 1987.
———. *Vino.* Atlantic/Little, Brown, 1980.
Belfrage, N. *Life Beyond Lambrusco.* Sidgwick & Jackson, 1987.
Belloc, Hilaire. *The Path to Rome.* Penguin, 1986.
Bentley, James. *A Guide to Tuscany.* Viking, 1987.
Berenson, Bernard. *Italian Painters of the Renaissance.* Phaidon, 1952.
Bugialli, Giuliano. *On Pasta.* Simon & Schuster, 1988.
Burckhardt, Jacob. *The Civilization of the Italian Renaissance.* Harper & Row, 1958.
Calvino, Italo. *Italian Folktales.* Harcourt Brace Jovanovich, 1980.
Clark, Kenneth. *Piero della Francesca.* Phaidon, 1951.
Dallas, Philip. *Italian Wines.* Faber & Faber, 1983.
d'Amato, Federico Umberto. *Guida ai ristoranti tipici regionali.* Rizzoli, 1987.
David, Elizabeth. *Italian Food.* Penguin, 1979.
Del Conte, Anna. *Gastronomy of Italy.* Bantam, 1987.
Dickens, Charles. *Pictures from Italy.* Ecco, 1988.
Goethe, Wolfgang. *Italian Journey.* North Point, 1982.
Guicciardini, Francesco. *The History of Italy.* Princeton University Press, 1984.
Hare, Augustus J. C. *Augustus Hare in Italy.* Ecco, 1988.
———. *Cities of Northern Italy.* Routledge & Sons, 1884.
———. *Walks in Rome.* Routledge & Sons, 1877.
Harris, Valentina. *Traveller's Guide to the Food of Italy.* Henry Holt, 1988.
Hazan, Marcella. *The Classic Italian Cook Book.* Knopf, 1976.
Hazan, Victor. *Italian Wine.* Knopf, 1982.
Hibbert, Christopher. *Rome.* Norton, 1985.
Hofmann, Paul. *Cento Città,* Henry Holt, 1988.
Hughes, Spike and Charmian. *Italian Food and Wine.* Simon & Schuster/Fireside, 1986.
Hutton, Edward. *The Cities of Umbria.* Methuen, 1905.
Huxley, Aldous. *Along the Road.* Ecco, 1989.
Italia (red ed.). Michelin, 1989.
Italy (green ed.). Michelin, 1983.
James, Henry. *Italian Hours.* Ecco, 1987.
Langdon, Helen. *The Knopf Traveler's Guides to Art: Italy.* Knopf, 1984.

Lawrence, D. H. *Lawrence in Italy*. Penguin, 1985.

Macadam, Alta (ed.), *Northern Italy* (Blue Guide, 8th ed.), Ernest Benn/W. W. Norton, 1984.

Manzoni, Alessandro. *The Betrothed*. Penguin, 1984.

McCarthy, Mary. *The Stones of Florence*. Harcourt Brace Jovanovich, 1976.

——. *Venice Observed*. Harcourt Brace Jovanovich, 1963.

Montaigne, Michel de. *Diary of a Journey to Italy*. Harcourt, Brace, 1929.

Pavese, Cesare. *Stories*. Ecco, 1987.

Piccinardi, Antonio. *The Gourmet's Tour of Italy*. New York Graphic Society, 1987.

Plotkin, Fred. *The Authentic Pasta Book*. Simon & Schuster, 1985.

Romer, Elizabeth. *The Tuscan Year*. Atheneum, 1985.

Roncarati, Bruno. *Viva Vino: 200 + DOC & DOCG Wines*. Wine and Spirit Publications, 1986.

Root, Waverley. *The Food of Italy*. Vintage, 1977.

Sharman, Fay, and Brian Chadwick. *The Taste of Italy*. Macmillan/Papermac, 1985.

Svevo, Italo. *The Confessions of Zeno*. Vintage, 1958.

Twain, Mark. *The Innocents Abroad*. New American Library, 1980.

Vasari, Giorgio. *The Lives of the Artists*. Penguin, 1982.

Wasserman, Sheldon and Pauline. *Italy's Noble Red Wines*. Sterling, 1987.

INDEX

Pinot Grigio del Collio di
    Mario Schiopetto, 240
Pinot Guarnazzola, 221
Pinot Nero, 237
Pinot Noir, 126
Pinturicchio, 241
Piperno (Rome), 114
    ranking of, 99
    review of, 277–278
Pisa, 251
    hotel in, 253
    Leaning Tower of, 251
    restaurants in, 113, 251–
        253
Pisano, Bonanno, 251
Pisano, Giovanni, 242, 251
Pisano, Nicola, 242, 289
Pizzeria, 24
    See also Restaurant(s)
Le Plat d'Etain (Cuneo), 106
Plaza (Padua), 238
Plaza (Rome), 282
Plotkin, Fred, 317
Polenta, 58, 209, 346
Polenta e osei, 136
Polo, Marco, 317
Pomiane, Edouard de, 59
Ponte a Moriano, 254
    restaurant in, 113, 254–256
Porchetta, 2, 242, 247
Porta Palazzo market (Turin),
    313
Porta Tessenaca (Gubbio), 108
Al Porto (Milan), 110
Al Portone (Scandiano), 116
Pound, Ezra, 2
Il Pozzo (Monteriggioni), 111
Prà, Enzo de, 8
Prà, Rossana de, 8
Prato delle Rose, 333
Price categories, 14
Primavera (Rome), 115
Principe di Piemonte
    (Viareggio), 344
Principe di Savoia (Milan),
    222–223
Propertius, 131
Prosciutto, 238, 239
Prosecco di Valdobbiadene,
    322

Protestant Cemetery at
    Testaccio (Rome), 267
Prunotto, Guido, 133
Puccini, Giacomo, 193
Puntarelle, 2, 265, 278

Quercia, Jacopo della, 193, 288
Quistello, 206, 257
    restaurant in, 113, 257–259

Radicchio, 35, 85
    of Treviso, 2, 303
Le Ragne, 171, 229
Ramandolo, 160
Ranco, 259
    restaurant in, 113, 260–262,
        297
Raphael, 241, 314
Rating(s), 11
    atmosphere, 13
    class, 12
    service, 13
    stars, 11–12
    wine, 14
Ravenna, 262
    hotels of, 264–265
    mosaics of, 262, 263
    restaurants in, 113, 263–264
Ravioli, origin of, 183
Reading List, 11, 370–371
Recco, restaurant in, 114
Recioto della Valpolicella
    Amarone, 333, 335
Recioto di Soave, 153, 335
Reggio nell'Emilia, restaurant
    in, 114
Regina Palace (Stresa), 298
Regional food and wine
    specialties, 10, 11,
    41–42
    Abbruzzi, 42–45
    Emilia-Romagna, 45–49
    Lazio/Latium, 50–52
    Liguria, 52–56
    Lombardy/Lombardia, 56–
        62
    The Marches/Le Marche, 62–
        65
    Piedmont/Piemonte, 65–71
    Tuscany/Toscana, 71–78

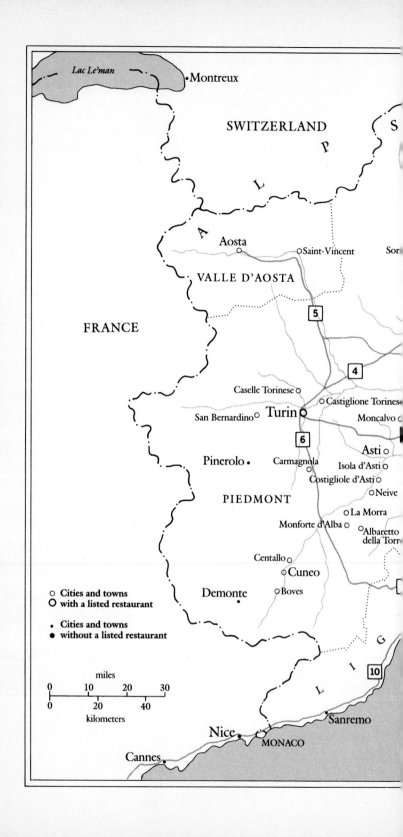

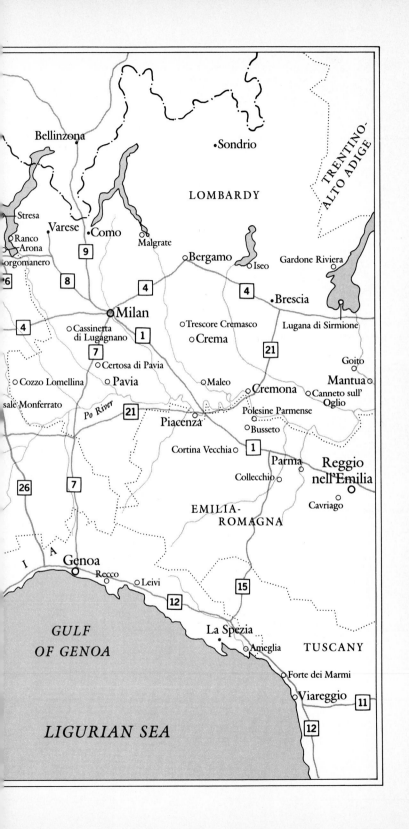

Bellinzona

Sondrio

LOMBARDY

TRENTINO-
ALTO ADIGE

Stresa

Varese   •Como

Malgrate

Ranco

Arona

orgomanero

9

Bergamo

Iseo

Gardone Riviera

8

4

4

Brescia

4

Milan

Trescore Cremasco

Lugana di Sirmione

Cassinetta
di Lugagnano

1

Crema

21

Goito

7

Certosa di Pavia

Mantua

Cozzo Lomellina

Pavia

Maleo

Cremona

Canneto sull'
Oglio

sale Monferrato

Po River

21

Polesine Parmense

Piacenza

Busseto

Cortina Vecchia

1

Parma

Reggio
nell'Emilia

Collecchio

26

7

Cavriago

EMILIA-
ROMAGNA

L I G U R I A

Genoa

Recco

Leivi

15

12

GULF
OF GENOA

La Spezia

Amiglia

TUSCANY

Forte dei Marmi

Viareggio

11

LIGURIAN SEA

12

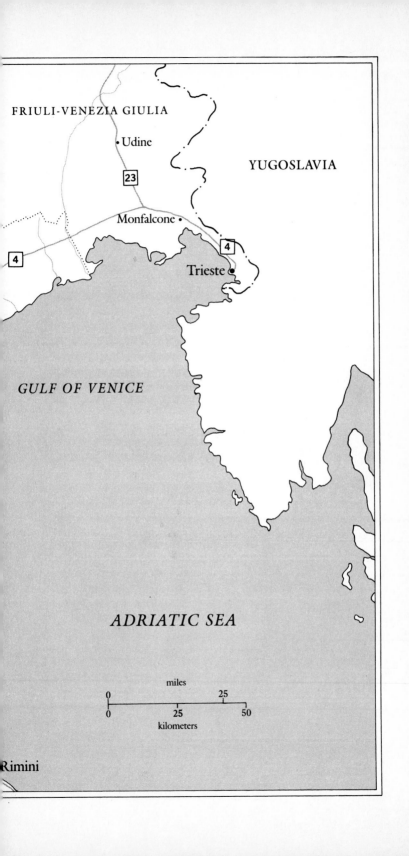

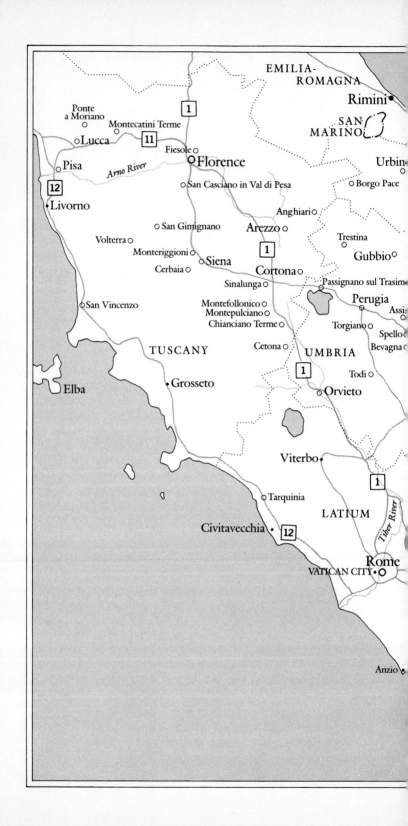

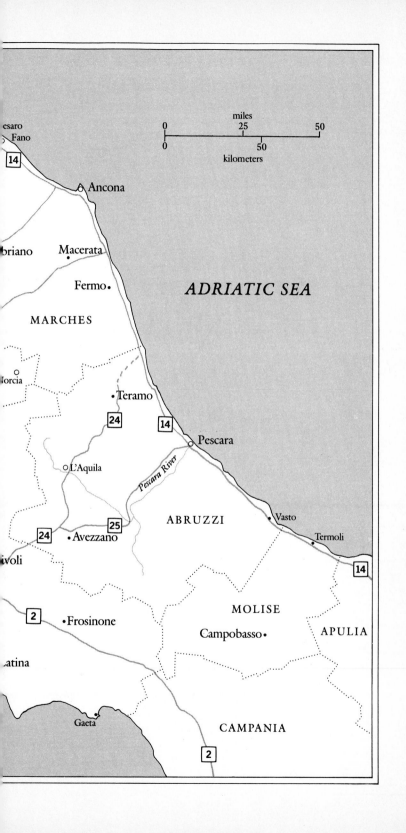